Margaret Drabble was born in Sheffield in 1939 and educated at Newnham College, Cambridge. She was awarded a CBE in 1980. Her many novels include *The Peppered Moth* and *The Seven Sisters*. Margaret Drabble is married to the biographer Michael Holroyd and lives in London.

THE RED QUEEN

Two hundred years after being plucked from obscurity to marry the Crown Prince of Korea, the Red Queen doesn't want her extraordinary existence to be forgotten. Her long and privileged life behind the Korean palace walls was not all it seemed, and the Red Queen (or her ghost) is still desperate to retell her tale. Dr Babs Halliwell, with her own complicated past, seems the perfect envoy — having read the memoirs of the Crown Princess on the plane to Seoul, Babs has become utterly engrossed in her story. But why has the Red Queen picked Babs to keep her story alive, and what else does she want from her?

Books by Margaret Drabble
Published by The House of Ulverscroft:

THE WITCH OF EXMOOR
THE PEPPERED MOTH
THE SEVEN SISTERS

MARGARET DRABBLE

THE RED QUEEN

A Transcultural Tragicomedy

Complete and Unabridged

CHARNWOOD
Leicester

First published in Great Britain in 2004 by
Penguin Books Limited
London

First Charnwood Edition
published 2005
by arrangement with
the Penguin Group UK
London

The acknowledgements on p.453 consitute an
extension of this copyright page

British Library CIP Data

Drabble, Margaret, 1939 –
  The red queen.—Large print ed.—
  Charnwood library series
  1. Hyegyonggung Hong Ssi, 1735 – 1815 —Fiction
  2. Channeling (Spiritualism)—Fiction
  3. Queens—Korea—History—18th century—Fiction
  4. Korea—Kings and rulers—Fiction
  5. Korea—History—1637 – 1864 —Fiction
  6. Large type books
  I. Title
  823.9'14 [F]

  ISBN 1–84395–907–0

Published by
F. A. Thorpe (Publishing)
Anstey, Leicestershire

Set by Words & Graphics Ltd.
Anstey, Leicestershire
Printed and bound in Great Britain by
T. J. International Ltd., Padstow, Cornwall

This book is printed on acid-free paper

The dead weep with joy when their books are reprinted.

The Russian Ark,
Alexander Sokurov, 2003

Prologue

This book was inspired by a volume of court memoirs written in Korea more than two centuries ago. Unlike the heroine of the second half of this volume, I did not read the memoirs of the Crown Princess on an aeroplane at a cruising altitude of 36,000 feet. I read them sitting in the sunshine in a London garden. But, like my fictitious heroine of modern times, I was utterly engrossed by them. I have tried to describe the nature of the impact that they had on me and on Dr Halliwell. It is sheer chance that the Crown Princess came my way at all, but, once I had met her, I could not get her out of my mind. She insisted on my attention. She made me follow her, from text to text, from country to country. She seemed to be making demands on me, but it has not been easy to work out what they might or could be. Several times I have tried to ignore her promptings and to abandon this project, which has been full of difficulties, but she was very persistent.

I have turned her story into a novel, of a kind. This is because I am a novelist, and, for better and for worse, writing novels is what I do. I do not know if this is what she would have wanted. She wanted something, but this may not have been it. It may well be that she would have utterly deplored the liberties I have taken with her story. Being dead, she has not had much say

1

in the matter. She has had no control over how her readers interpret or adapt or translate her story. All I can say is that my efforts are a homage to the power of her narration and to the bravery of her long life.

They are also, of course, a homage to the most recent and most scholarly translator of the memoirs, Professor JaHyun Kim Haboush, who has rendered the original into a vivid English, and whose pioneering studies of this period of Korean history are an invaluable resource. She has devoted many years of her life to this subject, and has succeeded in giving the Lady Hyegyŏng a new voice in our time. She too, I think, has been somewhat haunted by the Lady Hyegyŏng.

I feel some anxiety about the way in which I have appropriated this strange material. But appropriation is what novelists do. Whatever we write is, knowingly or unknowingly, a borrowing. Nothing comes from nowhere.

I have not given a detailed account of all my deviations from and elaborations of the original material. In some aspects I have been faithful to it; in others, not. I have supplied some invention, and added some interpretations, most of which are overtly displayed as interpretations, rather than facts. There are (and have been) many possible interpretations of the story, and mine is only one of them. You will find details of sources and a bibliography at the end of this volume. I must emphasize that Professor Haboush, whose work first introduced me to this material, does not endorse my interpretation, and has had no influence over the point of view or overall tone

2

that I have adopted, though she has offered various editorial suggestions, some of which have been followed. The responsibility for any historical mistakes or anachronisms, whether they be intentional (as some are) or inadvertent (as some will no doubt prove to be) rests with me alone. My admiration for her work is great, but I appreciate that she may wish to dissociate herself as a historian from this work of fiction and fancy.

What struck me most forcibly about the memoirs, when I first read them, was the sense of the clarity of the individual self, speaking clearly and directly and personally, across space, time and culture. This seemed even stranger to me than the sensational nature of the events described, and made me ask myself questions about our modern (and postmodern) doubts about universalism and essentialism. The Crown Princess speaks with dramatic urgency, as though willing posterity to listen to her. After death, she is no longer confined by the culture that imprisoned her. She speaks out from it. She represents a peculiar version of the phenomenon of life after death. Like Dr Halliwell, I do not believe in ghosts. But I do believe that in some sense the Crown Princess is still alive.

I think I am saying something more than the obvious, which is that some books outlive their authors. I do not think that I am speaking here of narrative skill, or of literary talent, although the Crown Princess had both. I believe that she was a prescient woman who lived out of time. In this postmodern age of cultural relativism, that should be an untenable belief. Nevertheless, I have felt the need to investigate it, and this book is the result.

Perhaps I need to spell out my intentions, for attempting to write across cultures is dangerous and liable to misinterpretations. This is not an historical novel. The voice of the Crown Princess, which appears to speak in the first person in the first section of the novel, is not an attempt to reconstruct her real historical voice. It was originally inspired by her voice and her story, but her voice has mixed with mine and with that of Dr Halliwell, and, inevitably, with the voices of her various translators and commentators, all of whom will have brought their own interpretations to her and imposed their personalities upon her. I have not attempted to describe Korean culture or to reconstruct 'real life' in the Korean court of the late eighteenth century. Instead, I have asked questions about the nature of survival, and about the possibility of the existence of universal transcultural human characteristics. The Crown Princess was my starting point for this exploration, but not its end. My Crown Princess is a woman who has read the works of Voltaire. It is my belief that something between the lines of her text suggests that she would have understood Voltaire's attitude to religion and the monarchy very well. But this is only my belief.

I do not know whether the Crown Princess loved her children, her husband or her father-in-law. I can only speculate. We know what custom dictated, but we do not know how fully

4

custom was followed. I do not think that anybody knows. I do not know whether or not the court ladies kept pet cats, as my narrative has supposed, though I have found no evidence to the contrary. I do not even know whether magpies (which appear frequently in this text) were regarded as lucky or unlucky in Korea at this period. I devoted some time to the puzzling question of the cultural significance of magpies, but arrived at no satisfactory conclusion. Some authorities say one thing; some another. The general consensus is that in China and Korea they are considered harbingers of good news, whereas in the West, traditionally, they bring bad luck. The Crown Princess seems to regard them as a bad omen. I really do not know why that should be.

In the earliest translation of the Crown Princess's memoirs, the ominous flock of birds that appears at a crucial moment in the narrative is said to be a flock of ravens, not of magpies. Ravens and magpies are related, but not identical. I do not know what birds flocked on that fatal day, but I have reason to suspect that the translation which described them as ravens was paying homage to *Macbeth*.

PART ONE

Ancient Times

When I was a little child, I pined for a red silk skirt. I do not remember all the emotions of my childhood, but I remember this childish longing well. One of my many cousins came to visit us when I was five years old, and she had a skirt of red silk with patterned edgings, lined with a plain red silk of a slightly darker shade. It was very fashionable, and very beautiful. The gauzy texture was at once soft and stiff, and the colour was bold. Woven into it was a design of little summer flowers and butterflies, all in red. I loved it and I fingered it. That skirt spoke to my girlish heart. I wanted one like it, but I knew that my family was not as wealthy as my mother's sister's family, so I checked my desire, although I can see now that my mother and my aunt could read the longing in my eyes. My aunt and my cousins were delicate in their tastes, and like most women of that era, like most women of any era, they liked fine clothes. They came to envy me my destiny and all its lavish trimmings — well, for a time I believe they envied me. But I was brought up in a hard school, and, as a small child, I had no red silk skirt, and I concealed my longing as best I could. This hard school served me well in my hard life. My mother, too, endured hardship in her early years. I used to wonder, childishly, whether it was my longing for red silk that brought all these disasters upon me and my house. For my desire was fulfilled, but no good came of it, and it brought me no happiness.

I was still a child when I received a red silk skirt of my own. It was brought to me from the palace, with other precious garments made for me at the queen's command. I was presented with a long formal dress jacket of an opaque leaf-green brocade, and a blouse in buttercup-yellow silk with a grape pattern, and another blouse of a rich pale foxglove silk. I had been measured for these robes by the matron of the court, and they were lifted out and displayed to me by a court official, with much ambiguous and bewildering deference. I think my response to these rich and splendid artefacts was lacking in spontaneous delight and gratitude, though I did my best to conceal my fear.

The red silk skirt was not a gift from the palace, although it was included in the fine royal display of gifts. I was to learn later that it had been made for me by my mother, as a reward and as a compensation for my elevation. She had made it secretly, at night, hanging curtains over her windows to hide the lights in her chamber as she worked. This is how she performed many of her household tasks — discreetly, quietly, modestly. My mother liked to hide her thrift and industry, and she avoided compliments on her domestic labours. At this time, I knew nothing of this special undertaking on my behalf. I stared at the red silk skirt in ungracious silence.

My mother reminded me that I had once expressed a wish for such things, and she watched my face for smiles of gratitude. I did not remember having expressed this wish, but I confess that she was right to have divined it in me. But now I was too sad and too oppressed to raise my eyes to look at my new finery. My illustrious future hung heavily upon me. I was nine years old, and I was afraid.

I have been dead now for 200 years, but I have not been idle. I have been rethinking my story, and my history. I am not dead enough or modern enough to adopt the word 'her-story', in place of 'his-tory', but I feel compelled to suggest that this false, whimsical and, to my ear, ugly etymology could, if ever, be appropriately invoked here, for I am a prime and occasionally quoted example of the new 'her-story'. I see that I have an honourable though not wholly adequate mention in the first Encyclopedia of Life Writing, published in the Year of the West 2002, where I am incorrectly named as 'Princess Hong', and my memoir, even more oddly, is entitled 'In Burning Heart'. I do not know who bestowed that inappropriate title upon my work.

I wrote various accounts of my story during my earthly lifetime, and I must say that they were well written. I am an intelligent and an articulate woman, by any relativist and multicultural standards that you may choose to invoke. But each of those versions was written as a piece of special pleading. I have had to defend to death and beyond death the reputations of my father, my uncles, my brother, my clan. (Our clan, in our lifetime, was known as the Hong family, and we were, of course, as should go without saying, of ancient and distinguished lineage. In some

11

versions of my story in the West, I am now given the title of Lady Hong: indeed, this name appears on the title page of what I believe to be the second Western translation of my work. This was not my name.) Above all, I have had to vindicate the tragic temperament and career of my unfortunate husband, whose horrifying end had such complex and painful reverberations for the history of our country, and for me. There were so many violent deaths in my family circle. I have even had to attempt to defend my immensely powerful yet deeply perplexed father-in-law, who seems to be the villain in some of these versions. Was he villain, victim or hero? With all my hindsight, and with the hindsight of many not always illuminating and often partial commentaries, I still cannot be certain. Death does not bring full light and full knowledge.

Many thought I was fortunate to die in my bed, an old woman of eighty years. Indeed, it is remarkable that I managed to live so long, in such turbulent times. But how could I have allowed myself to die earlier? Many times I wished to die, and sometimes I thought it my duty to die. But in universal terms, in human terms, it was my duty to live. My life was needed. My son and my grandson needed me. I could not abandon them. I survived for them. (I could even argue that my kingdom needed me, but that would be a grandiose claim, a masculine and dynastic claim, and I do not make it.) And now, 200 years later, with the knowledge of two centuries added to my own limited knowledge on earth, I intend to retell my story. I hope to purchase a further lease of attention, and a new and different readership. I have selected a young and vigorous envoy, who will prolong my afterlife and collaborate with me in my undying search for the meaning of my sufferings and my survival.

In life, I was called arrogant by many, and devious by some. I had many enemies. I suppose I was both arrogant and devious. And indeed I cannot look back on my past life without some sense of my innate superiority. Much ignorance and much stupidity and much fear surrounded me, particularly during my middle years. I was designed to be a poor and helpless woman, in a world where men held the power — and power was absolute, in those days — but I had eyes in my head, and a quick brain, and could see what was happening around me. At times I could make others dance to my tune. I myself survived, but I had my failures. The worst of them was this.

I lost my poor husband. I tried to save him, but, despite all my efforts, he had to be sacrificed. He was too mad, too perverse, too much destroyed by his place, his heritage, his nature. He was too hard a case for me. Even today, in these advanced and enlightened times, I think I would have been unable to save him. Even today, I think he would have met a similar fate, though in a different, to me unimaginable, but perhaps parallel manner. But that is a conclusion I have reached after many decades, after two centuries of reflection. And who knows, maybe even now some wonder drug is being

13

prepared, a drug that could have saved him and his victims from the extremity of his terrors and the horror of his end? Medication for such diseases of the brain grows ever more precise, or so we are told. We have become expert in tracing chemical imbalances and the defective activity of our myriad of neurotransmitters. But these discoveries come too late for him and for me.

Let me begin at the beginning, with my long-ago childhood. I have discovered that childhood is now widely considered to be a social construct, and I note that my written versions of my childhood have been knowingly or charitably placed by others as 'nostalgic' or 'idealizing' or 'self-serving'. I have thought much about these comments and interpretations. I will narrate what I take to be the facts, as I have been told them, and I will add some of my memories, though I am well aware that personal memories may be reinforced or undermined to the point of disbelief by family memory. None of us has full access to even our own stories.

I am rather surprised that some of my readers seem to have missed the cautious and disclaiming note of irony that is and has ever been my dominant mode. Here, beyond death, I will attempt to dispense with it, though maybe the habit of it is too deeply ingrained by now. I do not think of myself, with plaintive self-pity, as a tragic heroine. I think of myself as a survivor.

I was born, according to the Western calendar, on 6 August 1735. This year, 1735, was known as *ŭlmyo* in our calendar, but, for simplicity's sake, I will use Western terminology for

14

chronological terms, just as, in my own time, I chose to write mainly in the Korean *han'gŭl* alphabet, rather than in the less accessible though more literary language of Chinese. Some say I was born at noon, some say I was born at one o'clock in the morning, but all agree that I was born at my mother's family home in Kop'yŏng-dong in Pansong-bang, which was a western district of the large walled and gated city of Seoul, in the country now (and long) known as Corea, or Korea. (Corea is the older transliteration: I believe our traditional enemies the Japanese were responsible for altering it to Korea, on the grounds of Western alphabetical precedence. For J precedes K, does it not? And Japan wished to come first.) Seoul in my day was known as Hanyang or Hansung, taking its name from the broad river Han that flowed (and still flows) past it and down to the Yellow Western Sea, but for your convenience I will call it by the name by which it is now known. I was born in the house of my mother's parents. It was traditional in those days and in our culture for a woman to return to her mother's home to give birth (though I, of course, in my exceptional circumstances, was not to be allowed this comfort). When I was born, my parents were both in their early twenties: they had been married in 1727. In 1735, the Chosŏn dynasty, of the royal house of Yi, had already lasted for three centuries, and was to survive until modern times, until the year 1910. I was born during the reign of King Yŏngjo, the twenty-first king of Yi lineage.

15

In 1735, in Europe, the Enlightenment was gathering its strength, but few of the Western texts about the universality and perfectibility of human nature had reached us in Korea. News of Roman Catholicism and its Jesuit missionaries had reached us, but not, I believe, the works of Voltaire. Nevertheless, something of the spirit and the wider perspectives of the Enlightenment informed, I trust, my earlier texts, as they do this posthumous revision. It is my belief that the universal exists, and that in the end of time, in the fullness of light, we shall see it, and know all things. This is a foolish belief, but no more foolish than the temporal beliefs of many dynasties and many multitudes. If I continue to seek, I may yet find. If my belief can be justified, I shall find others who will collaborate in my quest.

Several members of my family were executed because they were suspected of sympathizing with Catholicism. Catholicism was violently repressed, and there are many Korean saints and martyrs recognized by the Catholic Church. I, in those years, had no religion. Outwardly pious, I prudently paid lip service to the ancient dogmas and tenets of Confucianism, but my mind went its own way. It went the way of survival. I make no apologies for this.

Were the early years of my childhood as happy as I once claimed that they were? No, of course they were not. They were overshadowed by anxiety, by strain, by fear. It is only in comparison with what was to follow that they could be described as happy. It is true that my

16

grandfather petted me and predicted a great future for me, and that my aunt — herself a very highly educated woman — taught me to read and write, and praised my mental abilities highly. But the burden of all these expectations lay heavy on me. I had an older sister who died when I was very small. I have no recollection of her, but I sensed that after her death my parents had invested many worldly hopes in me. But hopes of what? Were they already plotting my destiny, my downfall?

I was indulged as a small child. Was this in prospective recompense for the later sorrows, which they could hardly have fully foreseen? My older brother was brought up very strictly and coldly, but I was often permitted to share my mother's room at night. This was not usual, and perhaps it was not wise. I think First Brother resented the favours that he thought were shown to me.

From childhood, I was acutely conscious of family resentments. I was unnaturally attuned to them, to my sorrow. But this awareness kept me on my guard. And I was to have need of my guard.

My father claimed he had dreamed of a black dragon the day before I was born. It had appeared, or so he said, entwined about the roof beam of my mother's bedroom. My father had therefore assumed that I would be a boy, for a dragon portends fame and distinction in public life. Was it this dream that dictated my fatally favoured upbringing? I can hardly think so. Our legends and histories are full of dragon dreams.

(Even today, Koreans claim to dream auspicious dragon dreams.) My father may have invented that dragon. Our dreams do not lie, though they may deceive us, but we may lie about our dreams. In our culture, even so late in history, dreams could be cited in justification of or in explanation of strange acts. We had left behind the rites of our distant forebears, who superstitiously sought meaning in the cracking of turtle shells, but we dwelled still, when it suited us to do so, in the dark ages of the mind. We toyed with dragons and yarrow stalks and hexagons and magic books of jade; we saw messages written on stones and etched on leaves. We listened to oracles; we invoked spirits; we consulted geomancers and shamans. (As, I note with some surprise, you do today. There has been little progress there.) And some of us cast our minds forward, though perhaps not very successfully, to the more interesting speculations and interpretations of Jung and of Freud.

My father, during these years of my early childhood, was exhausting himself by preparing for his state examinations. Mysteriously, he at first failed his examinations at the Confucian Academy, but he received an official appointment nevertheless, as custodian of a royal tomb, and redoubled his intellectual efforts. Our society — or perhaps I should say our section of society — was obsessed with academic success and with the passing of these time-honoured examinations. Even those who did not seek public life, even those who became scholars of the woods and the mountains, were obliged

18

when young to share the obsession with examinations. You may think that your society lays too much emphasis on grades and tests and examinations, and some of you may argue that they cause much psychological damage — well, all I can say is that I believe that our society, in this respect, was even worse. You inherit only a shadow of the oppression. It was impossible to rise or even to survive in our world, if you were a man, without passing through a rigid sequence of military or civic examinations. You had to pass through them before you could escape from them by achieving the respected status of mountain-scholar — a path which one of my brothers was obliged to choose. But my father did not wish to retire. He was a very ambitious man, or so I have now come to think. During his life, he held many prominent ministerial positions. In his later years, he could rightly be described as the power behind the throne.

The time came when my parents began to quarrel bitterly. I think this was after the birth of Third Brother, the second of my younger brothers, in 1740 or 1741, when I was about six years old. (Second Brother, the first of my younger brothers, was born in 1739, an event of which I have no memory.) I do not know the reasons for my parents' disaffection, but I could see its results. My mother had recently lost both her mother and her father-in-law, and upon the birth of Third Brother she fell into a depression. I, too, was unhappy because of my paternal grandfather's death — I had been fond of him, and he had always made much of me. But what upset me most, I have to admit, was the fact that during his last illness I was banished to my great-grandmother's house. I hated it there. She was a stout, ill-tempered, tyrannical old woman, and nothing in her household seemed to run smoothly. And, of course, I missed my parents. But when I returned home, after grandfather's funeral, all was at odds there, too. As I have said, my parents were quarrelling, and my mother was insisting that she wanted to go home to her own family — and indeed she did leave my father for a while, taking me back with her to Pansong-bang. As I recall, my father was enraged both by her desertion and by her refusal to take some medicine that he believed would alleviate her depression. Her rejection of it he read as a rejection of him. He was also angry that I had been taken away; he came to collect me and took me home with him. (Strangely, I cannot remember what happened to my little brothers at this time. Were they with me and my mother in Pansong-bang, or with my father and the wet nurse? It is immaterial, but it is strange that I cannot remember. My memory is full of gaps.) Mother then returned home also, but for a while she and father were not on speaking terms. Angry messages were sent from one to the other from different parts of the house. The domestic atmosphere was cold and deadly, and I wished mother and I were back at Pansong-bang.

Mother wept day and night, and she developed an eating disorder that made her refuse all food. I suppose she was depressed. Was it a form of postnatal depression? Such a condition was not officially recognized or named in those days, though it was common enough. It was midwinter, and an icy wind blew through the eaves. The door frames and screens rattled, and icicles hung from the roof tiles. Soon my father's anger turned to sickness, and he too began to refuse food — and so, in consequence, did I. I had witnessed too much; I was too close to them. I could not choose but to partake of their misery. I could not stomach the meals I was offered: they filled me with nausea. Was this an imitative filial piety or a form of incipient anorexia? I remember that a lump of my thick black hair fell out: I had a bald white shiny spot on my scalp, the size of a large coin. I was fascinated and appalled by this physical manifestation of grief. So were my parents. They had been in the grip of a mutually exacerbating and competitive despair, but eventually, for my sake, or so they said, they were reconciled. My father claimed that he could not bear to see me in decline, so he began to eat again, and encouraged me to do the same. He even offered the spoon of ginseng to my lips with his own hand. My mother also rallied. They said they were reconciled for my sake, but how am I to test the truth of that? What was I to them? What of my brothers? Where were my brothers during this dark time? Am I so selfish that I have forgotten the part they played? Why was I the close and chosen one, the spy within the bedroom?

When this grim winter episode of marital conflict came to an end, and spring returned, my parents gave me a toy pan and a toy pot to cheer me, and to reward me for having been so sensitive to their misery. And it is true that by the end of this grief-and-anger period, I felt that they had transferred their misery to me. I had taken it into myself. One should not, I believe, expect so much of small children, though I note that, in this respect, even greater emotional burdens are now placed on children by parents than was common in my day. But I liked my new toys, and I played with them, dutifully, seriously, happily, as a small child should. I still remember them clearly, that little bronze pot and that little pan, because I did not have many toys. Busily I filled and refilled them with water and flower petals and pebbles and grains of rice. I arranged feasts for my dolls, in the courtyard, under the foxglove tree. Dried poppyheads were my pepper pots, and I shook the black seeds on to my cold little feasts. I begged to be allowed to heat my dishes on a real stove, but this was forbidden. I managed to warm them, slightly, to a tepid state, on the hottest corner of the heated wooden floor, and then I would raise them to my lips and pretend to eat. My play did not wholly convince me. Already I knew that play was a pretence, and that sorrow was real. An old head on young shoulders: that proverb from your language would have fitted me well, as it would have fitted my little sister. The Hong children aged fast.

My childhood, happy or unhappy, innocent or fearful, did not last long. Shocking things were soon to be expected of me, things that would now be forbidden by law in most nations on earth. I was to be the victim of advancement.

All these childish times came to an end when my parents put my name forward for the threefold royal selection ceremony for a royal bride. They justified this decision as their 'duty', for I was grandchild of a distinguished minister. They said they feared disgrace if I were not offered for the sacrifice, and claimed they were afraid to conceal me. My mother later swore that she hoped and believed that I would be rejected. I do not know how much truth there was in this: certainly she wept copiously when she discovered the way the wind was blowing, and even my father turned pale. I myself had no hopes, fears or expectations. I did not know what was happening. I was the youngest of all the candidates, and the most poorly dressed. I was sent to the palace in a skirt made from the cloth intended for my dead sister's wedding, and lined with fabric made over from old clothes. I was not quite a thing of rags and patches, but I did not see myself as a possible princess. I was not the material from which princesses are made.

It is impossible to exaggerate the significance of the rigid dress codes of this period, within the court and beyond it. Fabrics held destinies, and colours spoke of faction and fate. Seen now, from afar, from a world from which much ceremonial (though by no means all) has vanished, the rigidity of these rules of dress may seem a psychotic expression of a deformed society. No wonder so many of us went mad. No wonder my poor husband developed those strange and unnamed phobias that were in part

23

his undoing. It is more of a wonder that we did not all run mad.

Nevertheless, despite the poverty of my second-hand clothes, despite the fact that I was merely the daughter of a poor scholar, I was to be the chosen one. I was favoured at the preliminary selection by Lady Sŏnhŭi, the mother of the Crown Prince, my bridegroom-to-be. The favours of Lady Sŏnhŭi filled me with fear and panic. She was the king's most favoured consort, and she was an intimidating woman. She had been known when young as the 'Bright Princess', but by the time I encountered her she had developed a formidable manner. I was frightened of her.

The prospect of the second presentation and selection, which reduced the numbers of contenders to three girls, filled me with a worse terror. Once more I was chosen. Already the horrors of my new position were clear to me. My father's house was besieged with fawning relatives and begging servants, but the palace itself, on this second long visit, was certainly no refuge. I remember struggling, physically, with the lady-in-waiting who tried to measure me for my ceremonial robes. I was in a state of panic, and I am afraid that I tried to bite her. I had to be calmed by force. I remember waiting long hours in strange pavilions in the vast palace grounds, sometimes alone, sometimes being patted and stroked and caressed by strange princesses. (My bridegroom-to-be had several full and several half-sisters, some of whom play a sinister role in this story.) I was confined for hours, perhaps days, to the Hall of Clear Thinking, and I tried to think clearly, but it was not easy. His Majesty King Yŏngjo came and patted me, and flattered me, and pressed improving reading matter upon me. I felt sick, and could hardly control my bowels. Strange foods were offered to me, but I could not eat. I was robed in stiff and uncomfortable court clothes of green and violet, and a slave of the bedchamber painted my child's face into an adult mask with unfamiliar cosmetics. I did not recognize myself. I longed to go back to my parents and my nurse, but, when at last I was released from these tortures, I found that my palanquin was being carried home by palace servants, and I was attended by one of the queen's own women, robed entirely in black. In homecoming there was no escape.

My home itself was transformed: my parents were waiting for me in new robes, their manner subdued, anxious and unhappy, and they now addressed me in formal speech, not as their daughter, but as their mistress. They had prepared a formal and symbolic meal, laid out on a red cloth, of which the royal entourage was to partake. (Was there rice, cooked with chestnut and jujube, signifying long life, such as I ordered to be provided, years later, for the unhappy betrothal of my son? I cannot remember for I was half-blind with dread.) My father seemed to have sunk into a state of panic and fear. He sweated profusely in his unfamiliar ceremonial garments. He smelled of fear. Why had I been offered up to this strange fate? To appease what

25

gods, to gain what advantage? I overheard my parents, full of doubts, talking about me, and whether they had been right to present me. In these last days, before I left my parents' home for ever, my father was full of advice and foreboding. I was allowed to sleep in my mother's bed, for the last time, and I lay there sobbing, hiding my head beneath the kingfisher quilt, listening to the low murmur of their adult anxiety and grief. I wished to die, and so to avoid my fate. I cannot describe the intensity and the terror of my apprehensions. I felt like a criminal, though I did not know what offence I had committed. I cried and cried, and would not be comforted. I was only a child and had not learned the arts of concealment.

But fate marched towards me, with an army of regulations, and, as I have said, new garments, including the consolation of that red silk skirt, which came too late to bring me any joy. Rather, it reminded me of the obscure and relatively carefree youth that I was about to lose for ever. The codes of the court, its customs and rituals, were drummed into me. I was a quick learner, but I did not then understand the rationale that had constructed these elaborate performances, and I like to understand what I am doing, and why. I was only ten years old, but maturity had been thrust suddenly upon me. I could tell from my father's manner and his elaborate and often repeated warnings that a false step or a rash word would mean disgrace, perhaps death, not only for myself, but also for my family.

That red silk skirt has much to answer for. I

ordered another one like it, for my adult body, when I thought I was my own mistress. It gave me no pleasure.

I say that my husband was mad. And so I believe he was. But his son and my son — our son, the son who became king — could not admit this. Nor could we admit the manner of his death. Our lives have been full of so many denials. Intricate, politic denials. Our son devoted much of his adult life to the rehabilitation of the reputation of his mad father. But I lived through that madness. What and whom do I blame for it? Do I blame his father, my father-in-law the king, King Yŏngjo, for his excessive demands and excessive expectations? Do I blame King Yŏngjo for so oddly and unnaturally favouring several of his daughters and thereby deliberately and openly humiliating his only son? Do I blame the unnatural rigour and ceremony of court life? Do I blame the factional strife that tore our country apart? Do I blame the dead hand of Confucianism and its reverence for the dead parent? 'Filial piety' was the everlasting refrain of our culture. As you can well imagine, its rigid dictates were not always observed as faithfully as they should have been, and many a child rebelled against its parent, but nevertheless those who rebelled did so at a high psychic cost.

My father-in-law the king was suspected of gaining the throne through fratricide. His brother, King Kyŏngjong, was a man weak of mind and body, and, after a brief rule, he died, and Yŏngjo succeeded. Foul play was suspected, and many rumours circulated. This was ten years before I was born, but the rumours did not die away — they multiplied. My slave Pongnyŏ, who cared for me as a baby, and who came to the palace with me when I was married, was full of gossip about these old scandals. She loved to frighten me with her tales. Some said the feeble-minded king had been bewitched, and had died through the black arts — by powdered bones, by incantations, and by mystic writings on eaves and lintels. Others said that his garments had been treated with the venom of snakes. One story held that a eunuch had poured a noxious ointment of henbane and mandrake into his ear, as he lay sleeping in the royal arbour. But the most popular version was the one in which Prince Yŏngjo had sent his brother a dish of poisoned mushrooms. The king tasted them, praised them, went into a spasm, and died within the hour. And so Yŏngjo gained the throne. That was the version that Pongnyŏ liked best, though she could never offer any first-hand evidence for it.

I wonder what gossip she spread about me. She lived to a great age, and she had seen much and no doubt guessed at more.

At times of strife or uncertainty, the poisoned mushrooms and the accusation of fratricide were sure to surface again. King Yŏngjo was always in fear of threats to the legitimacy of his rule. Our country has a long history of such scandals. We are not unique in this. I now know that all monarchies in all countries produce scandals of succession and murmurs of conspiracy and murder. Against this poisonous backdrop of gossip and innuendo and occasional outright denunciation, we attempted to survive, and to appear virtuous. Later accounts of our country describe this century, the eighteenth century, as a period of peace and prosperity, and it is true that King Yŏngjo initiated many reforms, but it was not peaceful to me and mine, as you shall hear.

My husband and I were ten years old when we were married in 1744. We were children, and we had no say in that matter — or in any matter. We were fifteen when the marriage was consummated. This was in the first month of the year 1749.

I cannot remember the marriage ceremony well, though I do recall that my mother looked magnificent, in her high wig and her rich and courtly robe with a lemon-yellow top beneath a violet overjacket. I cannot remember clearly what I wore. I was sick with fear that I might make a false step. I have to say that my father-in-law the king was kind and indulgent to me at this stage of my young life: on this point my subsequent testimony, however diplomatic and indeed obsequious in intent, has not lied. I do not know why, but he seemed to favour me and to wish me well, and he encouraged me when terror overcame me. I was often speechless, often faint. He spoke to me gently, and gave me his advice about etiquette and court behaviour. I wonder, now, if he did not, in fact, prefer women to men. He was very fond of some of his seven daughters, particularly of the princesses Hwap'yŏng

29

(his third daughter) and Hwawan, who was three years younger than his only son, Sado. Perhaps from Sado's birth onwards the king saw my husband as a rival, as a potential parricide. Necessary though that birth was, for the survival of the dynasty, maybe he resented it. All fathers find a rival in a son. Maybe that is why we talk so much of filial piety, in an effort to restrain our natural impulses towards parent-murder.

King Yŏngjo was a strange man, a complex character. He was a powerful monarch, known as a reformer, but there was something vacillating and at times hysterical about him, something almost effeminate. I remember that he spoke to me about intimate details that shocked and surprised me. Never, he said to me when I was yet a child, a pre-pubertal child, never leave traces of red cosmetic on a white cloth. Keep your linen white. Men do not like to see the red smear, he told me. Do not let men see your artifice. It seemed a curious matter of concern for so great a monarch, and I was disturbed by his mentioning it. I still think it would have been more fitting for one of the three Queenly Majesties, my mother-in-law Lady Sŏnhŭi, or the Dowager Queen Inwŏn, or even the king's first wife, Queen Chŏngsŏng, to have spoken to me about these things. I do not know why he took it upon himself. His words shamed and embarrassed me.

I now think, with the benefit of maturity and an afterlife, and in light of my readings of nineteenth- and twentieth-century anthropological and psychoanalytical literature, that he was speaking of men's fear of menstrual blood. But did he know that? Did anyone, at that time, know that? I think not.

How eagerly we women may watch for the smear of blood. And how, at times, we, too, may fear to see it.

The king also warned me to be wary at court. He said I should pretend not to see some of the things that I saw. However strange I found them, I should ignore them. He did not say what these things were. It was a good and useful warning.

But he was also generous to me, in many ways, and gave me some lavish and delightful gifts. How I loved the eight-panelled painted paper *hwajo-do* screen that was installed at his command in my apartment in the Detached Palace. This *fleurs-et-oiseaux* screen was of a subject and style considered traditional for the lady's chamber, but it was of extraordinarily beautiful and delicate workmanship and muted subtlety of colouring, and I would gaze at it, entranced, for hours on end. It portrayed slightly stylized but familiar birds, in an idealized landscape of small rocks, slender flowering peach trees, pines, peonies, vines and ripe pomegranates; in the foreground and middle ground of two of the panels, plump spotted carp floated amongst ducks and herons. The soft tones were predominantly green and brown and rose and plum, against a natural ochre-brown background, though in my favourite panel a family of mandarin ducks, symbols of domestic happiness, took on a lighter blue-green as they swam amidst a bed of flowering lotus. It was a happy family

— a mother bird, a father bird, and three ducklings, above whose heads fluttered two little blue birds of happiness.

When we were little, the Crown Prince and I played games together. We played, like the children that we were. Prince Sado had toy soldiers and toy armies, and I had little toy horses to ride, as well as dolls and kites and shuttlecocks. Many gifts had been lavished upon him, perhaps unwisely, by the ladies-in-waiting of his late aunt, the widow of the late king, that king who was or was not killed by the poisoned mushrooms. The Crown Prince was much indulged — too much indulged — by the late king's faction. The palace matron, Lady Han, in particular, had encouraged him in his love of military games: she was good with her hands, and she made him swords and scimitars and bows and arrows of wood and paper. She also invented an all-too-thrilling game in which young ladies-in-waiting would hide behind screens and doors, then leap out at him, brandishing their paper weapons and crying martial cries. Naturally, he was enchanted by this sport, and at the time, when he described it to me when I was a child, I saw no harm in it. It was only later that I began to see its dangers. His father and mother had been remote and cold towards him, and had much neglected him during his boyhood, rarely visiting the nursery quarters. The prince had needed some boyish comforts. This is how I saw it, when I was younger.

Lady Han had been dismissed from her post

two or three years before our betrothal because the king and Lady Sŏnhŭi seemed at last to have become aware that her influence was unhealthy. But the damage was already done. The first seven years of life are the important ones, as I believe the Jesuits say.

When the revered sage Mencius was a little boy, he played at funerals. His mother did not approve, and took steps to divert him from these morbid preoccupations. She was quite right not to approve, in my view. She was a more attentive mother to her son than the Lady Sŏnhŭi was to my husband.

Although our lives were largely separate, some hours of contact were permitted to my betrothed and me, and we, too, played military games and fought little campaigns on the schoolroom floor. I think these contacts were against the strict etiquette of the court, but nevertheless they took place. Many things took place that were not in the rule book. There were many blind eyes at court.

These, too, were exciting and at times feverish games. The prince would rescue me from imaginary rival factions and carry me safely on his back, piggyback style, to his kingdom. I have to admit that I loved this game. I clasped him tightly round his waist with my legs. In 'real life', my family, the Hong family, was of the Noron faction of the Old Doctrine, which had long been in conflict with the Soron faction of the Young Doctrine, but in our game the crown prince and I made up other, more poetic names — I was of the Crimson Petal faction; my enemies were of the Black Bough. Occasionally the crown prince would take on the role of one of the enemy, and he would pretend to capture and then to torture me. He invented ingenious tortures of a pre-pubertal sexual nature, and I willingly complied. He would pretend to bind me fast, with silk sashes, and, while I was thus bound, he would caress me through my garments and insult me with mild abuse. Then he would make me kneel and lift my skirts, and caress me beneath my garments. Then he would pretend to behead me — our kingdom, alas, was only too familiar with beheadings.

These were forbidden games, and we would cease from them abruptly when interrupted. We were spied upon both overtly and covertly for most of our young lives. But he was the Crown Prince, and I was to be the queen, and we were married, so we were permitted some licence, and some private time together. My most intimate servant, Pongnyŏ, who had been with me since my birth, would occasionally turn a blind eye to our activities and let us frolic unseen. Pongnyŏ was only a slave, though she became my lady-in-waiting, and was many years later, after the tragedy, elevated to the rank of palace matron. In those early years of my marriage, those unconsummated years, she was my constant attendant. Another of my early attendants was Aji, the wet nurse who had breastfed me as a baby at my maternal home. She came with me also to the marriage pavilion. She, too, was discreet. Aji and Pongnyŏ tried to shelter me and the Crown Prince, and to prepare us for the ordeals ahead. Both lived to old age. Both outlived the Crown Prince.

I was to be the Red Queen. In play, the Crown Prince used to call me his 'little Red Queen'. He liked my red silk skirt. I liked the name he gave me. I was vain and I was theatrical, and I was fond of my status when I was a little girl.

The Crown Prince played with my younger brothers, too — those two little brothers who were so similar in feature and so close in age that some mistook them for twins. They enjoyed visiting the palace, though they always had to be on guard. My husband, who was not much older than them, used to tease them and encourage them to overstep the invisible mark that proclaimed him as a prince and them as commoners. They were cautious about his overtures, and careful not to be tempted into overfamiliarity. They were right to be cautious. The field around the prince was red with danger.

His name was Prince Sado. I will use this name because you will remember it, and because it is the name by which history and his people remember him, though in fact it was conferred upon him posthumously. During Prince Sado's lifetime, he had many names, reflecting his somewhat capriciously changing status. Prince Changhon was the best known of these, but Sado is the name that has endured. Korean nomenclature in the royal and affined families was very complicated. The names of the princesses his sisters are confusing to the Western eye, for they all begin with the letter H, and are difficult to pronounce, but Sado's

35

posthumous name is easy to remember. It signifies mourning. A sad name, for one who is mourned.

Prince Sado's name, as I discovered long after his death and mine, also has a quite arbitrary connection with the name of the Marquis de Sade, and of the derivative noun, 'sadism'. It is a meaningless and fortuitous connection, and as far as I know neither the Marquis de Sade nor Count Sacher-Masoch (who also was strangely obsessed with clothing) knew of the existence of the kingdom of Korea (or Corea, or Corée), let alone of the sufferings of my husband. Yet the connection provides a useful aide-mémoire.

So, remember Prince Sado. And remember his innocence. He was a child when we played these games of beheadings. He had not yet earned his title. He had not yet become the Prince of Mournful Thoughts, the Prince of the Coffin.

I have no name, and I have many names. I am a nameless woman. My true name is unknown to history. I am famous, but nameless. And I was never a queen in my lifetime, red or otherwise. I became a queen after my death. So much happens after death.

Sado told me once that he had thought my genitals would look like the udder of a cow, with four teats and four nipples. He was relieved by their neat simplicity, when he stole these covert, excited glances at them. Of course, in those times, I had no breasts. I was flat, and smooth of skin.

Children find the human body confusing. Even 'liberated' and well-informed children in

36

the twenty-first century find the human body confusing. Even children reared naked in villages of baked earth find the human body confusing, and are shocked by the drama of the events, both natural and unnatural, that inevitably overtake it. Small wonder, then, that the Crown Prince and I, so swathed and so enveloped in such rich symbolic fabrics, should have had false images of what is hidden away. The laws governing physical contact between the sexes were, in a Confucian culture, very strict and very complex. Contact between the sexes, except within marriage and amongst close kin, was in theory forbidden, though of course contacts took place. Rules are one thing, practice another. But in theory at least women took one path, men another, and those paths should never cross. There were many elegant and time-consuming debates at our court on small, not to say ridiculous, points of principle — for instance, was a man permitted to soil himself and pollute his kinswoman by holding out his hand to save his sister-in-law from drowning? This popular moral conundrum was not dissimilar from the predicament of the heroine of Bernardin de St Pierre's novel *Paul et Virginie*, one of the sensational successes published in Europe during my lifetime, though of course we in Korea knew nothing of this small volume. In this curious work, the virtuous heroine Virginie refuses to undress to save herself from shipwreck, and thus drowns within sight of shore and of her lover. Clothing has much to answer for.

The colour red was the royal colour of Korea.

(Yellow, we were told, was the colour of the Chinese emperor, the Son of Heaven, and we were subservient to him.) King Yŏngjo, my father-in-law, a man not without vanity, considered that the king alone had the exclusive right to wear it, but by his reign the wearing of red robes had spread through the court. He attempted to forbid it, just as he attempted to forbid the wearing of costly and richly patterned Chinese silk, and high, elaborately braided wigs of false hair, but he failed. He was a man of strange contradictions, veering from vanity to frugality, from abstinence to drunkenness, from histrionic display to extreme self-denial and retreat. Maybe this is what monarchy inevitably does to the human spirit. But I prefer to think that he had a unique and peculiar character, which resulted in the unique and peculiar fate of his son. I do believe that character affects history. That is no longer a fashionable view, but those who have lived close to power, even if themselves powerless, as I was, tend to hold it. And we were a small country, where one man's whims could affect many.

Confucius said that a man should not wear scarlet at home. I do not know why he said that — maybe as a passing joke, who knows? — but that, too, became written on tablets of stone.

I think men are afraid of blood, although they are attracted to it. I think King Yŏngjo, as I have said, was afraid of menstrual blood, though he did not know it. I remember that as a child I was particularly anxious, not about menstruation, but about excretion. Even when I grew older it

38

seemed to me strange that the organs of excrement and the organs of procreation should be placed so close to one another. When I was little, I must confess that I had thought them identical — it was small relief to me to learn that they were so narrowly divided. It is not so, I know now, with all species. May I be permitted to say that I find the human body not elegantly designed? We pay a high price for our higher intelligence. Our nearest relations, the apes, are not lovely either. They parody our defects, and we know that, though we are reluctant to admit it. I prefer fish, or birds, or flowers.

Like many children, I thought that women gave birth through the navel. This was no stranger a notion to me than my little husband's view that my genitals should resemble the udder of a cow. As for the penis — I thought it unsightly, asymmetrical. I did not like the way it flopped to one side or to the other. At least a woman's body could be cut into two neat halves. Sliced, like an apple.

You might be able to appreciate my childish ignorance better if you were to look at the illuminated manuscripts illustrating the court ceremonies of the period. Many of these survive, though I am informed that not all have yet been traced. No doubt some have perished, but I believe more will be recovered in time. Our country was much plundered, much invaded. I have sent my envoy to re-examine the manuscript commemorating the sixtieth anniversary of the consummation of my marriage to Crown Prince Sado: this grand and lavish celebration took place in the *kisa* year of 1809, when I was seventy-five years old, and my husband was long dead and buried (and indeed exhumed and reburied). With hands gloved in white cotton, my ghostly representative turned the pages of this valuable and handsome volume, beneath the sharp eyes of its custodians. You do not have to go all the way to Korea to see this manuscript, for, like the Elgin Marbles, it has come to rest in the British Museum in London, via a curious route involving a French admiral and a French bakery.

(I have discovered that it was purchased from the French by the British in 1891. I wonder if it will ever be restored to its native land? Perhaps I could make a nuisance of myself by persuading my envoy to agitate for its return? What right had the French then or the British now to this Korean artefact? Personally, I think that such narrowly nationalistic attitudes towards such rightly treasured artefacts are misguided, but it would be easy to play devil's advocate and make an inconveniently plausible case for the manuscript's return.)

Looking at these images through my envoy's modern eyes brought back to me many memories of formal court life, and of the more intimate scene of my defloration. My father-in-law would not have liked the sight of the red blood on the pale sheets of the nuptial bed, although the shedding of this blood signified the conception of an heir.

King Yŏngjo was fastidious and asthmatic, and at times he vacillated. But despite these weaknesses he had a strong will, and, unlike his son and his grandson, he lived to a venerable age. His was one of the longest reigns of any monarch in the history of the world.

I digress. I was attempting to recapture that vanished world of ceremony, but I find in myself an understandable reluctance to recall the day of the consummation. Oh, I had been well instructed. I knew my fate. The matron of my bedchamber had herself explored my body in preparation. She said that it would ease the passage. She was a sadist and a liar. I think she was perverted. I do not think these explorations were customary, as she claimed they were. I think they gratified her in some manner. But I was at her mercy. I knew no better. I submitted. As children do.

It would have been better to have left the task to Sado himself, for in those early days he was not without gentleness and ardour. I think, in those early days, he liked me.

The illustrated manuscript in the British Museum, captured from its hiding place by Admiral Rozé, shows in intricate documentary detail the grandeur and the expense of the reverence which my grandson the king paid to me, the survivor, the matriarch. You can see the screens of crimson lacquer; you can see the pale green roof ornaments; you can see the billowing cream silk canopies; you can see the hangings of vast pink painted peonies; you can see the serried ranks of courtiers in robes of carmine and sage green and peacock blue. You can see the gifts displayed upon tables, and the women with their parasols and their fans, and their intricate and elegant hair ornaments standing proudly a foot high. You can see the officials prostrated low upon woven sedge mats. There are the candlesticks and the flags and the pennants and the candles and the incense stands. There is the great orchestra, and the musicians with all their instruments — the drums, the bronze bells, the stone chimes, the iron chimes, the pipes and the flutes and the triangles and the ivory clappers. And there is my throne, the elegant delicate silver throne, with its frame of red lacquered wood.

(Red lacquer was once a royal prerogative, though by this time the merchant classes were beginning to appropriate it, despite the king's objections. Change was coming, even to our allegedly frozen land.)

The silver throne is empty. I am not depicted. I am not there. I have no name, and I am not there. It was forbidden to depict me. No queen could ever sit for a male painter. No men could dance before the queen, and the musicians who played in the inner court to the queen were blind — just as, in your day, I am told that only blind masseurs may obtain a licence to practise traditional massage in Korea. There were many absences, many prohibitions. Some linger after death.

But although my portrait could not be included in this empty scene, although no image of me at that ceremony or at any other ceremony survives, although my very names have perished, I was there. In that year, in the *kisa* year, in

1809, at the age of seventy-five, I was there. I was there for the presentations and for the dancing and the music and the speeches and the relays of banquets. They were in my honour. I sat immobile and with perfect decorum, with royal decorum, upon that slight throne. I received homage. How heavily weighed those elaborate and beautiful ornaments upon my head — the jade, the ivory, the blossoming and trembling sprays of jewels, the ebony combs. And as I sat there, through the long day of hardly tolerable ritual boredom and banqueting, I cast my mind back to those early days at court, when I was a little child, when I had to practise court behaviour. I rarely made a false step. I schooled myself towards perfection. I rose early, and rehearsed for hours in solitude, for I was afraid. Sixty years later, I remembered my husband in his childhood and that bodily consummation, so many decades ago. I sat on the throne and thought of him, so terribly tormented, so long dead, and now lying at last in a new city in his splendid shrine in state.

I visited that splendid shrine, on another, earlier state occasion, when I was a mere sixty years old. It was one of the few journeys I made in my imprisoned and privileged life. I will come to that. That, too, was well recorded, well documented. I will return to that. I will try to send my envoy to that scene.

As I have said, Prince Sado and I were married for five years before the consummation took place. It was five years of study for him, and of a different kind of study for me. We were both

43

precocious, and precociously placed. He had been more fully exposed to high expectations than I. I had been allowed a little space of carefree childhood, in my early infancy, but he had been allowed none. From the moment of his birth, he had been watched over. His every gesture was attended, first by wet nurses, then by nurses, then by tutors. He was attended by slaves and eunuchs and ladies-in-waiting and spies. Every sign and sound he made was interpreted as a sign of his princely genius. If he pointed at a written character and made a noise, it was greeted with cries of approbation. If he scribbled a baby's scrawl with a marker thrust into his childish fist, it was hailed as a prophecy, or as a miracle of the calligraphic arts. He was acclaimed as the most handsome, the most intelligent, the most robust, the most gifted of infants. His father the king, King Yŏngjo, disastrously doted upon him, looking to him to redress all the wrongs of the family, to make payment for all the crimes that he had himself committed. Having neglected him in his earliest years, he overcompensated in his later childhood. This was bad judgement.

King Yŏngjo had waited long for his son's birth, and he was forty-two when this male heir was born. He had lost his first son some seven years earlier, an event which had shaken the royal succession and caused rebellion, ferment, tortures, executions. Sado was destined to rescue the state from these divisions. He was to reconcile those deadly factions, the Noron and the Soron, and to bring in an era of Heavenly

44

Peace. There was much rejoicing, too much rejoicing. Too much was expected of this baby. He was expected to right the wrongs of his dynasty. He was expected to clear his father's name.

The fratricidal crime of the poisoned mushrooms was never far from King Yŏngjo's mind, although it had never been proved and was always denied. And in my view, I may now say openly, now that we are all dead, this crime had never been committed. My father-in-law King Yŏngjo had many faults, but I do not believe that he killed his brother. He lived to commit a crime far worse than that of fratricide, but I do not think he was responsible for the poisoned mushrooms.

Prince Sado was praised and adored as a baby, and surrounded by sycophantic palace ladies who tended to his every whim, picking up his toys, fastening his trousers for him, tying his laces, washing his face for him, and waiting on him hand and foot. There was no discipline in those early years. (He always hated washing his own face.) But as he grew older, as I have said, too much was demanded of him. As he grew out of the charmed estate of infancy and into boyhood, faults were constantly found in him. Those talents that he had were overlooked. I remember the days when he used to enjoy painting, which was considered an appropriate royal occupation. (I believe it remains an acceptable occupation, in the surviving royal houses of the West.) Prince Sado had a true talent for painting and calligraphy, which our son

45

and grandson inherited, but I believe that none of Prince Sado's works survives. He had a gift. Although he painted military scenes with castles and forts and armies, he also liked to paint mountains and waterfalls. He was an admirer of the new 'true view' school of landscape painting, though there were few true views that he was able to see with his own eyes, so circumscribed were his movements in his early years. It is no wonder that he wished, as he grew older, for the freedom of travel.

The claustrophobia of the court cannot be described. It was a closed world within a closed world. Sado wanted to see with his own eyes the Peony Peak, the Green Lotus Hermitage, the Magpie Bridge, the Cold Jade Pavilion, the Hot Crystal Springs, the Diamond Mountains. The very names of the places enchanted him. He painted them from his imagination, as he painted bamboo and chrysanthemums from life. Later, he destroyed most of these works himself. He was a great destroyer. All that we remember of him now is his destructive madness, and the manner of his death.

The curriculum of a student prince was punishing. Sado's father, King Yŏngjo, had been through many years of what I would now call indoctrination: he had been obliged to spend many hours and many weeks and many months studying the works of Confucius and Mencius, and the histories of the Chinese and Korean dynasties, and who knows how many other canonical and fossilized texts. He had to learn by rote and to repeat the texts word for word, and was chided for any errors. Tutors watched over him, and coached him, and examined him, and official reports were written of every success and every failure. His son Prince Sado was drilled in the same hard school. Fathers like to force their own suffering upon their sons. Although quick of intelligence, Prince Sado found his studies a great strain. When he became flustered, when he stumbled in his recitations, his father would wheeze and rant at him. Sado developed a stammer at this time, and, when he stammered, his father would yell at him, 'Spit it out, boy. Spit it out!' This was not helpful.

His father's name gave him particular difficulty. He always stammered when he had to use his father's name. Fortunately, there were many acceptable circumlocutions he could employ. But I noticed that he could not pronounce his father's name.

As I have said, our society was obsessed by examinations. As my father's life bore witness, we idolized scholarship, even the dead hand of dead scholarship. Sado, as heir to the throne, was not compelled to ascend the scholarly ladder to achieve position, but study was nevertheless demanded of him, and his failures were harshly criticized. Sado was afraid of his father. As he grew older, he would delay the daily moment at which he had to confront his father. He would refuse to dress. He would hesitate over his choice of clothes, like a woman. His fear of clothing became a mania. This became well known. His violence towards his attire passed beyond joke and gossip, and into the realm of terror.

47

I longed for red, and for many long years, as a widow, I wore white. Had I been born in modern times, were I living now, I might choose to explore the question of nakedness and dress. Of the body, and of clothing. I have now read and reread the globally disseminated Hebrew version of the sinfulness of nakedness — the story of how Adam and Eve saw that they were naked, and were ashamed — and I have compared it with other myths in other cultures. I consider that this matter has not been satisfactorily addressed. Yes, I sometimes think that, if I were to have another life on earth, I might choose to devote a few decades of it to the question of clothing and the perversions of clothing. My longing for a red silk skirt, Sado's fear of the jade beads. The golden dragon robe, the black vest, the butcher's hated bamboo hat with leather strings. How could these longings and fears have dug in so deep, with their white roots? How could they have caused so many deaths, of such innocent, lowly, harmless people? What are garments but the outer clothing of the spirit? And yet men have killed for them, and been cruelly abased by them.

When I was mortal, I stole most of my learning from books translated into the vernacular. I learned *han'gŭl* early and easily, encouraged by my learned aunt. *Han'gŭl* was the ingenious and scientific phonetic alphabet so brilliantly devised six centuries ago, during the Golden Age of King Sejong. We did not call it by the name of '*han'gŭl*', a name which was not given to it until the twentieth century, but we could all read it. It is much more accessible than classical Chinese, though that, too, I studied with some success. King Sejong did not, of course, create this script single-handed, but he was, I believe, personally responsible for appointing the committee of scholars who devised it, and to him goes the honour of the vision of a more widely accessible written language, which would not exclude the common people. (Careless accounts in tourist guides to our country credit King Sejong himself with the invention of the alphabet, just as, I note, North Korea now attributes the twentieth-century invention of massed dance notation to the Dear Leader, Kim Jong Il, the son of the Eternal President, Kim Il Sung. I think King Sejong was a cleverer man and a better monarch than the Dear Leader Kim Jong Il, but of course, I am a southerner, and I permit myself to retain some of my prejudices in death.)

When I was young, I read everything I could lay my hands upon. I stole learning from my clever young aunt, who was willing to teach me. I stole from Prince Sado, who in those early years was willing to talk to me about history and about literature and about the Confucian texts. I was an eager and a secret scholar. I stole and stored the scraps I thought I might need. Learning was not forbidden to women, but nor was it freely offered to them. I think, now, that my exemption from the masculine curriculum and the state examination system was a blessing in disguise: unlike my husband, I was able to sharpen my wits without fear of failure. But at times, when I was young, I envied those who had more access to learning. The luckiest women, in this respect, were the *kisaeng*, those courtesans of the *demi-monde* who were expected to be literate and well informed in the arts. In its treatment of women, our society and our civilization resembled most that the world has known. These days, women sift through the sands of past time for cultures when women were learned and held power, but they have not yet discovered much. They look back to the stone ages for lost matriarchies, but little has yet been revealed. There were powerful queens and empresses, even in our own land, long ago in the Silla period, and there are Korean fairy stories about powerful and adored princesses, as there are in every culture. But, for the most part, women's power was exercised through men. As mine was, for I lived in repressive times. I take no little credit for the survival of my son and my grandson. I fought for their lives. They owed their lives to me in double trust, by my blood and by my wit.

But, I repeat, I failed my husband Prince Sado. I could not help him. Nor could I help my third and perhaps my most loved brother, Nagim, who died in exile. So many died in exile. It was a common fate. Nor could I save my uncle Hong Inhan, who was executed, I fear through my fault. I saved my son and lost my uncle. These were hard times, hard choices.

Although I am dead and immortal, I cannot read the undiscovered past. I have to wait for some mortal human agency to dig it up for me.

50

It is slow, and at times I grow impatient. These mortal human agents were, through most of the nineteenth and twentieth centuries, called archaeologists and anthropologists and historians. They are joined now, in the exploration of the past, by geneticists and evolutionary biologists. Were I to have a second or a third time on earth again, perhaps I would choose to be reborn as an evolutionary biologist. But I am a ghost, and I am not free. I can speculate, but I cannot rend the veil that obscures the past. I have my envoy, and she has her envoys, but all these emissaries have their temporal and corporeal and local limitations. As a ghost, I am denied easy access even to some of the discoveries that have been made about my life and times. My life was full of prohibitions, and not all of them have passed with my death. Ghosts, too, have their restrictions.

Our system, the Confucian system, was a dead system. It was centuries dead long before I was born. It did not move forward, in the eighteenth century, towards the universalism of the Enlightenment, though, despite its rigid hierarchies, it had some universalist tenets and tendencies of its own. But the systems of belief that have succeeded it are also dead. All religions, all faiths are dead, though some still make a false show of survival. It is simply that Confucianism endured for more centuries than most.

I do not blame Confucius for the destruction of my husband. I could, I suppose, do so, if I wished to be ingenious, and to apportion blame far from where it must rest. But Confucius did not lay down the code and the manner in which the father must kill the son and the son the father. Nor did Aeschylus, who was a contemporary of Confucius, invent this code. Nor did their near-successor Sophocles. They neither prescribed nor proscribed. They simply described what was, and what had been, in the bloody history of our ugly species. There is no moral to the story of Oedipus.

We in the palace, of course, knew nothing of the ancient Greeks, and I still have much to learn about them. But, largely isolated though we were and chose to be, we were not entirely ignorant, even in those mortal days, of the arts and sciences and superstitions of the West. A hundred years before my birth, our Crown Prince Sohyŏn had spent some years in China, and he and his envoys returned with books and stories and artefacts and paintings that showed us something of life in Europe. He brought a terrestrial globe, showing us for the first time the Western view of the shape of the world. We saw the Western global view, though I cannot say that we liked it. I am told that none of these objects has survived the many anti-Western purges that followed, but I remember seeing with my own eyes an oil painting of the crucifixion of Christ, brought by the Jesuits to Yenching, and thence to our court in Seoul. And I remember that I wondered at the barbarity of the West, which devised such bizarre tortures, and I was puzzled that a culture which committed such atrocities should wish to export and advertise them. I also saw books of engravings, which were full of scenes of tortures and decapitations and castrations and other so-called martyrdoms. I did not care for these foreign images, as a child or as a woman. But it may be that the art that reached us was inferior art, second-rate art, export art. Cheap missionary art, for undiscerning foreigners.

I have since discovered that what I then in my ignorance took to be portrayals of the cruel ceremonial castration of a royal male baby were in fact portrayals of the circumcision of Christ, a subject for some reason particularly dear to the Jesuits. I knew nothing, when I was alive, of the religious significance of these images, but, as a mother of boys, I did not like the way the sharp metal instruments hovered over the infant's small and tender parts. Nor did I like the way that fat and naked cherubs improbably hovered in the sky, looking complacently down upon this unpleasant event. (In our country, in those days, the custom of circumcision was unknown, though I believe it is now very widely practised. It is one of our more curious twentieth-century American imports.) The only Western image which pleased me was a lacquered portrait of a royal mother and child, painted on gold-dusted wood and inlaid with mother-of-pearl. I liked this image of maternity, and I approved of the power invested in the mother figure.

I do not deny that we had our own atrocities. We had our decapitations and our castrations. But we did not celebrate them in art. Our aesthetic was fastidious. Our court art may have lacked the art of perspective, but it was refined and it was delicate. It did not portray gross carnal acts or crude painted idols. It was an art of flowers and fish and birds and butterflies and blossoms.

I was brought up in much bodily ignorance, and I dreaded the moment of consummation. I dreaded failure and rejection. Princesses who failed to conceive were often condemned to a hard and lonely life. As my fifteenth birthday approached, my mother and my aunt had tried to tell me the rituals of the marriage bed, and our slave Pongnyŏ and my wet nurse Aji had whispered and giggled and sniggered about these secret female matters to me. My mother told me my duty, and told me that it would be fulfilled if I were to submit silently to the act, and to continue to respect my husband. My mother respected my father. I had been witness to this. I knew my duty. It was my duty to conceive and to bear an heir. My small, soft, nubile body within its cocoon of silk and brocade was a sacred vessel, and it must be filled with the royal sperm and bring forth a son. The body of my husband in those early days was as shiny and smooth and yellow as a grub. What a dreadful metamorphosis awaited us both!

I think Prince Sado feared the event as much as I. Already he lived in fear of his father — not the violent terror of his later adult years, but an anxious, fretting, nagging fear of failure. His father's admonitory spirit accompanied us to the marriage bed. But we performed our duty to the satisfaction of all, and I duly conceived and bore

54

my first son, to the rejoicing of the court and, I am told, the common people — though who can tell what the common people think or feel? They may have nourished hatred rather than joy. I never saw the common people living their common life. I glimpsed them through the curtains of my palanquin when I was sixty years of age, as they lined the roads of my royal progress, and I was curious about them. But it was too late. Too late.

The act of sex seems to give pleasure to most men, and they seek it, sometimes to their peril. My father-in-law the king had more than one wife: this was his duty. (His first wife and primary consort, Queen Chŏngsŏng, one of the three Gracious Majesties who loomed over my marriage bed, was childless.) But I think the fact that he took a young consort quite late in life, and a young consort of a lower caste who bore children who were the age of our children, was deeply unsettling to Prince Sado. (Sado was very attached to the childless Queen Chŏngsŏng, his stepmother, who always took his part.) It must have seemed to Prince Sado that his father would live and procreate and dominate and criticize his son for ever. He would never be free of his father. This is what he must have thought. And he was right.

Prince Sado, after our marriage, took secondary wives and concubines, as was customary, and he also lay with nuns and prostitutes, which cannot have been his duty. It is even said that he slept with his younger sister, Madame Chŏng, the favoured daughter of their father. It may have

55

been so. Certainly their relationship was unnaturally intense, and some of the events towards the end of Sado's life might best be explained by such an involvement. But the rumour of incest may have been a malicious fabrication, like the story of fratricide. Such stories are common in royal circles, in all countries. It was clear that this sister hated me, but she had many other reasons to hate me. All I wish to say in this context is that the act of marital sex gave me no pleasure at all. Maybe it pleases some women of other social orders, or in other lands. But for me, the act was so bound, so circumscribed, of such a deadly importance. It was like an examination — like those examinations over which my father and my brothers slaved so diligently in the search for advancement and enlightenment. I passed, but at what cost?

I have observed, in the animal kingdom, that the female of the species seems to receive little delight from coitus. Who has not seen a cockerel mount a hen, or a dog a bitch? The female endures the indignity, shakes itself, and moves off. There is tenderness and fidelity, I am told, between some species of birds, and even of fish, but I have never observed it. Mandarin ducks are an emblem of marital fidelity and appear on many a painted screen, as well as on the one my father-in-law gave to me: they are said to pair for life and to grieve if a partner dies. I have not observed this phenomenon with my own eyes. I cannot read the expression of a grieving drake or duck. But the paintings are pretty enough.

Indeed mine, as I have said, was more than pretty. It was a painting of paradise.

When I was a girl of about twelve years old, a married princess but still a maiden girl, I had a pet kitten. She was a gift from some emissary from a foreign kingdom of the west; I forget its name. Siam, perhaps, or Burma? We were not distinguished as a cat-loving or cat-worshipping nation, but I was allowed to keep this kitten as a pet. She was such a pretty creature, cream and beige in her colours, and gentle and soft in her ways, and affectionate towards me. One day, as we were playing in the palace compound, a large, wild, black-and-white tomcat leaped down from the roof tiles into the courtyard, and chased her and cornered her and mounted her.

I cried because I thought he was killing her, but Pongnyŏ told me that no harm was being done, though the act had appeared to me to be an act of aggression. And indeed there was no harm, for the cat conceived and bore three of the most charming kittens you could ever have seen. The expression and demeanour of bored and subdued indifference with which she had endured the tomcat's crude and rude assault was succeeded by such purring, such delight, such pride, such pleasure! Even as she gave birth, she purred in ecstasy. She nudged and licked and caressed her little blind blunt-headed babes, and taught them how to nurse from her teats. She was the most tender and gentle of mothers, although she was little more than a kitten herself. Her motherhood gave both her and me great delight, and watching her kittens play was

57

one of the happiest memories of my early married life. The kittens would chase one another round the garden amongst the stalks of the chrysanthemums, and climb up the cherry trees and the gnarled junipers, and hide behind the big leaves of the foxglove tree. They would stalk sparrows on the gravel, and try to pounce on butterflies. They were fastidious in their manners, cleaning and grooming themselves diligently. They would neatly bury their small messes in the earth. They were so clean that I allowed them to sleep upon my bed in a small bundle, and they would nestle in the silver ewer or the white porcelain vase in my chamber. They charmed even Pongnyŏ and Aji. I smile now, to think of them. Who *taught* their mother to teach them? My little cat was gentle, motherly and wise. She loved her kittens. Her love was inborn. It was her nature.

I was that mother cat. When my first son was born, in 1750, such a passion of adoration and love broke in my breast, like the breaking of the waters of my womb. I was suffused with warmth. I reached out my arms to him and wept with joy. I was very young. I was in my sixteenth year.

I tell you this because it has been said that my love of my sons was politic. It has been said that all my conduct was governed by personal ambition and family pride, and by a selfish will to survive. And so in part it may have been, for it was indeed my duty to survive. I had to survive for my son. How could I separate myself from him? He was of my body; he was of my lineage; he was my future; he was the future of his country; he held in his fists the future of his maternal grandparents and uncles and aunts. Both the Hong family and the Yi dynasty depended upon him. He was the heir to the heir. But it was not for this that I loved this poor, helpless little scrap of being. I protest that I loved him with a love that was pure and spontaneous and unselfish, as my little cat loved her kittens. He was the first joy and the first love of my life. He was my own.

And his father loved him, too. I could weep now as I remember the broad smile of paternal pride on Prince Sado's face, as he picked up the little tightly swaddled bundle and gazed into its sleepy, half-closed eyes. Prince Sado, now formally designated the prince regent, was like a child in his delight. He hoped that the birth of little Prince Ŭiso would conciliate his father the king, and prove a new bond between them. He attended the ceremony of the ritual burial of the placenta and navel cord, and reported that it had been attended by many good omens. He was full of hope. He was sure that his father would relent and treat him more affectionately. He was aware that he had been a disappointment to his father, and hoped now to win his trust. I, too, now hoped for better times.

But things did not turn out as we expected and desired.

His Majesty King Yŏngjo was not appeased by the birth of my first-born. His irritability and fits of anger with Sado continued. I think this anger was connected with the recent death of his third daughter, the much-favoured Princess Hwap'yŏng, who had died in childbirth a little more than a year earlier, but whose death he still bitterly and very publicly mourned and lamented. It had been a hard year for the whole nation, the year of her death, a year of famine and epidemics, during which many of the common people died. The birth of our son Ŭiso merely rekindled his grief over this earlier loss, and not one word of good will or congratulation did he send to his only son or to me on the birth of our first child. I concealed my sense of indignation, but Prince Sado was deeply hurt, and had a right to be so.

Princess Hwap'yŏng had always been kind to her little brother Sado, and to me, his child bride, and had tried to mitigate the effects of her father's marked and unusual partiality for her. She had spoken up boldly for her little brother on many occasions, but to little avail. She had been motherly to me, and would have been my friend had I not been so much in awe of her. Her death had caused terrible distress to her father King Yŏngjo, who went into deep mourning. He had himself been in ill health this year, there had been unrest in the court, and he had been threatening after twenty-three years on the throne to abdicate.

I believe his threat was rhetorical, for he loved the flattery of those who pleaded with him to remain at the helm of the ship of state, and made many empty threats of this nature. But I concede that there was an exhaustion in him in these times, and I observed that the death of Princess Hwap'yŏng exacerbated his tendency to asthma. Nor do I believe that the traditional medicinal

60

concoctions of blue-flower campanula root prescribed by his secondary consort, Sado's mother Lady Sŏnhŭi, were beneficial, but that is another matter. Asthma, in my view, is often a temperamental affliction, and responds poorly to medicines. I do not wish to suggest that the Lady Sŏnhŭi was a poisoner, despite my grievances against her at this time, but by this stage in my court life I was beginning to suspect that she might be a dangerous influence. It is in the nature of courts to be full of suspicions, and it is in the nature of a daughter-in-law to distrust her mother-in-law. Relations between mothers-in-law and daughters-in-law in our country have always been notoriously difficult, and I believe remain so.

I could have survived the neglect of little Ŭiso by his grandfather had it not been for my growing sense that this tiny and beloved first-born child of mine was not robust. The birth was easy enough, for a first delivery — my mother was able to be with me, although she was seven months pregnant herself, and was soon to give birth to Fourth Brother — and I benefited from her help and her experience. But then she had to leave the palace, for her own confinement, and I was left to make my own decisions. The baby seemed to do well in his first two months, but after this period he failed to thrive. I hired a new wet nurse, having formed suspicions about my first appointment, and for a while he seemed a little better, but I could tell that there was something amiss. He was given to little shaking seizures, and often vomited up his food.

61

His bowels became affected, and he did not gain weight. I protested against the administering of dried frog broth, which was considered a sovereign remedy for malnourished infants, but in the end I was overruled, and spoonfuls of it were fed to him. I do not suppose it did him either harm or good.

How to tell of my despair at his sickness? I cast my mind back through the annals of the royal house, seeking precedents, and naturally I found them. There was evidence of both physical and mental disability in the Yi dynasty, and it is my belief that King Yŏngjo's brother, Sado's uncle, the King of the Poisoned Mushroom, had suffered from a mental condition that had unfitted him even for the brief rule he enjoyed. (To be frank, I believe he was even madder than his near contemporary King George III of England: some of his reported utterances suggest a complete lack of grasp of reality, though of course, as he was king, people did not like to contradict him.) And although Prince Sado's mother, Lady Sŏnhŭi, came from stronger stock, she had lost two brothers in infancy. There was sickness also in my family line. The Korean aristocracy and gentlefolk — the yangban class, as we were called — were naturally much inbred, as a result of our policy of national isolation. We on our peninsula were almost an island folk. Hereditary illnesses were common. We loathed the Japanese, who had invaded us, and we had no respect for the usurping Ching dynasty of China, who had overthrown the Ming. (We remained devoted to the memory of our earlier allies, the gracious and cultivated Ming, and considered ourselves to be their true and only heirs.)

I think now that my first baby Ŭiso suffered from a weakness of the immune system. We did not then know that such a system existed. There was nothing that could then have been done to save him. Even had this diagnosis been possible, no cure would have been available. Cures for these weaknesses are not readily available now, even though so much more is known about genes and heredity. Even in this age of transplants and gene therapy, some weaknesses remain incurable.

It is now my belief that Ŭiso inherited his weakness from his paternal side.

I spoke to nobody of my fears for Ŭiso, for I did not wish to alert jealous and vindictive attention to my son's delicate state, but within myself I nursed a deadly fear. I would hold him against my breast and feel the beating of his frail heart against mine. His little chest was so small and thin, and his heart beat and fluttered against his ribs. His ribcage was like the ribcage of a starved rabbit. He smelled of sour milk, poor thing, however often his clothes were changed and freshened. I had a premonition that he was not long for this world. I would whisper poems and lullabies to him, and sing little songs of my own composition, and croon him to sleep in my arms. His soft black hair grew from a whorl on the back of his head, in a concentric circle. So sweet, so neat, so perfect. I had bad dreams, in which I saw the jealous ghost of the late princess, falsely smiling. She came to my bedchamber during the night to claim my child, to carry him away to the Yellow Springs of the underworld. She had died in labour, and she envied me my son.

I think I was somewhat paranoid, at this time, imagining harm even where there was none.

Prince Ŭiso was a sad and serious infant. His fingers were long and thin and delicate. He rarely smiled. But he would gaze at me intently when I spoke to him. His eyes were very large in his small face. He seemed to question me, as he gazed at me, but I did not know the answer.

He survived his hundredth day, and we celebrated it in the correct manner, but I was not sure that he would reach his second birthday, which would mark the next landmark in his life. I tried to hide my fears from him, but I think he could see into my thoughts.

A little after this hundredth-day ceremony, when Prince Ŭiso was about five months old, his paternal grandparents King Yŏngjo and the Lady Sŏnhŭi unexpectedly came to my quarters to visit the baby. King Yŏngjo, who rarely left Seoul, was about to depart on a diplomatic and ceremonial visit to the celebrated hot spring resort of Onyang, forty miles south of the capital. He seemed at this time to wish to be reconciled with Sado and myself. I wished to protect my darling from them, hoping they would not notice his weakness, but they insisted not only on seeing him, but also on stripping him of his clothes to examine his body. Their reaction to what they saw was curious and wilful, although in some ways not unwelcome. Prince Ŭiso had distinctive birthmarks on his body — one on his shoulder and one on his belly — which I had noticed while I was bathing him. These were marks of no great import, and in my view of utter insignificance in comparison with the sadness of his wasted little frame, which weighed less than that of many a month-old child. But the king and his lady, in their ignorance and their stupidity and their superstition, did not notice his bodily weakness — no, they seized upon these as signs that he was a reincarnation of his aunt, the late Princess Hwap'yŏng, who, they claimed, had borne similar marks upon her body! Have you ever heard the like of such nonsense?

From this moment, however, their attitude to the baby changed, and he became much favoured. This was not to my advantage. He was moved from my apartments to the Hwan'gyŏng Pavilion, which was lavishly refurbished to receive him, and every attention was showered upon him. When he was ten months old, Prince Ŭiso was designated Grand Heir and Royal Grandson by Yŏngjo. I was dismayed when this was announced, but I was obliged to mouth my gratitude. I knew this elevation spelled ill luck, and so it proved. My baby was doomed. In their folly, they ignored the symptoms of his frailty and continued blindly to promote him as a royal marvel. The mother cat in me could have scratched out their eyes.

The Grand Heir, poor little mite, died in the spring of 1752. For all his pompous titles and rich garments and prostrated slave attendants and subservient eunuchs, he died, as sick babies do. Mercifully, he died peacefully, in his sleep. I was by his side. As he lay on his crib, he breathed his last, a long, shuddering last breath, then passed silently away. I was plunged into silent and private grief, for I chose not to compete with the public pomp of desolation that greeted the news of his death. I had learned to conceal the depths of my emotions, and maybe my attendants thought me cold and unfeeling, but in truth I was in despair. Believe me, I mourned my little son, and not my place at court, or my status as mother of the Grand Heir. He was my baby, and the first great love of my life. My nature grieved, and not my dignity.

Prince Sado said a kind thing to me at this sad moment. 'My little Red Queen,' he said, 'you bear no blame for this sad event. You have been a good mother to our little one, whatever they may say of you, and our next child shall be blessed.' Those were his very words. How could I forget them? How could I ever be made to believe that Prince Sado was nothing but a weak and evil man?

Evil, in my view, is a word that has been much abused.

Mercifully, Prince Sado's prophecy was fulfilled. I was already pregnant when Ŭiso died, and my second son, of glorious and majestic memory, was born that autumn. He was born on an auspicious day in an auspicious year, sixty years after the birth of his childless step-grandmother Queen Chŏngsŏng, who claimed that he was an answer to her prayer. Sado and I greeted his arrival with joy. We have all heard tales of mothers who have turned against their surviving children through the loss of one, and who have grieved rather than rejoiced over new births. And I understand these reactions, for the loss of a child is like no other loss and can drive one to irrationality, to wildness and despair. But my second son, Chŏngjo, was from the moment of his birth a joy to me, and a compensation for his brother's death. I used to dream that the two little brothers played together in the garden, and these dreams comforted me. I induced these benign dreams. I learned to dream them at will. I was never to forget Ŭiso — now, even in eternity, I remember him — but I did not turn my face or my breast from Chŏngjo. My bondswoman Pongnyŏ brought me rice and seaweed soup, traditional fare to build up the strength of a nursing mother, and I in turn nursed my baby. I nursed him myself for some weeks, which might perhaps have been considered improper, had it been widely known. A ceremonial presentation of the royal nipple was all that was usually expected of a princess, but I wanted to feel the baby at the breast, and now I have that memory, though it was soon, and for good reason, snatched from me. I had always suspected that Ŭiso's wet nurse, despite my careful choice of her, might have carried some infection to him, and I wished to avoid any repetition of this possibility. Maybe, I wondered, it had been worse than an infection — who knows what may happen in the jealous byways of a palace? My mother, who was able to be with me for some of this period, supported me in this decision — though I have to say that my mother's mental and physical health were not good. She was always anxious, always sickly, always full of apprehensions.

But I need not have feared for my second-born, for Chŏngjo was a sturdy and robust child from birth. He was as strong as his brother Ŭiso had been weak. He latched on to the teat boldly and took his food greedily; he never regurgitated one drop or morsel. He was put early to the test. When he was only three weeks old, there was a serious health scare, for a measles epidemic broke out in the city and the palace. Measles, in those days, was a much-feared illness. Although strict etiquette forbade me or the baby to leave our quarters for twenty-one days after my confinement, the court physicians of the Medical Bureau insisted that the baby prince be moved, and he was taken to Naksŏn Hall, in another part of the palace compound. There I arranged for him to be tended by an elderly lady-in-waiting and by my own wet nurse: I was not too anxious for him, for already in his short life he had shown a firmer will to survive than Ŭiso had ever manifested. That very day, despite our diligent efforts to appease the measles spirits with rice cake and herbs, Prince Sado himself was also taken very ill. (If you address the spirits of measles or of smallpox politely, as 'distinguished guests', and feed them properly, they are supposed to take pity on their hosts and move on to other

68

dwellings — that is our superstition, and it is one that for some reason, rational though I am, I have always been tempted to observe. Why should we not be polite to microbes? We lose nothing by courtesy.)

I, still weak from childbirth, caught the disease, too, though my case was not as severe as that of my husband. Baby Chŏngjo's case was very mild, and he recovered before either of his parents. He was a tenacious child.

My father conducted himself heroically during this epidemic, dividing his attention between Sado, myself and his new royal grandson Chŏngjo, on whom all our hopes depended. We were all housed in different residences in the palace compound, and the distances were not short: he was our go-between, tirelessly trudging from one to another across the lawns and up the steep steps and granite slopes. He always said that it was the crisis of the measles that made his beard turn white, but as far as I can remember, to be honest with you, it was prematurely white before this episode. Many of the palace servants fell ill and some died. I recovered first, and, in the absence of his usual attendants, I was able to go to nurse Prince Sado myself; I remember sitting by his bed with cool rice water and vinegar, and herbal infusions, as my father read to him, hour after hour, from the old Chinese histories, of campaigns and victories and defeats in centuries long ago. It was through such hours of eavesdropping that I acquired much of my knowledge of the past.

Prince Sado's sister Princess Hwahyŏp, the

seventh daughter of His Majesty, died of the measles at this time — in fact, she had been the first to catch it, and she was blamed by some malicious gossips as the source of the infection. She had brought it into the palace from the town, and there were dark hints as to where she had contracted it. Measles was a killer then, as it can be now, and we knew nothing of vaccination. There was no such practice in our time. It is true that the Turks had long been acquainted with the practice of vaccination against smallpox, which was already being introduced to the West, but measles was still an uncontrollable disease. We were right to fear the illness. Princess Hwahyŏp, like Sado, had not been loved by her father. She was a great beauty, but for some reason her father was always cold towards her. Their disfavoured and rejected status had been a bond between brother and sister, and her death was a blow to Sado, leaving him more lonely than ever. Another sister, another ally gone.

Our son Chŏngjo recovered from his illness rapidly, and put on weight fast. I always remember my little sister, who was then about six years of age, coming into the bedchamber and saying, when she first saw him, 'What a *huge* baby! He's *enormous*! He's not going to cause you any trouble, I can tell you!' (She was obliged to address me formally, as 'Your Ladyship', but she could be quite irreverent, even while employing the courtly rules.) Chŏngjo, who was then about three months old, smiled and chuckled when she tickled him, and all the ladies of the bedchamber laughed. And it is true, he

70

was very plump. After the wasting illness of my first-born, this was a great relief, as you can imagine. I had feared, for a while, that I was a bad vessel, a transmitter of poor health.

But I must also record that my little sister, who herself was also to meet a sad fate, had wept silently over her baby nephew Ŭiso's death. I would not like to suggest that she was insensitive, poor girl. I fear that my fate overshadowed hers, and added to her sorrows, but that is another part of the story, which will not be told here. Then, she was young and bright and cheerful, though precocious for her years. We were a gifted and confident family. Our gifts attracted much resentment.

Yes, our son Chŏngjo seemed set to reinstate his father and myself in the good books of His Majesty. He was a fine-looking baby, handsome and strong like his father. I watched over him carefully, for all our fates, as well as my own happiness, depended upon him.

But the birth of Chŏngjo did not reconcile Prince Sado and his father, as I had hoped and expected. After the measles epidemic, things grew even worse between them. I have often heard His Majesty say that it would have been better if Sado had died of the measles. He wished his own son dead. What cruelties there are in words! These words had a truth in them, but they should never have been spoken.

At this time, a rumour began to circulate that Prince Sado had given new currency to that old story about the fratricide and the poisoned mushrooms, and was spreading slander about his

71

father, and plotting against him. There was not a word of truth in this cowardly attack, but King Yŏngjo took it upon himself to go through a ludicrous parade of prostrating himself in denunciation at the Sŏnhwa Gate of Seoul, crying out against his son the prince regent and the accusing memorial sent by a censor to the court.

It was by now bitter winter and the snow was deep. Our city is surrounded by steep mountains: their bare grey rocks look down upon us coldly even in summer, and in winter their peaks are clothed in white. Sado, compelled by court etiquette to attempt to outdo his father, went to the gate and awaited his punishment there in the open air, in an exaggerated display of remorse and penitence. He knelt on a straw mat, and beat his head upon the stones until it bled. The snow fell thick upon him, until he became a man of snow, white with rime, like a ghost from the mountains. And he had but lately recovered from the measles. My fury with both father and son was boundless. I despised their childish, empty, theatrical displays. I, of course, stayed at home in the palace, well wrapped in layers of padded garments and a fur-trimmed gown, with my feet tucked under the table and warmed by the comforting heat that rose through the brown polished floorboards from the stoked furnaces below. The modest glow of a charcoal brazier kept me company: my attendants faithfully fed its soft dull red heart. I tucked myself into my bed that freezing night, 'warm on my duck-embroidered pillow, beneath my kingfisher quilt', as the old poet has it. I kept myself safe.

I hid away in my warm winter retreat, and while Sado and his father played deadly games at the city gate, I, within, played childish games with my little boy. I rolled a pomegranate, and he crawled after it. The charms on the little golden bracelets round his dimpled, chubby wrists and ankles made a music that pleased us both. He laughed with delight when I hid my face behind my fan, then revealed it. These are the games of all children of all ages of all the peoples of the earth. The descendant kittens of my first little cat (she now being dead) would play with the little prince, and pounce and bounce around him. Let those grown men play their stupid games, I said to myself in the bitterness of my fearful heart, we in here, in this safe place, will try to keep ourselves warm, and guard our innocent spirits from the demons of pride and hatred.

Ah, my little prince, how beautifully in the end you justified the promise of your boyhood! My heart's darling, you were so gifted and so beautiful. It breaks my heart to think of the unmentionable tragedy and wickedness that you were forced to witness. You were exposed to horror, you were led into temptation and disgrace, you were manipulated by those you thought your friends, yet you survived and triumphed over them, and I am here to tell and to retell your tale, as I told and retold it upon earth.

The dim glow of the charcoal, the oiled veneer of the polished floor, the gold-red sheen of the tender veins of the living rosewood, the soft secret road of the silk, the cool green of the jade.

So your father Sado crouched in penitence in the snow, and the snow drifted down upon him and coated him and clothed him with the white robes of mourning. The flakes settled on his royal robes. He became a cold statue of grief. And still he was not forgiven. His father was a remorseless, relentless man. Has any father ever so tormented his son? And yet to the end of his long life on earth I had to sing the praises of this wilful old man, your grandfather. Our history remembers him as a great monarch, but he was also capricious, vindictive, unfatherly. Our society laid such stress on the filial virtues: the child must honour the parent, no matter how ill that parent has conducted himself towards his child. How could Sado not run mad? He was spurned and rejected and tormented. How could he honour such a cruel father? He was caught in a trap from which there was no escape. I thought bitterly of these paradoxes, as I watched you take your first steps. You were so eager to please, so full of unwary smiles. And I, too, more wary, was also eager to please. One false step, one unwise word, and you would be taken from me as too precious for my care. You tottered over the reed mat, and fell, and laughed, and heaved yourself up again, and tottered bravely on. I walked on ice, on knives, on dragons' teeth.

My father tried to be a comfort to me, during these difficult years, but he was delicately placed. He had to watch his every step. Intrigue surrounded him, and his motives were always suspect, for it was widely and not wholly wrongly believed that his first concern was not for the kingdom, but for the prosperity and survival of his own family line. How often in dark moments he must have regretted my selection as bride of the Crown Prince! Now I was learning to interpret the deep gloom which had overcome both my parents when I had passed through the last of those three bridal selection processes, when I had passed, as it were, the first grades of the examinations of my life. No wonder they feared for me and for themselves. But they had chosen to allow my name to be advanced, had they not? My fate was on their heads.

Some of my family chose — or were forced to choose — to live as scholars of the cave and the mountain, hidden from the eyes of envy, tending their gardens and writing poems about herons and flowering reeds and moons and butterflies and waterfalls. But my father had a restless ambition and a desire for the glories of this world. And in me there had been a desire for that red silk skirt.

Did my parents ever love me, as I loved my children? As I loved my dead little first-born, my surviving son and my two daughters? I cannot tell whether they did or did not. Politics intervened so early in our lives. For me, maternal love was a consuming passion, and in vain do the wise and the cynical point out to me that in my case the interests of maternal passion coincided with the material interests of myself and my family. Yes, it was so. But still, I remember the mother cat. Over the decades since my death, I have thought much of these matters, and I have made many comparisons of my fate with the fates and life stories of others. It now seems to me that it may be that all my passions were driven, as it were, into one narrow channel. Driven by circumstance of history, of family, of character. The force of my nature was very considerable. We human creatures are not born equal. We are not blank slates or lumps of putty. We are born with unequal passions and attributes. I was born with a powerful spirit, and it was dammed up in me. In other societies, it could perhaps have flowed more evenly, less violently. But in my time, in my lonely place, it could find no other object but my sons. I was driven back into a primitive maternal obsession, a fierce white cataract to which I gave the name of love.

And yet it was love. I can still recall the distant sensations of earthly love. I remember watching Chŏngjo's small, earnest face as he bent intently over his piece of rice paper, as he dipped his brush in the black ink or prepared his ink stone: I remember his childish grief and despair when his hand could not reproduce the beautiful imaginings of his brain and his eye. Again and again I had to comfort him for a botched page, for a human imperfection. He was such a fierce and serious little child, and my heart went out to him. He was as sensitive as he was strong. I yearned to him. My whole body yearned to him. This was love. Was it not?

My nature was channelled, maybe, but it was not distorted. It was not broken, like a bound foot. We women in Korea did not bind our feet:

much as we aped many Chinese manners and fashions, we never followed that absurd and dangerous practice. We did not adopt the embroidered lotus shoe and the provocative tottering step on the three-inch toe. A bound foot is an unnatural distortion, but maternal devotion is not. Do I make my point? Or am I revealing myself as a Confucian casuist, descended from a dynasty of casuists?

My little boy was doomed to see what he should not have seen, to hear what he should never have heard. I could not protect him from these things. He was caught in a chain of terrible consequence.

As he grew and flourished, his father's mental health deteriorated. This and other forces came between us. Other powers struggled for possession of my son, for it was clear, even during his father's lifetime, that he, Chŏngjo, was to be the next king. No wonder that I look back to those early days of motherhood with a mixture of pleasure and grief. We were close, then. I had him to myself. We were surrounded by a small army of slaves and nurses and ladies-in-waiting, but I could still call him my own.

I tried during my earthly life to describe the progress of Sado's illness, and now I find I must address it again. As I have recorded, in my memoirs, his symptoms began to become noticeable round about the year 1752, at the time of the death of Ŭiso, our first-born son. But maybe there were earlier signs? The illnesses of the great are often misleadingly recorded. There are strategic illnesses, and strategic concealments of illness. I myself often claimed to suffer from ill health when in fact I judged it diplomatic to withdraw from the public eye. I was occasionally ill, and surely had a right to take to my chamber from time to time, but in truth when young I had a remarkably strong and resilient physical constitution: how else, after so stressful a life, could I have lived so long and seen so much? It was only at the time of the great crisis of the Imo Incident that I succumbed, for a while, and even then I did not wholly surrender.

Sado, too, unlike his older brother who died before his birth, unlike some of his sisters, had a strong constitution. In this, he resembled his father. Unlike his father, he subjected his naturally fortunate constitution to severe trials of indulgence and excess. King Yŏngjo was, by the time I came to know him, ascetic of body, if not of temper, and on the whole lived simply: he wore light clothing and preferred cool chambers even in our cold wintertime. He rationed the underfloor heating in his apartments, and complained if too much was spent on royal fuel. He visited the hot springs not for his health's sake, but in order to placate and show himself to his people. He was notoriously sparing in his diet, eating little and cautiously, as though fearing every mouthful might be of poisoned mushroom. He was a skinny, stringy old man. He looks plump enough in his portraits, but portrait painters are always liars, and leave out the shadows. That is their trade. Yŏngjo was asthmatic, but I have always considered that his breathing difficulties were of the type that reflects troubles of the mind, not of the body. There were times when the very sight of Sado made him catch his breath in pain and anger.

King Yŏngjo had tried to curb his nation from indulging in excesses of alcohol, imposing various laws to fine both nobles and commoners who drank intemperately, and prohibiting the unlicensed distilling of wines and beers. (We drank a lot, as a nation, and I am told we still do.) Of course, these laws were flouted, as such laws always are, in every kingdom on earth. The policy of prohibition has a bad record. And Yŏngjo himself was not at all certain about the wisdom of trying to implement his attempted reforms. He vacillated.

I remember one incident, at court, during the era of the strictest prohibition, when King Yŏngjo manifested a characteristic and almost ludicrous inconsistency. It was the day of some annual ceremonial, to pay tribute to the longevity of the elderly — we were very insistent on paying tribute to the old. A feast had been ordained, to which all couples who had been married for more than thirty years were invited. Songs were composed in their honour, and long speeches about the acquiring of wisdom were delivered. Little gifts of carvings of turtles and cranes, and other suitable symbols, were handed out, with small, embroidered flags attached to them. Delicacies of rice and honey were prepared, and foodstuffs in the royal colours were lavishly displayed and indeed consumed. But, because there was a royal edict in force against the serving of wine, only herbal infusions were offered, in vessels usually reserved for wine. The king himself took one of these cups of anodyne liquid, thinking and evidently hoping that it was wine, and sipped from it, but, when he discovered that it was not what he expected, he flew into a terrible rage and threw the liquid to the ground, letting out a violent storm of abuse against the kitchen staff who had dared to insult the elders of his kingdom with such feeble, spiritless stuff. Nobody knew quite what to do — would it be safe to remind him that the feast lacked alcohol because of his own decree? A brave retainer bustled off towards the kitchens and returned with a great jar of strong, well-fermented liquor (for there was always plenty available), and poured a beakerful for His Majesty, proffering it to him, with some inspired phrase like 'Your Majesty, please accept our newly created virgin brew, prepared especially for our new era!' Yŏngjo sniffed at it, sipped it, and drank it back, with evident satisfaction, then asked for more, and authorized its lavish distribution to all the old folk, who enjoyed it as much as he did. It was, by all accounts, a very merry festival. I was not there, for it would not have been seemly for me to attend, but I heard many reports of the incident. My woman Pongnyŏ, who was something of a mimic, enjoyed recounting this incident immensely, and her rendering of the behaviour of some of the old ladies lost nothing in the telling.

The retainer of the royal household who took this bold initiative risked execution, as did all illicit brewers. He gambled on the king's connivance, and won.

Looking back, in my old age, this tragic farce seemed to me to characterize the inadequacies of our despotic yet bureaucratic regime. After many years of watching the whims and vagaries and weaknesses of monarchs, I began to yearn for a more consistent, more enlightened, less petty system of government. Yet now that I am immortally old, I see that even so-called enlightened systems cling to absurdities and inconsistencies. The surviving monarchies of Europe offer a strange commentary on progress.

Yes, the king could be personally inconsistent, as well as inconsistent in his office. Although he praised temperance, there were other occasions, even later in his life, when he himself was spectacularly drunk in public. He had a violent, erratic personality, as excessive in his privations as, on occasion, in his indulgences. But he had a reputation for abstinence, and, by and large, it was deserved.

My husband Prince Sado, in contrast, was not by nature a temperate man. He was given to alcoholic excess, and to sexual excess. These are not uncommon faults for princes in all kingdoms in all time, and at first they were not harshly judged. Prince Sado, like his father, was given to excessive histrionic display: the rituals and ceremonies of court life encouraged this kind of behaviour. We were fond of pageants and processions, and moments of public drama. But Sado also had weaknesses of his own that were rare, and as far as I know, unprecedented. No physicians could rescue him from himself. I watched the growth of his symptoms with great alarm.

You should know that, after the consummation of our marriage, Sado took two secondary consorts, by both of whom he sired children. There was nothing unusual in this: it was our practice. I will not say I did not suffer some jealousy and resentment, for I did, but I did not indulge them inwardly or reveal them outwardly. The first of these consorts was a lady of the court, but of the Lower Second Court rank, Lady Yim Sukpin, who did not present much of a personal threat to me — she was not very clever, and her two sons by Sado were, to be frank with you, quite stupid. I felt some contempt for this liaison. I suppose what one feels in such a situation is a jealous contempt for an unworthy rival. It is not a very dignified emotion, but it is not very distressing. Confucian doctrine forbids jealousy in wives, and in this instance the doctrine provided a good cover for my true feelings. The lady's first son was born in 1754; the second a year later. Although it was beyond the call of kinship and duty, my father and I tried to protect these boys in later life, when they were left fatherless, but both came to bad ends.

Much more problematic was to be the addition, a couple of years later, of Pingae, or Lady Pak, as she was sometimes known. She was a wit and a beauty. In taking her as a consort, Prince Sado caused much offence, for she had been a lady-in-waiting to the Dowager Queen Inwŏn, King Yŏngjo's stepmother and the most favoured wife of Prince Sado's grandfather. Pingae had worked in the dowager queen's sewing department. The dowager queen had been a powerful presence in court during the early years of my marriage, and she was a handsome and intelligent woman: she was kind to me, after her fashion, when I arrived at court as a child, and I was fond of her, in my undemonstrative way. It was very shortly after the dowager's death in 1757 that Sado took Pingae to his bed, though I believed he had had designs on her for some time. This caused much indignation because there was a prohibition against such intergenerational sexual relations: Pingae's daily physical proximity to Sado's late stepgrandmother should have rendered sexual contact with Sado forbidden, for it was construed as a kind of incest, but Sado paid no attention to this taboo. Nor, I must say, did I see the force or logic of it, as they were not blood relations. Had I known Pingae's eventual fate I might have pretended to great moral objections and invoked, for her sake, the strictures of palace protocol. But I was ignorant of the future.

My husband set Pingae up in some splendour, in her own detached apartment within the palace grounds, with expensive screens and hangings, and ladies-in-waiting to attend on her. He gave her costly gifts of jewels and fans. On that level, at first, he treated her well. She had some influence over him, at the beginning of their affair.

This new liaison was successfully kept secret from his father for some time. King Yŏngjo did not know Pingae personally, of course, and would not have recognized her had he seen her, but we knew that the very fact of this contact would enrage him. As, when he discovered it, it did.

Pingae's late mistress, the Dowager Queen Inwŏn, was much honoured during her lifetime and after it by her stepson King Yŏngjo, who showered upon her more weight of honorifics with more resounding syllables than any other woman in our recent history had ever bowed beneath. We were great counters of syllables in the palace. And I have to say that, as palace matrons go, she was an impressive character. She was also, by the time I knew her, a little deaf, but she always seemed able to hear me when we spoke together privately. I think sometimes she pretended to be more deaf than she was. I much preferred her, at this period, to my mother-in-law, Lady Sŏnhŭi. I never forgot how kind she was to me when I knocked over the rice jar. I wept and wept, I was so ashamed, but she comforted me, and told me that she herself had once tripped over the corner of a carpet and nearly fallen in the presence of His Majesty, her husband. These were serious matters, at court, these small accidents and trifling misdemeanours.

King Yŏngjo bestowed many titles upon her, and he also addressed to her a great deal of conventional and second-rate poetry. Composition was not his forte, but the composing of poems was a social necessity in our time. His calligraphy was impressive — you may still see examples of it adorning the gates of his palaces, as the guide books will tell you — but his literary ability was, I fear, limited.

I believe the dowager queen was tolerably kind to Pingae, when Pingae waited upon her. Nevertheless, Pingae clearly had ambitions beyond the confines of a sewing chamber.

I was ignorant of the shape of the future, and I respected Pingae when she entered Prince Sado's life. Unlike the dismal and complaining Lady Sukpin with her everlasting crocodile tears and her foolish fondness for her plain and stupid boys, Pingae was clever, well read and sharp-witted. Her formal education was as sound as mine, though more directed towards the pleasing arts and the promiscuous arts of pleasing. Unlike me, she did not come from a respected family of scholars, but she had attended an academy before entering the palace. And she had an artistic talent. She taught me new embroidery stitches, which helped to pass the time pleasantly. (She knew a pretty and novel version of the Chinese knot.) She wrote poetry, and she would read me her *sijo*. Prose was to become my forte, and I was never happy with the constraints, economies and subtleties of verse, but Pingae was an artist in the shorter form. Unlike the king, she could write. I admired and envied her talent. She wrote mainly in the melancholy *kisaeng* tradition, short three-line pastoral lyrics of love and loss, of green willows and red leaves and blue mountains, of lakes and bridges and separations. They were conventional, derivative, elegant little pieces, elegiac and gentle

85

in tone, but genuinely accomplished.

But she also composed, unusually, some longer poems with urban themes, in which one could detect a strange note of what I would now describe as social protest. This was a period when the strict divisions of society outside the walls of the palaces were showing some signs of erosion, when rich merchants were beginning to buy their way into the great *yangban* families of the nobility, when even peasants began to dream of the possibility of a new freedom. Ours had long been a society that paid lip service to merit, to an education open to all, even though in practice it was so firmly closed against all comers. But there were now some signs of change. New notions from what was called the School of Practical Learning began to infiltrate orthodox Confucianism. New scientific theories from China and the West were being discussed, new construction and engineering techniques were being developed, and genre paintings of common life became popular, even at court. I see now that Pingae's urban fairy tales spoke of the coming of a more open order. I liked her versions of the tales of the road sweeper who married the moon princess, the silk spinner who was snatched up into the Milky Way to live amongst the king's sons in the heavens, the bird of the streets that perched upon the emperor of China's throne and sang subversion in his ear.

Yet she, like me, was dependent upon the favours of the Crown Prince. She, like me, had to watch her every step and every word. And by this time Prince Sado was deeply unpredictable and often violent in his behaviour.

She was stylish, the Lady Pingae. She wore her silk jacket cut higher on the bosom than any other lady at court. I would never have dared to wear so extreme a fashion, yet I admired it. I can see her now, with her sloping shoulders, her long, elegant swan neck, her firm young breasts, and that pert, proud little silk jacket, riding high above the high waist of her long, full gauze skirt. She had a lovely line. Her eye for colour and weave was faultless: those years in the sewing department had not been wasted, and now that she had money lavished upon her she was able to command some beautiful and extravagant garments for herself. I remember in particular an enchanting little jacket of dull yellow-gold, a sandy gold, with a pattern of fishes, which she wore with a turquoise skirt with a moiré wave design woven into it. It was like a seascape. And the waistband was of thin, dark blue gauze, embroidered with flowing green fronds of seaweeds.

I had never seen the sea.

I told Pingae about the red skirt I had longed for as a child, and we sighed and murmured and smiled as we exchanged confessions of our little vanities. It had been dull for her, attending on the dowager, sewing and embroidering endless yards of cloth in the queenly wardrobe. Who could blame her for catching the eye of Prince Sado, and for wanting royal robes of her own? I did not blame her.

Was I jealous of the Lady Pingae? I do not know. The attitude towards wifely jealousy in our polygamous society was confused and confusing. On the one hand, jealousy was disapproved, for the wife was supposed to be entirely subordinate to her husband's wishes; on the other hand, a total absence of jealousy was construed as an unseemly and disloyal indifference. Degrees of jealousy demanded subtle shading. (Two hundred years before our time, a queen had been so unsubtle as to scratch her husband's face in a fit of possessive jealousy: she died for the offence.) I do not think I was envious of Pingae's beauty or of her talents, and I do not think I resented Prince Sado's attentions to her. But I have to admit that I coveted one of the gifts he gave her. You may remember that I mentioned the screen of *fleurs-et-oiseaux* that my father-in-law gave to me. Sado gave to Pingae a screen that was as lovely, and more strange. It was of *fleurs-et-rochers-et-papillons*, of flowers and rocks and butterflies, and it showed a sequence of strange little pointed rocks with sheer, sharp geometric edges, jewel-like, crystal-like, each rock accompanied by a different flower, and above each flower a pair of butterflies. The colours were bolder than in my subtle, muted screen: the tiny rocks were azure blue and malachite green, the flowers were crimson and yellow, the butterflies of a fantastic glowing brilliance of scarlet and tortoiseshell and yellow, with swallow-tails and swirling patterns of ribs and veins and peacock eyes.

Maybe you have heard of the conceit we nourished, the conceit that these tiny crystalline rocks and pebbles, as small as the flowers that grew by them and the insects that hovered over them, could grow into mighty rocks and mountains? Pingae and I used to make little trays, à la japonaise, with miniature landscapes and seascapes, with silvered water, and amethyst hills, and coral trees hung with gem-like fruits. We designed forests of freedom, and lakes of deliverance, and mountains of escape, where our free and tiny spirits could wander in a miniature paradise.

When Pingae was in a good mood, she had such a winning way of dressing my long hair. She would wash it in water scented with the leaves of the chang-po plant, and brush and comb it. In those days, when it was loosened, it fell in a thick cascade down to my waist. I was proud of my shining hair. We would laugh, as we sat together of an evening, and she would brush my hair and smooth my brow and temples with her long, white fingers and long, pink nails. She would shape my hair and sculpt it into soft, dark raven wings. She used a magical perfumed lacquer, mixed from peony oil and wild sesame and some kind of resin, which made the structure keep its shape. Then she would polish my nails with an infusion of Lady Slipper and burnt alum, and tint my lips with safflower and cinnabar.

She had some fine cosmetic secrets, though she herself appeared to have little need of them. Her skin was like ivory. She glowed with a pale, rich, precious light. I assume this translucent glow was natural. If it was cosmetic, it was discreetly so. Discretion was then in vogue. In our day, the earlier fashion for bold, colourful and extravagant make-up had given way to a more refined and subdued look. We prided ourselves on our unassuming good taste; on our austere aesthetics. My little ceramic pots of oil were priceless, but they were of the plainest white.

There was a woman's hour every evening, in our country, when women were allowed to walk the streets of the city, and men were forbidden by a strict curfew to leave their homes. After nightfall the women had the streets to themselves, and were free to walk and joke and wander. I, of course, as a palace lady, as a crown princess, was not allowed such licence, but I heard stories of this magic time of liberty from my sister, from my young aunt and above all, now, from Pingae. Pingae would tell me of the tearooms, and the sweetmeats, and the silk merchants, and the chestnut vendors, and the disreputable Buddhist nuns, and the washer-women, and the gossip, and the little dogs, and the monkeys, and the smells of spring and autumn. She would speak, and I would stitch with my gold and crimson threads. Seoul was a great and busy city, and Pingae was a city lover, but she would also tell me of the river and the hills and the mountains beyond. She herself had paid a visit to the legendary temple of ten thousand peaks. She would tell me stories of the countryside and of the villages, of the games of kites and swings and seesaws, of the festivals and picnics and pleasures of country people. She had a quick eye and a quick tongue. I would have said that she was a born survivor. But it was I that lived on into old age.

I remember that Pingae was curiously and paradoxically fond of the melancholy story of Queen Min, otherwise known as Lady Inhyŏn, one of those popular true stories of a virtuous wife that our Confucian culture was much disposed to produce. Lady Inhyŏn was the wife of King Sukchong, who put her away from him because she was childless, and took a concubine, who produced an heir. He sent his wife into banishment, where she pined faithfully for six long years in a lonely, ruined house, or so it is said, until the concubine in turn fell out of favour and the king attempted to woo back his first and former love. Eventually, after much persuasion, she returned to court, but shortly after died, at the age of thirty-four, amidst much royal grief and penitence. I do not know why Pingae liked this story so much. One might have expected her to take the part of the wicked rival, Lady Chang, the upstart concubine, and maybe secretly she did. According to the 'true story', the jealous Lady Chang murdered Lady Inhyŏn by witchcraft. It is a grim, ghostly story of ground bones and buried skeletons and envenomed garments and portraits pierced by wicked arrows. A chamber of horrors story, a Jacobean story of palace villainy fit for one of your playwrights of revenge tragedies, a story that I would have thought fanciful had I not lived to see worse with my own eyes.

Lady Chang, accused of the murder of her reinstated rival, was forced to swallow poison. She said that, if she were made to die, she would

91

kill her son the crown prince, too, and she and the heir would die together. But she died, and he survived.

Lady Chang was the mother of the crown prince who became the King of the Poisoned Mushroom whom King Yŏngjo supplanted. She was not the mother of King Yŏngjo himself: his mother was a woman called Ch'oe Sukpin. King Sukchong had many wives and many concubines. There is no need to remember their names. This is not a history book or a work of genealogy.

What a strange mixture our palace lives were, with their mixture of fear and violence, of boredom and elegant inertia.

It was perhaps wrong of me to have enjoyed the company of Pingae, and I know that there was malicious gossip about our association. The Dowager Queen Inwŏn, her one-time employer and my stepmother-in-law, would have disapproved of it because she had been very strict about these matters: she had introduced a new rule that concubines and the daughters of concubines should not sit together with the wives and daughters of princes, in order to try to prevent such friendships and liaisons. But the dowager queen was dead, and I was lonely.

I loved Pingae's stories because she had seen something of the world. At times, how I longed to escape and to see this other world. I had been trapped young, and imprisoned. Women of our time and of my rank led claustrophobic, indoor lives: our gardens were large, but they were walled and indoor gardens. Outdoor exercise was considered unseemly, un-Confucian. It is said that the little girls of the court were fond of swings because, if they swung themselves high enough, they could glimpse the world that lay over the compound wall. I was too grand and too noble to play on the swings, but my daughters used to sail into the sky in their coloured butterfly skirts.

I watched the marker of the round bronze sundial, as it caught the slowly moving shadow of the sun.

I watched the wind streamer, as it fluttered in the breeze that blew towards us from the granite mountains.

I watched the ginger dragonflies, as they hovered over the grasses.

I heard the rain drops, as they fell on the broad leaves of the foxglove tree.

I watched the kingfishers, as they darted through the reeds.

I watched the white herons, as they stood on guard at the water's edge.

I listened to the cry of the cicadas.

I gazed at the silent golden fish in the lotus pond in the secret garden, and wondered if they knew their confines. Occasionally a fish would leap, hopelessly, upwards, into the dangerous air.

I liked this verse, by a *kisaeng* poet of the past century, whose name I forget. I often thought of it.

> Who caught you, fish, then set you free
> Within my garden pond?
> Which clear northern sea did you leave
> For these small waters?

I have seen more of the world now, and it is confusing. But I will make sense of it before time itself dies.

Despite her bright and worldly ways, Pingae was more superstitious than I was, and occasionally she would ask me if I wanted to consult a wise woman about Prince Sado's growing illness. It was forbidden for us to consult these women, but, of course, the practice lingered on, particularly amongst the lower and merchant classes, and it was not unknown for ladies of the court to make contact with them. (I am told the practice still survives, even in your time. I am told the great spirit grandmothers in suburban Seoul are still greedy for the sacrifice of food and dollar bills.) These approaches to the spirit world were made through shamans (or *mudangs*, or *mansins*, as they were variously described), and most of them were harmless. Not all court ladies were intent on murdering their rivals by smearing the cotton lining of their robes with poisoned pastes. Some merely sought remedies for complaints and sicknesses, and these wise women knew of good herbal remedies. But bad advice was also given: one former queen was advised to propitiate the evil spirits that were attacking her son by bathing daily in a cold stream. Not surprisingly, this did her and him little good, for as a result of this practice she caught cold and died. Or so the story goes.

I resisted Pingae's suggestion that we consult a shaman because I had little faith in a cure through such means, and because I wished to

94

protect Prince Sado from gossip, and to conceal his affliction. But as I watched him deteriorate, I began to think we had nothing to lose, and at times I think I would have tried any remedy, however wild or primitive, or unlikely. All who have loved a person driven into insanity will know where this desperation can lead. How can one minister to a mind diseased? One will try any witchcraft, any newfangled or old-fashioned form of healing. But by then it was too late. He was beyond reach, and it was dangerous to approach him.

They say that these wise women, these *mudang*, are themselves mad, or possessed. And Prince Sado was now mad. Can one mad person cure another? I suppose it may be so. Some say that one cannot understand the ways of our country without understanding the ways of the *mudang*. But you must understand that, although a woman, I was a member of an educated elite, and I believed in reason. The madder Sado became, the more I believed in reason. I took refuge in reason and in the life of the mind. Posterity is witness to my rationality.

I say I am not superstitious, and I have always been suspicious of these conveniently auspicious dragon dreams that we claim to have. I have never dreamed of a dragon in my life, despite the dominant dragon imagery of our culture. I think most of these dreams are politic fictions or literary conventions. The father of the ill-fated and faithful Lady Inhyŏn, of whose sad story Pingae was so fond, claimed that he saw shimmering lights hovering like a rainbow over her washbowl when she was an infant — a more original conceit than a dragon, I concede, but I fancy just as retrospective. My father even admitted, in later years, that he had embroidered the black-dragon dream he claimed to have had before my birth: he had based its graphic details on an old painting that used to belong to my grandfather, and which mysteriously reappeared in the Bridal Pavilion when I became betrothed to Sado. The reappearance of the painting was rather strange, I admit, but I am sure it owed more to human than to supernatural agency. Valuable objects did tend to wander round the palaces, disappearing and resurfacing without much official explanation, but we need not credit ghosts with these removals.

I must, however, confess to one common though by no means universal (nor indeed Korean) superstition, to which I have been subject all my life. I am afraid of magpies, and I say secret childhood rhymes to placate them whenever I see them. I think of them as birds of ill omen. I do not know why. I now know that in some cultures the magpie is feared, whereas in others it is treated with respect. Fear of magpies is neither innate nor universal, but it certainly afflicted me. Maybe I was already foreshadowing the Western superstitions of my Western ghost. In our culture, the magpie was seen as a harbinger of good fortune, as a herald of guests. It is strange that I felt this fear. Was I already moving out of the conditioning of time and place? Had some process of ghostly permeation already begun? It seems a trivial and harmless phobia, but it is not without its interest, and I have devoted some posthumous time to its study. I have not finished with it yet.

Magpies are a very adaptable species and, I note, increasingly widespread. *Pica pica* has colonized the world. They have become dominant in many neighbourhoods, including the one that my ghostly representative now inhabits. They have driven out many other species, including the small songbirds. I always feared them, in whatever numbers or manifestations they appeared. I know that in some parts of the East they were regarded as wise birds of good omen. They were famed in Korean legend for their benevolence in forming the Magpie Bridge that linked those star-crossed lovers, the herd boy and the weaving maid, on the Seventh Night of the Seventh Moon. I know that in China they are called the 'birds of joy'. But from early childhood, I believed they were unlucky. Maybe a magpie threatened me in my cradle. They are large birds, and can be aggressive. Naturally, I cannot remember any such incident. I am somewhat ashamed of this small irrationality. I wonder what superstitions besieged Voltaire. None of us is immune to such weaknesses.

Even as I composed those words, one of these ill-omened birds came down and landed on the window ledge. It had its evil eye upon me. I saluted it with the rhymes, as one should, and off it flew. Had I neutralized its malice? What ill can one suffer beyond the grave? It was glossy and

97

cocky, and it strutted boldly and offensively in my sight. Magpies are baby-stealers and jewel-snatchers. A gathering of magpies heralded the death of Prince Sado.

Prince Sado himself was deeply superstitious, despite his strict indoctrination into Confucian rationalism, and he consulted all manner of charlatans who nursed and encouraged his growing illness. In the year of the measles epidemic, there was a great storm, remembered in the countryside for many years, and it was at this period that Sado began to succumb to his terror of thunder. I know that many weak mortals fear thunder and lightning, and not without some cause, but in Sado the fear became utterly irrational. I am no mathematician, but I do know that one's chances of dying in a thunderstorm are, in ordinary circumstances, remote. But Sado dreaded the thunder. He thought it was the voice of vengeance. It was at this time that he became obsessed by that dangerous and pornographic book, *The Jade Pivot*. This was in our day a very popular work, which described the god of thunder and the various punishments he inflicted upon sinning mortals. The god of thunder is a hideous blue creature, winged and clawed, furnished with a chisel and a mallet, and his role is to punish undetected crimes. This book was full of horrifying images and vivid descriptions of tortures and torments in various particularly violent forms of hell. It was a stupid book, fit only for superstitious simpletons amongst the common people, but Sado took it with a deadly seriousness. He began to tremble at any loud noise, and he imagined that he saw people that were not there. He thought that people were watching him, and would send his servants out to arrest these ghosts.

He also developed a fear of objects made of jade, which of course was in our culture (even more than in most cultures) a much-prized precious stone.

The August Personage of Jade rules the Court of Heaven. He is the father figure and emperor of the palace of the higher world. Or so the vulgar believe.

I did not fear jade. One of my favourite possessions in my life on earth was a beautifully carved jade duck, carrying in its beak a lotus bloom: I was fond of this solitary duck of soft green and russet tints. I liked the subtle colours of jadestone — the creams, the pale greys, the mauves, the browns and, above all, the greens. Apple green, spinach green, lettuce green, seaweed green, sage green. Jade was considered a lucky stone, and it was said to have healing properties. It would cure complaints of the kidney. In some countries it was known as the colic stone, or *lapis nephriticus*. I did not myself believe in its curative powers, but I was fond of my jade duck.

But Sado had quite other thoughts and fears. The very sight of the Chinese character that means 'jade' made him wince and cover his eyes in horror. At first I thought this was a pretence, an exaggerated reaction against the Confucian rigour of pragmatic, this-worldly rationalism, but

I began to see that, even though it might have begun as a game, a real fear had taken a deep hold on his poor brain. There was a period when he avoided contact with all jade objects. When he had to handle one, or found that he had handled one inadvertently, he would then go through elaborate washing and cleansing procedures.

His father was not without some oddities in this direction — he was forever washing his ears and rinsing out his mouth after speaking to certain disfavoured family members — but in him the fear of such pollution had not reached the stage of an obsessive phobia, as it did with Prince Sado. But maybe Sado inherited the tendency. It may have been a genetic fluke, a family tic. I am ignorant about these matters. Most people are ignorant about them. These issues remain unresolved. The long march of enlightenment is slow.

King Yŏngjo was certainly what you would now call neurotic. He had several obsessive-compulsive disorders which verged on the ridiculous. The rinsing of the mouth and ears after speaking to Prince Sado was odd in itself, but even odder was the way he would then try to throw the dirty water over the wall into the courtyard of the Princess Hwahyŏp next door — it was a high wall, and the water often used to splatter back at him. This was not dignified or rational; and naturally it offended the prince. The king was also very particular about which doors he used for which purposes — he would go through one door on a pleasant enterprise,

100

through another for an unpleasant one. Superstitiously, he avoided the words 'death' and 'return', and held it particularly unlucky to return to a room to retrieve a forgotten object. He would not even send a servant on such an errand. This, of course, caused him some inconvenience. And he, too, changed his robes compulsively, though not as frequently as his son was to do.

There was one day a dreadful scene about a jade helmet that Prince Sado was supposed to wear for some tedious and unpleasant ceremonial occasion — I think it may have been an interrogation or an execution. I should mention that Sado's sadistic father never allowed him to undertake any pleasant official or ceremonial duties, such as attending archery contests or graduation parties, but insisted instead that he assist at various unpleasant public events at the Board of Punishment. He seemed to take a particular pleasure in summoning Sado to these events in winter, when it was snowing. (There were always conspiracy trials in progress in our country: we lived in a culture of denunciation and counterdenunciation.) The unfortunate effect that this had upon Sado was eventually, to my mind, all too clear, though his father never admitted the connection. In any case, on this occasion Sado reported for duty with his helmet lopsided and as if it were deliberately misplaced. His father mocked and sneered and shouted, and Sado grew defiant, and flung the helmet to the earth, with some stream of sad nonsense relating to his ill fortune and the powers of the accursed jade, and the gods know what demented rhetoric. This was one of the first episodes of the clothing sickness to be noted in public, though I in private had already begun to observe his extreme anxiety, his worse than anxiety, about his dress. There was to be a repetition of this incident before long, at the betrothal ceremony of our son Prince Chŏngjo. I will describe that when I come to it.

To be truthful, I find it hard to recollect the exact sequence of events that revealed the growing sickness of Prince Sado. During my lifetime, I wrote over a period of ten years four distinct memoirs, each time with a slightly different aim, each with its own revelations and evasions, each with its own agenda. I am trying to be truthful now, though I am not sure what agenda beyond truth a poor ghost might have. Perhaps even ghosts deceive themselves and others. However it may be, I find my ghostly memory is faulty and at times confused. Matters are made more complicated by my posthumously acquired awareness of psychology and psychological terms. I remain convinced, however, that my awareness of the nature of Prince Sado's sickness was keen even during his brief life on earth: it did not depend on a posthumous vindication either of him or of my own actions during my own much longer lifetime. Evidence for my sympathy and understanding is there, in those memoirs, for anyone who troubles to read them in the right spirit. Of course, I may be represented as a manipulative survivor, promoting the fortunes of the Hong family and my offspring. You can think what you like about that. But I tell you it was not so.

The pursuit of truth is a noble aim. One lifetime is too short to discover truth. Therefore I persevere.

Many misfortunes had come upon Prince Sado in the year that he attached himself to the Lady Pingae. He was recovering from an attack of smallpox during which he ran a very high fever in a winter of bitter cold. (Smallpox, like measles, was an ever-present threat, and no respecter of persons or place: at this point in the eighteenth century, it was responsible for wiping out royal lineages round the world.) He had a subsequent bout of malaria, and his tonsils were inflamed. The death of the Dowager Queen Inwŏn, as I have recorded, was a blow to him, for she had always set herself up as his protector and tried to defend him from his father's criticisms. (Thus, by extension, she was my protector also.) She tried to negotiate between father and son, between king and crown prince. But there was another death earlier in the same year that also affected him profoundly, and this was the death of Queen Chŏngsŏng, the childless first wife of his father, King Yŏngjo. This queen, the primary consort, had long been estranged from the king, and she, like the dowager queen, had also taken Sado's part. These two Queenly Majesties had always done their best to support the young prince, and he had responded to them with a respect and devotion that showed how keenly he missed his father's love and approval.

The death of Queen Chŏngsŏng was terrible.

It was natural, unlike so many of the deaths that followed, but it was terrible. She had been ill for a long time, but the climax of her sickness was horrifying. Anticipating death, she had already moved from her usual residence in the Great Pavilion to Kwalli House in the western wing of the palace, saying that she did not wish to pollute the grandeur of the Great Pavilion by her death rites. There, her condition rapidly deteriorated. Her fingernails turned a deep purple blue, like nails bruised in a vice, and one night she vomited enough blood to fill a chamber pot. The blood was not the clear red of a patient suffering from lung disease: it was thick and black. It seemed to us as though many years of poison had been gathering in her body and were now being spewed out. Sado and I were present when this happened, and Sado himself seized the chamber pot and carried it off, in tears, to the administrative office of the queen's residence to show it to the physicians. But it was too late, and they could do nothing for her. The queen herself urged Sado to go to bed and rest, and not to wait by her bedside, so with great reluctance he left her, and returned to his pavilion. During the night his stepmother fell into a deep coma. This was announced to Sado in the morning, and he immediately went round to her bedside, where he cried out to her again and again 'I've come, Your Majesty, I've come!' and pitifully attempted to raise a spoonful of ginseng tea to her crooked mouth. But she was past all response. She never opened her eyes again.

News of her approaching end had reached the king, who, although long estranged from her, came that same morning to her chamber. His arrival had an appalling effect on Sado. Sado had been behaving with such courage and such proper and properly apparent filial devotion until that moment, but at the approach of King Yŏngjo he seemed to collapse. He retreated from the bedside and crouched on the floor in a corner, like a guilty child. He looked frozen with horror. His tears dried, and he was unable to speak or move. Nobody could have guessed from this dishevelled, unseemly bundle how correctly he had been behaving until that moment, nor how much genuine grief he had displayed. And, just as I feared, King Yŏngjo began at once to criticize his son. He criticized his behaviour, his silence, his crouching attitude — he even criticized the way the bottoms of his trousers were tied. It was a grotesque scene. There lay Queen Chŏngsŏng unconscious, breathing painfully upon her deathbed — she died between three and four in the afternoon on the following day — and all that Yŏngjo could do was to berate his son for the way he tied his trousers!

Is it any wonder that Sado developed a clothing phobia, a clothing disease? I have searched the records for parallels to Sado's obsession. I have pored over stories of mad kings and legends of crazed priests in the Occident and in the Orient, but so far I have found nothing in history to resemble his mania.

'Himatiophobia', I have seen it called, in English, in one of the translations of my works.

But I do not think that this is a word commonly recognized in the medical or psychoanalytic lexicon.

I had my own theory about Sado's phobia. Its source lay in his father's wrath. To me this followed, as the night the day. The craziness with which Sado slashed his clothes was caused by King Yŏngjo's incessant criticisms of his son's appearance. I suppose it is more common for mothers to demean their daughters over matters of dress, but in our court, as I have explained, the significance of apparel for both sexes was immense. Perhaps all courts have such rules, but I feel that ours was particularly exacting. Etiquette prescribed distinct clothes for distinct occasions. Sometimes, in one day, many changes of costume were required, and these were complex garments, not easy to don without assistance. Sashes and ribbons had to be tied in the correct order and direction, from left to right, and it was not uncommon to see the ankles of a pair of trousers so badly tied that the trouser legs became twisted in a ridiculous fashion. So the prince was not alone in making mistakes with his appearance when he was left to attend to himself. I myself, as Crown Princess, had a magnificent wardrobe of robes of many styles and colours, of rare silks and gauzes, in which I could not have encased myself without expert assistance. Teams of seamstresses laboured for me, week after week, month after month. Records of their toil survive, for we were a bureaucratic society, and liked to make lists and inventories. Clothes were made for me that I never wore, that no one ever wore. Where are they now? Do any scraps of those rich fabrics still survive?

I know that small children have strong and what seem to be instinctive objections to some styles of clothing, to some textures. I never cared for a certain kind of embossed and shiny satin — it set my teeth on edge; I do not know why. (Nor do I much care for the coarse white gloves that the readers of manuscripts in the British Museum are obliged to wear.) Sado as a child is said to have preferred cotton to silk, but I am not sure if this was true, as the story was told to illustrate his natural princely modesty and dislike of ostentation. My own son, little Chŏngjo, never liked the obligatory white socks of childhood. They had to be forced over his reluctant feet. But he submitted because he had to submit. Children can form strong and seemingly irrational opinions about what they like to wear. But normal children grow out of these fads, not into them. A florid madness like Sado's I have never known. Yet, when I witnessed Sado's father's incessant reproaches, when I saw him at the very deathbed of the queen shouting at Sado about his trousers, I was aware that I was witnessing an unnatural scene, one of many unnatural scenes, and I knew that these scenes would have an unnatural outcome. How unnatural, I did not yet suspect.

After much thought, I have come to the conclusion that my husband would now, in your age, be likely to be classified as a paranoid schizophrenic. I mention this in passing. It is

107

only a suggestion. I am no expert in these matters.

The queen died in the afternoon of the following day, as I have said. I was present. But the formal announcement of Queen Chŏngsŏng's death and the preparations for the mourning were delayed because King Yŏngjo was distracted by news of a rival death — by the death of his young son-in-law, the husband of his most favoured daughter, the dangerous Madame Chŏng, the daughter who hated me so much and loved Sado so unnaturally. The death of Madame Chŏng's husband was an unlucky death for all of us. Had Madame Chŏng not been widowed so young, had she borne children of her own, she might have meddled less with my affairs. She might have kept herself at a proper distance from her brother Sado, instead of entering into that dangerous and possibly incestuous intimacy with him that was shortly to cause so much scandal. She might have left my son alone, instead of practising upon him and playing with him and making him dance to her tune. After Sado's death, she transferred all her lust for power to her manipulation of my son, the Grand Heir. But that is another, later story. I will come to that.

Death followed death. Shortly after the death of Queen Chŏngsŏng, the Dowager Queen Inwŏn also died, as I have narrated above. She was buried in the seventh month, in pouring rain. Prince Sado was a sad sight at this time, in his mourning robes of unbleached hemp, with his dishevelled hair and his wooden staff cut, as custom dictated, from the wood of the foxglove tree. The long process of mourning weighed heavily upon him. He wailed loudly and ostentatiously in the mourning procession, again as custom dictated, but the tears he shed in the courtyard at dead of night, gazing towards the shrine where the blue and white mourning tablet of Queen Chŏngsŏng was to be placed, were not mere ceremonial tears. 'I wish I were dead,' I heard him cry, again and again, unobserved by all but myself. 'I wish I were dead, I wish I were dead, I wish I were dead . . . ' It was the repeating cry of a dreadful bird of night. He meant it. I feared for his reason. With reason, I feared for his reason.

Death followed death. It was shortly after the deaths of the two Queenly Majesties that the killings began.

I digress here for a moment. Leafing through an academic periodical the other day, in an attempt to refresh my aged and ageing memory about the composition of the eighteenth-century Chosŏn Court Orchestra, I came by chance across an article by a twentieth-century scholar on the subject of 'Korea and Evil'. Koreans, he had concluded, after conducting some hundred or so interviews, do not believe in Evil. They believe in evil acts, but not in the abstraction of evil. His sample was small, and he interviewed through an interpreter, but nevertheless I think he had hit upon an interesting distinction.

I can put off the evil moment no longer. Let me now try to describe the first killing.

I find I do not know whether to aim for

109

suspense or simplicity at this point in my narrative.

I was reading, quietly, in my apartment, and intermittently stitching away at a panel of yellow satin: I remember the illustrated text I was reading; I remember the pattern of blossom and butterfly; I remember the gilt thread; I remember even the vermilion and turquoise of the cloth spool on which the thread was wound. It was a tranquil domestic scene. I enjoyed embroidery: I know that clever women all over the world were beginning, at this period, to revolt against the constraints of a life spent pointlessly embroidering useless hangings and useless garments, but I confess that I enjoyed the activity. Perhaps surprisingly, I much preferred it to book-binding, which some of the princesses adopted as a hobby. I liked reading, which I have to say some of the princesses did not, but I was not overly particular about grains of paper and colours of inks. I preferred the content to the form. But embroidery was different — I found it soothing, harmlessly soothing.

So picture me, innocently employed, sitting on my low, silk-cushioned rosewood couch. Then suddenly my husband Prince Sado burst in, through the outer chamber, past the ladies-in-waiting, carrying before him a strange, round object stuck on the end of a short spike — it looked to be about the size of a large cabbage. I heard the muffled sounds of the consternation of the ladies as he passed, but was at first unable to identify the object he was carrying, as I was wearing my tortoiseshell-framed reading glasses

110

(I was growing short-sighted by this time), and my eyes could not see what was in front of them. They had no focus. Trembling, I removed my glasses, and then I saw what I saw. Sado was bearing before him a severed head. It was not a papier-maché mask from a peasant puppet show, but a real head. My husband's hands were red with blood, and red blood dripped on to the oiled wood of the floor. At first I could not make sense of what I saw, even when I could see it clearly, so horrible was the vision that confronted me. I do not remember if I screamed or not. Later, my ladies assured me I conducted myself with dignity, but I cannot remember what I did or said. I had never seen a severed head. I was to see many.

I recognized the head. I knew its features. It was the head of Kim Hanch'ae, the eunuch who had been on duty that day. There were his full, broad cheeks, his bald, domed pate, his slightly jaundiced eyes, his full lips. The grimace of death did not disguise him. The transfixed gaze of his dead eyes met mine.

This was the first of Prince Sado's killings. Of course, there was nothing in law to prevent him from killing a eunuch, for Sado was the crown prince, with powers of life and death. He could dispose of slaves and eunuchs as he chose, without much fear of reprisal. But I knew, and the ladies knew, that this was a terrible event. He had crossed a bridge into another kingdom. Why had he done it, and why, having done it, had he brought the head to us? What was he asking of us? What madness, what despair had possessed him?

At the time, I was too stunned with horror to ask myself why he had selected Kim Hanch'ae as his victim. In fact, it is only now, two hundred years too late, that it occurs to me to wonder if Kim Hanch'ae had provoked or thwarted him in any particular way on that fatal evening. Eunuchs in our court, as in the Chinese court, could easily work themselves into positions of power, for they were privy to many secrets, and Kim Hanch'ae was an intelligent, academy-educated man. Had he been attempting to curb Sado's excesses, or to offer unwanted advice? I do not know. I did not on that evening seek any rational explanation for this bizarre and barbarous act. My mind at once rushed to an unhappy conclusion — that Sado had killed for some kind of perverse pleasure. And I still think my first instinctive guess was right. Prince Sado was never a politic man. I do not think he killed Kim Hanch'ae through policy.

You will remember that as a small child Prince Sado had played military games, unfortunately encouraged by Lady Han. As an adult, too, he had liked these games, and he had returned to them to play them on a grander scale. He enjoyed playing soldiers with parades of uniformed servants in the woods of the secret palace garden, and was sexually aroused by mock beheadings. He liked weapons and armour, and horses colourfully caparisoned in the finery of war. He had a fine sword made by a famous craftsman of which he was immensely proud. Its blade was sleek and curved and thin and dangerous. Even I could see that it was a thing of beauty, a work of art. And he had a little toy sword made for me, in imitation, a miniature sword such as ladies used to wear as a fashion accessory. At first I treasured it, as a gift, and wore it at my belt. But after this killing, I wore it no more.

Never had I thought he would turn from play to the real thing, from art to execution. He had deeply disliked the occasions when his father had obliged him to preside at real trials and witness real punishments.

I knew that he had behaved sadistically towards some of the ladies-in-waiting. He had threatened them with violence when they tried to refuse his overtures, and he had taken them without their full consent. Nobody spoke to me directly of these abuses, but I heard whispers, and I had eyes in my head. I knew these actions and tendencies were not good, but at this stage I had not known how far they had gone. Sado's favours were much feared, and Pingae alone seemed able to control him. Towards her, he behaved with some discretion.

He had not troubled me with sexual demands for some months when this first killing took place. As his primary consort, I had by now borne him four children, three of whom had survived, including the all-important son, the Grand Heir Chŏngjo, who was at the time of this first killing some five years old. (Pingae by now also had a child by Sado, and was to bear him one more.) I had done my duty to the Yi dynasty and to my husband, and he had done his duty to

113

me. He treated me always with respect, as the mother of the heir. I think he treated me with more than respect. There was a guilty pleading sorrow at times in his demeanour, as though something in him remembered the days when we were two married children, playing seriously together at being man and wife, at being prince and princess. I had known him as a child, and he had known me as a child, and together we had been frightened of the future. Never in his life, even until the last days, did he threaten me with death, though he did on one occasion injure me. I think he relied on my support and my understanding. Or do I mean that he relied on my collusion and my collaboration? Was I a party to his crimes?

When I describe us as 'two married children', I seem to be sentimentally invoking your pity. But in truth I do see us, as from afar, like two dolls in a distant pageant. Two small, over-dressed, unhappy, innocent dolls.

At this stage, at the time of this first killing, I did not speak up about his crime. I did not think of approaching either his father or his mother. I spoke only to Pingae and, in secret, to my older brother, who at that time, having passed his examinations, had become a court official — he was eventually to be appointed as tutor in the Office of Lectures to my son Chŏngjo, the Grand Heir. My father was at this time far away: I think it was in the preceding year that he had been appointed magistrate of the province of Kwangju. Pingae, of course, knew the true state of affairs, for the ladies-in-waiting spoke openly

114

to her. My older brother was appalled when I told him of the murder, and at first wanted me to leave the court altogether. But how could I leave my children? They needed me and my protection, I told him, and he could see the force of this argument.

First Brother and I would talk into the night, discussing my plight and Prince Sado's illness. First Brother was himself an austere, cold, clever man, the very opposite in temperament from Sado, and he was able to look with a detached eye upon the bizarre pattern of behaviour that I described to him and of which, of course, he heard unconfirmed rumours from others. By now, there was no concealing Sado's illness. First Brother and I agreed that though the killings (and one followed another) were the most horrific manifestations of his illness, the clothing phobia was the most mysterious. I find it very hard to write about it, even after all these years. I think it fills me with shame as well as with anxiety.

As I have said, Sado had increasing difficulty in dressing every day. Some days he would order me to have ten, twenty, thirty outfits to be laid out for him, and then he would reject them, one after the other. At first it seemed like a monstrous parody of childish pique or girlish indecision, but soon it took on a more sinister light, for he started to burn the rejected garments, or to slash them to pieces. With his finely honed sword he destroyed them, and with other lesser weapons. His chamber would be full of rent cloth, of soft mountains of ribbons of

115

black and of red. Then he would order these rags to be bustled away out of his sight, or burned, as he mumbled about ghosts and demons. And fresh suits would be brought, until at last one pleased him — and then he would don it, and wear it perhaps for days, sometimes for weeks, until it was filthy and began to fall to pieces. His servants and valets were in mortal terror of this strange behaviour — with good cause, as it proved, for he began to turn on them, and to attack them if anything went awry in the elaborate robing process. Some were even killed, I regret to record.

You are wondering if the clothing allowance of even a crown prince could provide endlessly for such destruction, and you are right to ask because the answer is that it was not easy. Such reckless consumption stretched his allowance and gave rise to much malicious speculation — for, of course, those near to him tried to conceal his madness. My father would secretly obtain bolts of cloth in the city, and supply them to his tailors, hoping to guess what fabrics, what colours would please, and trying to substitute cotton for silk. But this had been a great expense for my father, and moreover it was impossible to guess right, for Sado's sudden loathings and likings were capricious and irrational, or so they seemed to us. When Father left for Kwangju, it was even harder for us to conceal the problem, for Sado took to raiding the palace supplies, and there was much comment.

First Brother and I speculated in vain about this phobia. I think I voiced my view that Sado was reacting against the over-regulation of court life, and against his father's strictures, but First Brother thought this was an overly psychological interpretation (though that is not the word he would or could have used, of course).

We were past fearing for Prince Sado's reason: we knew he had already lost it. He was not only murderous: he was also suicidal. We felt helpless. Our only relief lay in the imminent return of Father from the provinces, though there was not much he could do either.

The emotional state of the court at this time was extraordinarily tense. Our house had become a house of horror, a charnel house, where everyone feared for his life. And it was not only Sado's madness that disturbed the dignity and tranquillity of the court. His father King Yŏngjo also was in a highly unnatural state, which came to a head several months later, at the winter solstice. King Yŏngjo had at last discovered, as we knew in the end that he must, that Sado had taken Pingae from the royal sewing room to be his concubine. He was outraged, and summoned Sado into his presence at Kongmuk House, where he was staying for the duration of the period of mourning for the Dowager Queen Inwŏn. He berated his son, and, more dangerously, he demanded that Pingae be brought to him at once. Sado refused, with violent oaths and violent abuse, and I hit upon the device of deceiving the king with a substitute. I sent in her stead another lady-in-waiting from my own sewing department, a young woman of much the same age as Pingae, and sent Pingae away to Sado's sister's residence outside the palace, where I advised her to stay hidden for a while. The king vented his wrath on the false Pingae, and arranged for her to be sent into exile.

At least he did not chop off her head. Well, perhaps he did, but not to my knowledge, and not in my sight. I absolve myself. As far as I know, he did not order her execution. She disappeared. So many disappeared.

I had saved Pingae, my rival and my friend. For a while, at least.

Then, for the first time in my life, the king turned on me, and shouted at me in a most undignified and uncontrolled manner, banging at the ground in his fury, and demanding to know why I had not let him know of what he described as a shameful and prohibited liaison. I defended myself as best I could, saying that it was not my wifely duty to inform on my husband. He went on shouting about Pingae, and about Sado's earlier concubine (that court lady of the Lower Second rank), and about Sado's insubordinate attitude, and about my deceit. Then he insisted that Sado return to see him and that I depart from his presence.

What happened next I did not witness, though my father did, and so did the whole bureaucracy, including the wretched president at that time, the devious and two-faced Kim Sangno, who was always critical of my husband. There ensued, it seems, another violent and blustering shouting match between father and son, which ended in Sado's rushing from the building and throwing

118

himself down the low stone-bordered well in front of Yangjŏng House. He might have been killed, but for the fact that there was very little water in the well, and what there was, was largely frozen. Sado was rescued by the palace guard Pak Se-gun, who managed to climb in and carry him out on his back. Sado was dreadfully bruised and soaked when he was heaved out, but the public humiliation was worse than any injury. The king became angrier than ever, and, when my father tried to intervene on Sado's behalf, Yŏngjo turned on him, too, stripped him of his ministerial office and sent him to await his punishment at a place outside the city. What a night! I prudently removed myself to the servants' quarters, where I hid myself away for some days, waiting for the storm to blow over.

Eventually King Yŏngjo forgave me, and summoned me back to my apartment. I expressed excruciating gratitude and prostrated myself before him, but alas, Prince Sado did not follow my diplomatic example. He refused to see his father and left me to do all the work of a go-between. They did not meet for many weeks, and in the end it was left to the father to descend to seek the son in his apartment. He cannot have been pleased by the grim and squalid conditions in which he now found Sado to be living, but some paternal feeling was left in him, and he shortly summoned him to a meeting in Sungmun Hall, at which the strangest of exchanges took place. Both father and son gave me their own accounts of this bizarre encounter, which took place in the spring of 1758, and to some extent they tallied. I believe this to be more or less the truth of what happened.

According to Prince Sado, his father now asked him directly about the killings, and, being unable to lie to his father. Sado confessed to them. According to King Yŏngjo, however, Sado began to speak of them of his own accord, believing his father knew all about them anyway. I do not know which of these versions is more accurate. Whoever spoke first, the outcome was the same.

Prince Sado explained himself to his father in these words:

'It relieves my suppressed anger, sir, to kill people or animals.'

'Why is your anger aroused?'

'Because I am so hurt.'

'Why are you so hurt?'

'Because you do not love me, and also I am terrified of you because you constantly reproach and censure me. These are the causes of my illness.'

Then, by both their accounts, Sado began to outline the killings — of eunuchs, attendants, prostitutes, ladies-in-waiting — and his father listened to this catalogue of crimes in horrified silence. I do not think Sado spoke of the clothing disorder. How could he have found the words to describe it?

It seems that Yŏngjo was moved as well as horrified by this catalogue because he promised to be more lenient and considerate towards his son in the future. Yŏngjo even came to me, in some emotion, and made the same professions of concern. I confirmed the view (which I also believed) that it was the king's lack of loving care that had so disturbed his son. The king then asked me to report on Sado's health, and to take good care of him. I did believe for a while that his heart had been touched and that he intended to try to show more affection to his son. I encouraged him with smiles and tears to be good to Sado. All our lives, literally, depended on some kind of rapprochement between king and heir. But it was too late, it was far too late.

There was such an accumulation of sorrow in our court at this time, such rivalry of grief. It was during the period between the surrendering of the supposed Pingae and Sado's confession that yet another of the princesses died, and by her own choice. Lord Wŏlsŏng, Princess Hwasun's husband, died of a fever, and Princess Hwasun starved herself to death in order to follow him. She died thirteen days after her husband, like a dutiful model Confucian wife. But instead of admiring the exemplary devotion of his second daughter, a devotion which the history books have praised so highly, King Yŏngjo did his best to dissuade her from fasting, and when she died he refused her the proper honours, on the grounds that she had been unfilial — in short, he accused her of preferring her husband to her father. No vermilion gate was erected in her memory. She was expelled from her father's affections. I wonder if her death played any part in Yŏngjo's attempted reconciliation with Prince Sado?

It was clear by now that the succession to the

throne was in serious doubt. Nobody thought Prince Sado fit to rule, although there were some who supported him for their own ends. I was almost the only person, apart from Pingae, who witnessed his moments of sanity and remorse. To others, he appeared by now to be wholly demented. The idiot President of the Council flattered Sado to his face, but schemed against him behind his back. He plotted and whispered and scribbled secret messages in the dust. Lady Sŏnhŭi stuck by the king night and day, trying to keep guard and to prevent the president from poisoning Yŏngjo's mind about her son, Sado. The mood in the palace was one of dire uncertainty: nobody knew what would happen from day to day. I lived in terror that some harm would be plotted not only against Sado, but also against our son, now proclaimed the Grand Heir. This proclamation was made in the third month of 1759, amidst much rejoicing, but I feared for the future. Prince Chŏngjo was only a child of seven. And three months after this proclamation, King Yŏngjo remarried.

The king embarked on this new marriage correctly, according to protocol, through the three-stage selection process, and with the apparent approval of Lady Sŏnhŭi, but this time he married a woman very much younger than himself and from a family that had always been enemies of my family. This did not bode well for us. The bride was only fifteen. I knew that no good could come of this marriage, though, of course, like Lady Sŏnhŭi, I was obliged to express delight. And I have to say that Prince

122

Sado in public managed to behave in a proper manner towards his new young stepmother during the three-day wedding ceremony, which was soon followed by the Grand Heir's formal investiture.

In theory, all should now have been well with us. In the public domain, Prince Sado was recognized as crown prince and regent, and our son Chŏngjo was firmly established in the direct line of succession, as the Grand Heir and Royal Grandson. But in private, things went from bad to worse. The clothing mania, if anything, intensified, and I had to provide chests full of silk for his military uniforms. I was sick with anxiety most of the time, and my digestion, which hitherto had been good, now began to trouble me a great deal. I could not keep my food down — I now think I may have developed an ulcer. King Yŏngjo did not keep his promise to be more tolerant towards his son, but continued to find fault with him, and even encouraged others to criticize him.

I remember in particular the terrible scenes on Prince Sado's twenty-fifth birthday in 1760. Birthdays had always been a torment to Sado, for his father had for years used them as an excuse to haul him before an interrogatory court of tutors, and this year was no exception. Sado lost his temper most violently, and I cannot say I blame him. He hurled abuse at both his parents, and threatened yet again to kill himself. He yelled even at his own children, who had dressed themselves up for the occasion in dragon-embroidered robes and formal blouses. When they came into the room to make their congratulatory bows, he shouted at them to get out, crying out that he knew neither father nor mother, nor son, nor daughters. They were frightened by this and turned white as ash. His mother, Lady Sŏnhŭi, was appalled: I think she had been reluctant to recognize how bad things were, but now there was no hiding from the evidence. I felt completely impotent, shrunk to nothingness. I wished to turn to stone, to vanish from this world. Poor children, poor little dolls in their best clothes. What harm had they done to him? They tried so hard to please.

Our lives, I repeat, were claustrophobic. The palace compound was large and had many pavilions, halls and apartments, but it was full of gossip and of echoes. The walls were paperthin. We felt enclosed, but we were spied upon. Sado felt impotent, despite, because of his violence. He felt his life was useless — as indeed I fear it was. Playing heir to a throne that you know in your heart you will never inherit is not an easy role. His frantic military games in the back garden of our compound were no substitute for action. He said he could not endure living so close to his father, spied on by day and by night. Although by nature a strong young man, he was developing physical disorders as well as mental, which I put down to our unnatural lives — it was at this period that his skin began to flake and erupt, particularly on his legs and ankles. I think his skin condition was what is now called psoriasis, or possibly some form of eczema, but I am certain that, like his father's asthma, it was

124

largely caused by his living in a perpetual state of nervous irritation. I sympathized with Sado when he said he wanted to get out of the city of Seoul altogether, to escape and to see a little of the outside world. I was resigned to my cloistered fate, but Sado was a man, with a man's needs. A change of scene would, I felt, do him good.

But how could we achieve this? His father had always wanted to keep him on a short leash, under close supervision. I could see no way of persuading King Yŏngjo to agree to his release, even on a short journey, and frankly I feared to arouse his wrath by even making a request. One of us had to keep on the right side of him. I suppose I was a coward. Sado accused me of being a coward and a double dealer, and at one point during one of these domestic rows he threw a chessboard at me, which hit my left eye and caused a hideous swelling. This was the first time he had struck me, and I do not think he really meant the board to find its mark, but I was lucky not to lose the sight of the eye. The skin turned purple, then a deep orange-yellow. The bruise bloomed like a peony through my delicate olive skin.

Despairing of my intercession, Sado turned to his sister Madame Chŏng, who was bolder than me, and better able to manipulate her father, King Yŏngjo. (I was not bad at manipulating the old man, or I would not have outlived him as I did, but I had my son as my priority: she, as I have said, was by now widowed and childless, and had fewer hostages to fortune.) Sado

125

appealed to his sister in desperation and with threats of violence. He went to her with his sword in his hand, telling her that if she did not effect some release for him he would kill her. Such a threat from him, already a seasoned killer, was not to be ignored. He also threatened to kill her adopted son, a wild and rebellious boy called Chŏng Hugyŏm, who was at this time aged about twelve. Sado got hold of him and locked him in a cellar and threatened to murder him if Madame Chŏng did not fix this excursion, on which he had set his heart. The boy himself had seemed wholly undisturbed by these threats, although he must have known of Sado's dangerous reputation, and hurled back abuse at the Crown Prince. I suppose I have to admit this child was spirited, but he grew up to be a little monster, and a bad influence on my son.

Madame Chŏng, afraid for her protégé, alarmed by her brother's mad violence, agreed to plead with their father, and she did so with some success. She laid much emphasis on Sado's ill health and the possible benefits of the medicinal waters for the skin disease on Sado's legs. Under pressure from his daughter, Yŏngjo reluctantly gave permission for his son to travel south to Onyang, to the healing wells and hot springs.

At the same time, she achieved a double coup. As well as persuading King Yŏngjo to authorize Sado's journey to Onyang, she, even more surprisingly, managed to persuade Yŏngjo and Lady Sŏnhŭi to move for a while out of the large palace compound where we all lived, and to spend some time in another of the five royal palaces of Seoul. She hoped, I suppose, that this might reduce the growing tension between king and regent. This 'Mulberry Palace' stood about three miles to the east of our Ch'angdŏk-Ch'anggyŏng Palace Compound, and it was far enough away to lift some of the sense of daily oppression and surveillance that caused Sado such irritation.

(This palace was later destroyed, and I believe that no traces of it survive in modern Seoul: the other four ancient palaces, although many times partially destroyed by fire, sacking and invasion, have been as many times rebuilt, and some of their original fabric remains. You may visit them, if you are so minded. My envoy has wandered round them in search of me, and so may you.)

Prince Sado was delighted by the respite of the royal removal. He had suggested it himself, on several occasions, but we never thought King Yŏngjo would agree to so unorthodox a proposal: the suggestion came better from Madame Chŏng, who was a devious woman, expert in flattery. I do not know what arguments she used to persuade King Yŏngjo to move, but we were grateful to her for this temporary remission. I know that many of the court officials were gravely surprised by this change of residence, and shook their heads over it: it foreshadowed, some muttered, the fall of the Chosŏn dynasty and the house of Yi. For myself, I was also delighted. I did not see it as a permanent solution to all our troubles, for I rightly suspected that eventually the king would return to the upper palace, but at least it gave us a little more privacy at a time when we needed it. Those with dark family secrets need privacy more than most.

My bruised eye looked so shocking that I was unable either to pay my respects to King Yŏngjo in his new residence at the Mulberry Palace or to see Sado's entourage off on its way. I pretended, of course, that the contusion was a self-inflicted wound — the old story about tripping on a reed mat and falling against a sharp-edged cabinet — and people pretended to believe me, but I do not suppose they did. Anyone can recognize a battered wife. And the relief that swept over me when Sado was safely out of the way and on the road to Onyang was overwhelming. I was pleased for him, but I was even more pleased for myself. I felt I could breathe freely again, and I gathered the children to me for their evening hour with a sense of reprieve. Our little family circle seemed almost normal once Sado had gone. The strain of living in perpetual fear while appearing outwardly calm is almost intolerable.

In some ways, I had seen far more of my husband than many wives of my class because I had been obliged to set myself up as his warden and his protector, as well as his wife. In some *yangban* families at this period, there was a very considerable separation of roles and of domestic life, and wives and husbands rarely met, but Sado and I, for better and worse, were closely bound to one another. One of the curious features of Yŏngjo's court, I now realize, was its inbred, overheated emotional intensity. King Yŏngjo himself was an unstable, passionate man,

128

perpetually demanding a strong emotional response from others, and despite myself I had been sucked into this whirlpool of demonstrative and competitive display. My response to this feverishness, in contrast to Madame Chŏng's, had been to appear cool and excessively submissive: she was by temperament far more confrontational than I. But, cool though I hope I managed to appear, I had been obliged to remain close to the emotional turmoil, in order to monitor its dangers. It was very exhausting.

So those were happy and precious evenings with my son and daughters, when Sado was on the royal road to the hot springs with his modest entourage of a thousand attendants. We sat at home, playing a new board game for which there was a craze at that time throughout the palace — you know how such crazes come and go. I forget the rules now, but it was a peaceful, gentle game, with pretty counters and tiles of ivory and bamboo, representing chariots and horses and elephants and knights and soldiers. I suppose it was a version of *changgi*, adapted for multiple players. A spirit of peace descended on our little gatherings. You could hear the difference in the children's voices. We felt safe together when he was not there. I knew that my sense of relief was a perversion, a distortion of my primary duty of marital loyalty, but even at the time I thought that nobody could blame me. I was merely seeking a little comfort with my own. Those closest to me knew exactly how I felt. A visible sigh of relief, a susurration of relaxation rose from our quarters. The evening air thickened with goodness like soup. The very flowers exhaled relief. The ladies — those that lived — began to smile again, as they went about their daily tasks. They had had a reprieve, a stay of execution. I began to taste my food again and to sleep less restlessly, less fearfully.

As we quietly rejoiced, Prince Sado made his way southwards, with his entourage, towards Onyang. He had wanted to set off in great splendour, with rank upon rank of soldiers in uniform, with a band and a procession of drummers, and brightly clad heralds proclaiming his progress. And in fact, though he expressed himself aggrieved by his father's curtailing of these grand plans, he was well enough attended. He was accompanied by his tutors, by 120 people carrying his luggage, by an escort of soldiers and a full military band — not as flamboyant a display as he would have wished, but by no means as demeaning as he claimed. And by all accounts he behaved properly en route, compensating farmers for damage caused to crops and property by his large train, and distributing largesse as he went.

I believe he set off in some hope of escaping from himself, and of finding some kind of peace. I think, also, that he secretly wanted the people of Korea to acclaim him as he passed. He longed for affection, for admiration, for recognition. He was tired of his secondary, submissive role as heir apparent: he was tired of being scolded for his shortcomings. He wanted to be loved. And he was excited, like a child, by the tourist attractions of Onyang, then as now a lodestone for pilgrims in search of health and refreshment. He was thrilled by the notion of the natural wonders of the hot springs and the legendary beauty of the landscape he had never seen. Oh yes, he set off in high hopes. His anxious mother, almost as demented as I was about his state of mind, arranged for his favourite meals to be sent along the route for him and cooked for him at each staging post — I think she was very worried, by now, about the scenario of the poisoned mushrooms. I was beginning to feel more sympathy, at this time, for Lady Sŏnhŭi. She was growing old, and she, like me, was devoured by a daily fear for Sado.

At home, in our nest, we tried to forget about poison, and even attempted a little merriment. It was my son Chongjo who suggested that we should invite Fourth Brother to come to stay with us for a few days, while the coast was clear. Fourth Brother was only eighteen months older than his nephew Chongjo, and they were good friends. I readily agreed, and indeed took the opportunity to invite all my brothers and their wives to stay at the palace for a while. I was so uncertain of the future that I was not sure if I would ever see them again, and the notion of one last family gathering seemed irresistible. First Brother was, of course, *au fait* with the whole situation, having been a court official, and Fourth Brother was too little to know about it — though who knows what information passed between him and his royal nephew? Information unsuitable for children, as were the scenes they were later to witness. But Second and Third

Brothers, both of whom were younger than myself, and both of whom were working towards their civil service examinations in the ineluctable *yangban* family tradition, had been kept at a distance, and I looked forward to this opportunity of confiding in them. The burden was too great for me to carry alone. I needed their help. They were only young men — very young men — but I longed for their sympathy and understanding.

Do not think that I complained about Prince Sado. I had too much pride to complain about my husband, and too much true loyalty. But I had to tell them of the facts, in case the worst should happen, so that they would at least understand my conduct. Also, I suppose I had a sense that I should warn them for their own sake — a family connected by marriage to the royal house lives dangerously. Already I could see that Second and Third Brothers would react differently to my story than First Brother, who always put his public role first. Second Brother was a scholar and a dreamer who did not care much for court life: he would bide his time, then go his own way, and thus survive in his own manner. But Third Brother, even at the age of nineteen, was something of a rebel. He thought nothing of denouncing Confucian contradictions, and even made open mock of our reverence for our ancestors. On one occasion, I remember that he said that it was foolish to offer wine and meat to blocks of wood, for the dead could neither eat nor drink. It was an insult, he said, to our grandparents' and our mother's memory, to honour them in this meaningless way. What he said was, of course, reasonable enough, but it was also heretical. In the privacy of my home he spoke forcefully against the double standards by which King Yŏngjo expected his son and indeed all his people to live. I remember his declaring, 'Why should Sado be filial towards a father who takes a bride ten years younger than the son? Has the father no respect for the son? And why has the father remarried into a hostile family? Is he intending to take revenge upon all the Hongs?'

While the children played their childish games — and I trust they did not play at funerals and beheadings — we adults sat in conclave over our rice wine. (Wine was always readily available in the palace, despite all my father-in-law's edicts against alcohol consumption.) When I described the clothing phobia and the agonies I had suffered in trying to conceal it, Second Brother turned pale, and said quietly, 'But this is nothing but madness. He is deranged.' First Brother blamed the illness on the indulgence of his princely childhood, and brought up the infamous memory of Lady Han and her military toys. Third Brother took a different line — prompted, perhaps, by my supplementary account of Sado's superstitious fears of the *Jade Pivot* book and thunder and ghosts and the terrors of hell. He said that we ought to attempt some sort of exorcism, some sort of spiritual appeal to salvation. I was surprised by this, but Third Brother argued forcefully that one of the principal weaknesses of our Confucian system

133

was that it made no place for the spirit. It was too rigid, too material, too insistent on place and function and ritual, and did not consider the inner individual being. Clearly Sado's spirit was in torment, said Third Brother, which is why he saw malicious ghosts everywhere and in everything, and could find calm only in violence.

Third Brother, I believe, was beginning to develop a concept of what other cultures had long called the 'soul'. He had been reading foreign books, and talking to advanced neo-Confucian thinkers.

We, in Korea, did not believe in the soul. Now, nobody believes in the soul. We have come full circle.

I listened to these ideas, intently, and stroked the fading bruise on my brow. What was the spirit? Were there good and evil essences, and did they pertain to people, or to acts? Could one separate Sado's evil acts from his being, and rescue his true self from them? You think we were a shallow and frivolous court, and I have said that we were an hysterical court. But we thought deeply, and talked deeply, at times. Think of us. We were at the long end, the dying fall of thousands of years of tradition, trapped like insects in the solidified mass of the past. To struggle out of that was painful, laborious. Third Brother struggled, and died for it. I, woman-like, was well trained in the arts of disguise and discretion, and I hid my efforts and my dissent. There were some, of course, who truly believed in the traditions — who believed that we Koreans were the only true inheritors of

134

Confucian wisdom, that we alone, now that the Ming dynasty of China had been overthrown, were keeping alive the true path and the proper way. But there were many more who were frightened to think freely, frightened to question the nature of the straitjacket that confined us.

I underestimate, perhaps, the genuine reforming efforts of King Yŏngjo. I had been too close to him, from my early years, and I could not see him in his role as a successful statesman. I acknowledge now that maybe he tried to move his country forward, but I did not at this time understand his politics or his statecraft. My father and First Brother attempted to explain these matters to me, and I have subsequently, posthumously, made efforts to study them. It seems that King Yŏngjo introduced new accounting systems, and distributed books in *han'gŭl* script to the peasantry. According to the history books, he established a state examination for older people, and organized the dredging of riverbeds by massive mobilizations of the workforce. The Military Taxation Act of 1751 was an important reform, and his attempts to abolish factionalism (his so-called *'t'angp'yŏng'* policy) aimed to establish a coalition bureaucracy including both the Noron and the Soron. It is now, in your day, argued that he was not unresponsive to the demands of the common people: one twenty-first century scholar tells us that he went out of the palace fifty-five times during his fifty-two-year reign to listen to their demands and appeals. And it may have been so. But these, in the long view, were mere tinkerings

135

with a failing system, intended to placate powerful enemies and appease public unrest. A little pitch, a little tar, a little glue. The great ship was sailing to nowhere. Our peninsula was stranded out of time.

I look back now, from my longer perspective, and I think about Europe, the Americas, Russia, India, Indonesia, Malaysia, Australia and all those discovered and undiscovered continents of which we then knew nothing or next to nothing. Of China we knew much, and of Japan something, to our cost, but we knew nothing of those lands towards which Captain Cook was soon to set sail. And of the Western powers themselves, we still knew little. This was the dawning age of Enlightenment, in Europe. Great waves of new thought were swelling up like molten magma from beneath the earth's crust. During my long lifetime, the French Revolution would come and go, and the king of France and his Austrian queen went to the guillotine. Did we sense the power of those eruptions, far away in our distant fragile earthly shelter? I think perhaps we did. Our perspectives were changing, slowly but inevitably. The art of perspective itself was on its way towards us.

And yet barbarisms and ceremonials persisted, persist. By chance I have been reading a life of my contemporary on earth, Catherine the Great of Russia, who married the Grand Duke Peter the year after I was married to Prince Sado — she was a little older than I was at the time of this union. My marriage was not consummated for five years, hers to Peter possibly never, though she did manage to produce a child who was recognized as her heir. The court life she knew as a young woman was, by her own account, in many ways as strange and unnatural as the court life of the kingdom of Korea. And her husband, like mine, played at toy soldiers. He had an army of them. He is said to have court-martialled, convicted and ceremonially hanged a rat because it had been caught gnawing at one of his toy soldiers. Such are the games that archdukes and crown princes play.

As we have seen, even wise children play strange games. It is when adults play these games that we should fear them.

When Peter was murdered, his wife's faction seized the throne, and Catherine became empress. She ruled Russia triumphantly for many years. She, too, was a clever woman. At her coronation in Moscow, she was more over-dressed than any woman in our country has ever been, and in far heavier and more unbecoming adornments. The fabric of her robes would have clothed an entire family. Four thousand pelts of four thousand of those pretty ermine rats were stitched together to make her robe, and she was so weighed down with precious stones that she could hardly move. She changed her dress and the styling of her hair ten times on that day of imperial celebrations. She ascended the throne in the year 1762, the *imo* year in which my husband was to die. I did not ascend the throne in Prince Sado's place. Yet I was, in my own way, a great lady, and princess of an ancient kingdom. I was not a handmaid. I never became the Red

Queen, but I was for many years the Crown Princess.

I told a lie when I said that I had been reading about Catherine the Great 'by chance'. On the contrary, I now suffer from a morbid and somewhat demeaning obsession with royal biographies, particularly of my own period, and have been making my way through lives of the Romanovs, of Louis XVI and Marie Antoinette, of Frederick the Great, of Napoleon and his Josephine, and of other potentates — lives that were unknown to me in my lifetime, restricted as we largely were to Chinese history and the Chinese tradition. Frederick the Great of Prussia, also my contemporary, was renowned as a great and enlightened ruler, yet he, too, nearly went mad in his youth, when he was crown prince. His soldier father put him under arrest for treason and conspiracy, and forced him to witness the execution of his dearest friend. The body of his friend lay on the sand in the sun for many hours. The crown prince, obliged to watch from an upper window, was forbidden to avert his eyes from this spectacle. The past is barbarous.

The last emperor of the Ming dynasty of China hanged himself. Louis XVI of France was executed. Marie Antoinette, his wife, was executed. King Louis was executed in the year that the English 'barbarians', led by Lord Macartney, attempted to enter China and were contemptuously rebuffed.

I repeat, the past of every country of the globe is barbarous. By telling this story, my story, I am

138

not accusing my country of any special barbarity, of any unique cruelty. I have read of the unfortunate wives of Henry VIII. I have read about the Star Chamber, and about the Inquisition, and about the French Revolution. America today has its Death Row and its electric chair.

Marie Antoinette was not nearly as intelligent and articulate as I am. She was a poor scholar and a muddled thinker. She blotted her books. Yet one cannot help but be moved by her sad story, for she was a devoted mother to her little ones. (She was falsely accused of incest with her son, a disgraceful and I believe unfounded allegation.) She, too, was a child bride, married by proxy at fourteen to a man she had never seen. The marriage took seven difficult and humiliating years to consummate. Prince Sado and I did better than that. Her wretched and sickly sons died. One of mine survived and became king.

Oh yes, alas, we compete beyond the grave.

In 1817, two years after my death, an Englishman, Captain Basil Hall, briefly sailed to my country, on a vessel called the *Alceste*: he wrote a fair and popular account of his visit, describing honestly the muted and distrustful but not wholly unfriendly welcome he received here. (We were very suspicious of foreigners, and with good reason: the *Alceste* and her companion sloop, the *Lyra*, were engaged in spying out and mapping our coastline.) Captain Hall executed some sketches of the volcanic Sulphur Island and of various other islands and harbours round our shores, and drew portraits of several of the gracefully dressed dignitaries whom he encountered. (He left behind the body of a young English sailor, who died at the age of twenty-one, and whose sad grave is still to be seen in the cemetery on the island now well known to you as Okinawa.) Like my husband and my son, Captain Hall had an artistic talent: his drawings were good. He later showed these sketches to Napoleon in exile on the island of Saint Helena. Napoleon expressed some interest in them. Captain Hall's father, Sir James Hall, had studied with the boy Napoleon at the Royal Military School in Brienne in France.

I do not know why I find this record of such an inconsequential contact between East and West so haunting. Maybe it is because so many of my family, like Napoleon, spent so much time in exile upon barren rocks and islands. I never in my lifetime set eyes on the yellow peak of Sulphur Island, nor on the Great Loo Choo islands. I saw them only in Captain Hall's pleasantly tinted sketches, which I saw in the Rare Books Department of the British Library. I saw so little, in my long life.

Was I plotting, with my brothers and their wives, against my husband and my father-in-law during Prince Sado's absence in Onyang? Some would have said — many did say — that we were a wicked and treacherous cabal. 'The Hongs of the Noron are up to their tricks again' — that no doubt was a rumour that spread around the compound. Yet I would swear that there was nothing disloyal in our discussions. We were trying to save Sado from himself. It is hard to describe the pity I felt for this violent and unhappy man. Great unhappiness and torture of the spirit compel our pity. And I was the first bride of his bed, and the mother of his first-born child.

My pity was much in demand on poor Sado's return from Onyang. He came back much disappointed, and much earlier than we expected him. Onyang, he complained, was small, dull and provincial. Onyang was a bore. The society was undistinguished and largely octogenarian — as, indeed, it is in many watering places, as I had tried to tell him — and the buildings were unimpressive. Even the landscape, he said, was dull. (I was disappointed to hear this as I had long cherished a secret desire to travel south — a desire, as you will hear, that was long after to be most strangely fulfilled.) The radium hot spring and lightly alkaline water had done nothing for his skin eruptions, he said. He wanted to set off again at once on another trip, to P'yŏngsan, but we managed to persuade him that he would find this even smaller and duller than Onyang. We knew that his father would never permit another outing so soon, so we did our best to put him off the notion of any further journeys. He was strangely submissive to our advice, at least for a while.

Prince Sado brought back a present for me. It was an amethyst sceptre, in a gross natural shape which I would now describe as phallic. The region was and is famous for its amethyst, so there was nothing particularly surprising or suggestive in the nature of the memento — apparently the tourist booths were full of these objects, though the piece that Sado brought for me was of princely quality. But I remember being slightly shocked by its form. The ladies-in-waiting sniggered at it, though not in my earshot, and I could see why. I pretended to be pleased with it, and created a little artificial garden for it, with a small lake of silver and flowers of jade and a tree of coral. He was pleased with my attentions to this ambiguous gift. There was so little I could do to please him that I was pleased, too. I wonder what happened to my amethyst garden. It was still at the palace when I died.

Sado came home in discontent, and soon resumed his military games and equitation exercises in the garden, in a hopeless, desultory yet persistent and superstitious manner. Meanwhile, during all this period, the king was paying more and more attention to our son Chŏngjo, the Grand Heir, clearly now depending on him for the future of his dynasty. And Chŏngjo, being mature and bright, responded well to these attentions. He devoted himself eagerly to the royal lecture sessions, and answered his grandfather's questions with a wisdom beyond his years. He was a serious child who expected a great deal of himself, and, unlike his father, he actively enjoyed the intellectual challenge of a cross-examination. Unfortunately, King Yŏngjo was not satisfied simply to accept the good fortune of Chŏngjo's aptitude and eagerness, and could not restrain himself from praising the grandson at the expense of the father. These ill-judged remarks and signs of discriminatory preference were transcribed into the accounts of the royal lecture sessions that Sado ordered to be recorded. This favouritism was very stupid of King Yŏngjo, but who was in a position to tell him to desist? I was so frightened that these reports might enrage Sado against his son that I persuaded the eunuchs in charge to delete any prejudicial comments from the copies of the proceedings that were shown to Sado. On the whole, this discreet system worked quite successfully, and I managed to moderate the tone of Yŏngjo's praises so subtly that Sado did not suspect that I was censoring the reports. But this deceit required incessant vigilance on my part.

It was during this period that Prince Sado began to leave the palace compound at night in disguise. This was completely forbidden, and very dangerous, but what could I do to prevent it? He could no longer be contained. He was a grown man, in the prime of life, and used to indulgence as well as to severity. I know that my father tried to speak to him, but without success. There was nobody who could manage the prince. I had despaired of my own influence over him, but I still had some faith in Lady Pingae, who for some time now had been the only person whom he permitted to attend him when he was getting dressed. I saw her as my ally, and considered that we had a common cause. I think she shared this view. I think she was my true friend. It may seem strange to some, this friendship between legitimate wife and favoured mistress, but, believe me, it was not so strange. Such alliances were not infrequent. I have to confess — I have already indirectly confessed — that I found Pingae attractive. She was beautiful.

Then, suddenly, one evening, in the first month of the *sinsa* year of 1761, as he was getting ready to go on one of his incognito outings into the town, Prince Sado was seized with one of his violent tantrums, and he attacked Lady Pingae as she tried to remonstrate with him. After that first death, the death of the eunuch Kim Hanch'ae, this was the greatest shock our circle had suffered. I was not a witness to this scene, but I had heard terrible cries across the moonlit garden, and the news of his assault on Pingae came to me swiftly. I do not know if he knew that she was dying when he stormed out into the night, but she died soon after, within hours. I reached her before she died, but she was already speechless and insensible from head wounds and loss of blood. I was not able to bid her goodbye. Despite my grief and shock, and the knowledge that Sado might return at any moment, I kept my presence of mind and managed to behave rationally. As soon as the night was over I had her body removed to Yongdong Palace, where I arranged for her funeral to take place. This was as correct and dignified a ceremony as I could manage, within the limits of discretion and finance. I felt I was becoming Sado's undertaker as well as his wife.

When Prince Sado returned from his rampage, two days later, he said nothing. He did not mention Pingae, and he never asked after her again. It was as though she had never been. This was the woman he had loved above all others, the woman for whom he had braved his father's fury. I never mentioned her again, of course. Did he know what he had done? I cannot tell. The news of the murder spread, despite the silence of myself and Sado, and I think it was no coincidence that the three chief ministers of the State Council — the President, the Minister of the Right, and the Minister of the Left — died in quick succession in the second and third months of this dreadful year. It was not a question of poisoned mushrooms. I believe they died by their own hands, in recognition of their inability to control Prince Sado, or to save him from himself. They saw it as their duty to die. Our culture had, at least in principle, a high regard for the dutiful suicide. My father was appointed to replace one of them on the State Council, a place that he accepted despite his deep misgivings. He had not sought advancement: he had had it imposed upon him, and for Sado's sake, and for my sake, and for my son's sake, he dared not refuse.

Sado continued his nocturnal wanderings, dressed in common clothing, consorting with blind fortune-tellers, prostitutes, *kisaeng*, nuns, monks, shamans and other lowlife and expendable characters. At the end of the third month, he went on a longer excursion, to the province of P'yŏngyang, in the north-west — we had tried to dissuade him from this in the previous year, but he had clearly set his heart on it. Although Prince Sado was travelling under a false identity, the governor of the province — Governor Chŏng, who was the uncle of Madame Chŏng's late husband — knew perfectly well who this mysterious and troublesome stranger was, and took it upon himself to wait on him and make sure that he had proper provisions. Governor Chŏng dared not report Sado's whereabouts to King Yŏngjo, but he kept in touch with my father, who found himself in an insoluble dilemma. My father was equally reluctant to alert the king to his son's transgressions because he feared the consequences for the rest of our family, in particular for the Grand Heir. So he, too, had to play a double game, concealing Prince Sado's absence and his increasingly uncontrollable dementia. We were all compromised by Sado, all complicit in his crimes.

The Outcast Prince, the Prince of Rags, the Prince of Mournful Thoughts. His fate was closing in upon him.

At the palace, in the prince's household, we played a new double game. We had to disguise his absence somehow, so we pretended that he was indisposed through illness. The head eunuch, Yu Insik, a clever and faithful friend, lay in the inner room, speaking and giving orders in the manner and voice of the prince, while another tended to him exactly as though he were the prince. Perhaps it is better not to discuss the terror and shame this duplicity produced in each of us who participated in it.

Others, less loyal to the Hong family, and playing for different stakes, were not slow to pick up on and to report the prince's aberrations. Denunciations and critical memorials, particularly about the visit to the north-west, were presented one after another to the prince, by those who quite rightly insisted that it was their duty to admonish him. The king did not come across these official memorials in the *Records of the Royal Secretariat* for some months, so there was a period of respite after Sado's return to the palace from the north-west — he had only been away for some twenty days, but these had been days of constant anxiety for us, knowing as we did that his father had not approved his absence. How different from the happy days of the permitted journey to Onyang! And yet, mysteriously, the secret P'yŏngyang visit seemed to have had a more calming effect on Sado. On his return, he seemed quieter, more in control, and he conducted himself in a more decorous way during his regular audiences and lecture sessions. How pitiably we searched for signs of improvement! We still thought that maybe, if he could lead a more normal, a more active life, he might yet recover. He even managed to make himself pay his first visit to offer his respects to his parents at their new residence in Kyŏnghŭi Palace, a visit that, despite my apprehensions, passed without mishap. A few days later, I too went to Kyŏnghŭi Palace to pay my respects to His Majesty and Lady Sŏnhŭi, taking with me the Grand Heir, their grandson. It was an awkward encounter. There was so much on all our minds, and so little we could say.

Inevitably, King Yŏngjo soon discovered about the unauthorized trip to the north-west. It was in the ninth month that he read the official records that mentioned it, and, predictably, he at once flew into a violent rage, ordering the banishment of certain eunuchs and the demotion of various tutors and royal secretaries. My father was at this time stripped of his post, though he was later reinstated. His Majesty threatened to descend in wrath upon Sado in the palace, and we fully expected his arrival and some dire consequences because on this occasion he had every right to be angry, for he had been deliberately deceived by all of us. Sado confided his fears to me. He said that he knew that his father wished to get rid of him. He believed his life was in danger. I tried to reason with him, telling him that the king loved the Grand Heir and would never harm the Grand Heir's father: 'He who respects the son must also respect his father, for father and son are bound together and share the same destiny,' I reminded him, deploying an old Confucian platitude. But the prince, with much prescience, declared that it would be easy for his father to depose him and declare the Grand Heir the adopted son of his half-brother who had died at the age of ten, before Sado was born. Thus the succession would be assured, and Sado himself would be annihilated and written out of the record. There were plenty of precedents in our history for such strategic false adoptions.

I protested that this was impossible, even while it struck me that it was horribly possible, but

148

Sado said, 'Wait and see! Even though you belong to me, he has always treated you and the children well. You will all survive, all of you. It is me that he hates, and me alone. His hatred has driven me into this illness, and now, because of this illness and his hatred, he will not let me live.'

He spoke prophetically, with the clear wisdom of despair.

However, the threatened royal visitation to our palace was suddenly cancelled. It seems that his inconsistent Majesty, who could fly into a rage about the tying of a pair of trousers, had as yet no stomach for dealing with a real confrontation over a serious issue. So we were spared this crisis, at least for a while.

The next drama involved the selection of a wife for our son the Grand Heir, and another miserable story of a jade headdress. It was time for Chŏngjo to be betrothed, and, as was customary, various names were put forward for the first selection for a child bride, including that of one young person much favoured by my father and by Prince Sado. The daughter of Minister Kim, she was persuasively described to me as 'a beautiful and elegant young girl' — poor child. Sado was too ill and too much out of favour to attend the selection process, so of course I could not go either, which seemed very hard to me. Luckily, the girl was chosen anyway: unluckily, both children contracted smallpox soon after the second selection. My father, now fully reinstated in King Yŏngjo's favour, was asked by Yŏngjo himself to stay with their grandson during his illness, to attend to him and see to his needs. My father was indispensable. He had made himself indispensable. Both of the children recovered, but it was an anxious time.

So all seemed well, and the final presentation approached. It even seemed as though Sado and I would at last be allowed to meet our future daughter-in-law. I was full of apprehensions about how Sado would conduct himself, and I was right to be so. Sado found it almost impossible to decide how to dress for this important event, and, when he had finally settled on a suit of clothes, he could not find an acceptable cap. He would not wear a hat suitable for his princely status, but instead he elected to put on a large and heavy cap of a military cut decorated with jade beads of the third rank. Even I have to say it was neither flattering nor appropriate, but nevertheless there was no call for His Majesty King Yŏngjo to become enraged by the very sight of this cap. He ordered Sado, in front of everybody, to leave the room. And Sado left, as it were, in disgrace.

I should have left with him, I suppose, but I was overcome by a natural desire to see this girl who was to be one of my family and the bride of my son, so I stayed. But I knew that Sado must be wild with humiliation and disappointment. I quietly suggested to Madame Chŏng and Lady Sŏnhŭi that there might be a possibility of taking the bride-elect to visit Prince Sado privately in our palace, which was on the way to the bride's pavilion. This unorthodox proposal threw them into a panic, and they were still discussing the issue, in much confusion, when I decided to cut

150

through their hesitations. I took the liberty of ordering an attending eunuch to make sure that the bride's palanquin and mine were brought into the palace together. And so we two veiled and hidden women were carried through the gate, and entered the adjoining lower palace to which my husband had been banished.

When we arrived, my daughter-in-law elect and myself, we found poor Prince Sado lying in great dejection and depression, nursing his sense of grievance and a small warm bowl of clear *ch'onju* wine. He had taken off that hideous helmet, and was dressed in an embroidered black silk gown. I entered the room boldly, with a theatrical flourish, followed by the poor little mite of a girl — how well I remembered my own terrors, and how justified were hers! — and announced with as much panache and respect as I could summon, 'Here I am, ready to present to you the royal grandson's consort and future bride!' Sado was pleasantly surprised, and struggled to his feet to pay his respects to the little lady. He was smiling foolishly all over his face. Goodness knows what she made of the somewhat dishevelled grinning figure of her future father-in-law, but she did her best to greet him in a proper manner, and somehow we managed to pass a pleasant hour or two together. Sado was very reluctant to see her go, and tried to detain her: he was on touchingly good behaviour with her, trying to make her laugh, and pressing her to take a sip of his wine. She struggled bravely with her natural shyness and terror, and endeared herself to her future father-in-law by speaking well of the Grand Heir. 'Such a fine young person!' she said. 'And so handsome, just like his father!' Sado, who had at times such childlike innocence, smiled with naive delight at this diplomatic remark, and paid her many compliments in turn. So pretty, a face like a flower, skin like fine porcelain, hair like the raven's wing, and such lovely dark eyes — and how fortunate that the smallpox had left no mark upon her lovely complexion. (Actually, she was still slightly scarred, but one can do wonders with cosmetics, and Sado was not very perceptive about such matters.)

One would never have thought, watching the two of them together, exchanging compliments, that Sado was a psychotic and a murderer. At such moments, I found it hard to believe myself. But within an hour of her departure, he was again reviling his father and shouting blasphemies.

I hoped and prayed that he would manage to control himself well enough to be able to attend the three days of the marriage ceremony at the beginning of the *imo* year of 1762. He was struck down, in the first month of the year, with another attack of very severely inflamed tonsils, and I did not know whether to wish for a timely recovery or not. Maybe, I unworthily thought, it would be as well if he were kept out of sight. In fact, with the help of acupuncture and moxibustion, he did get better quite quickly. The wedding itself took place on the second day of the second month, and Prince Sado and I were both able to be present for all the processions and the ceremonies. Grandfather and father were able to put on a show of unity as they saw the Grand Heir off on his way to present a carved duck wrapped in a dark blue embroidered and ribboned cloth to the little bride.

Sado was very anxious to be allowed to spend all three days of the celebration in King Yŏngjo's residence in the upper palace, near the newlyweds, and indeed spent one night there before his father ordered him to return home to the lower palace — an order Yŏngjo issued as soon as strict protocol permitted. I would have been allowed to stay on in Ch'angdŏk-gung, but I thought it was unfair (and unwise) to be so favoured, so I managed with many excuses to slip away. I was relieved, in a way, to leave the presence of King Yŏngjo's most recent wife, the young Queen Chŏngsun: I am sure the sight of her there with his father had exacerbated Sado's resentments. I am afraid Sado often used to shout abuse about the young queen, his new stepmother, in his drunken outpourings, though he made efforts to behave decently in her presence.

Sado had taken more and more heavily to alcohol after Lady Pingae's death. Having been unjustly and publicly accused six years earlier by Yŏngjo of excessive drinking, he had now taken up drinking in earnest, as if to fulfil his father's prophecy. And after the wedding of our son, after his brief attempt to behave correctly and in accordance with protocol, he again began to sink into real excess. He drank both wines and spirits: he was particularly addicted to a fierce form of

153

fired liquor which is still marketed under the name of *soju*. He found a companion in his drinking bouts in his sister, Madame Chŏng, with whom he held many disreputable parties within the palace compound, in the T'ongmyŏng Pavilion or outdoors in the gardens. Madame Chŏng, who was, you may remember, a young widow, was at this period widely lampooned as the incestuous partner of her brother. I do not know if they ever slept together, but they certainly drank together. At the end of the orgies, late at night, everyone, highborn and lowborn alike, would fall asleep over the tables, which were covered in leftover food and overturned bowls. These were scenes of unparalleled abandon and indulgence and excess.

Prince Sado's own residence now looked more like a funeral chamber than a home for the living. He had red flags made that looked exactly like funereal flags, and had them set up in every room, including his bedchamber. Obsessed by fear and the expectation of his own imminent death, he summoned blind fortune-tellers to his macabre court, and, when he did not like what they foretold, he ordered them to be executed. Many medical doctors, astronomers and servants were also killed or injured. Dead bodies were carried from the palace nearly every day. His paranoia increased as the killings continued, and, in the fifth month of the year, he ordered the construction of a kind of living tomb in an excavation beneath the palace. It had three small rooms with sliding doors between them, just like the inside of a grave, and there was a passage to the outside world through a small door in the ceiling. The door was nothing more than a wood panel of the same size, which had earth and grass planted over it, so that there was no sign that there was anything underground. The prince spent many hours alone inside this subterranean chamber, which was lit by a hanging lamp of jade.

He said that his intention was merely to have a place in which to hide all his military weapons and equestrian equipment in case His Majesty should come to the lower palace to ask for them, but understandably this underground tomb and the living death of the prince who hid there gave rise to dark suspicions. Some thought he was plotting against his father's life, though anybody who observed him as closely as I did would have known that he was beyond any such organized attempt; others, more reasonably, thought that he was insane, and wedded to death. This was certainly my interpretation of his behaviour. I can now see that in some ways our culture might have been thought to encourage a form of necrophilia, through its emphasis on ancestor worship, on offerings to the dead, and on prolonged and precise mourning rituals, but I hope I have made it plain that Sado's obsessions surpassed even the most devout or exhibitionist displays of normal or conventional mourning. He was consumed by death. In the prime of his youth and strength, he courted death. This was not a charade, though it may have begun as a charade.

Just after the digging of this underground

vault, his mother Lady Sŏnhŭi came to the lower palace of Ch'anggyŏng to visit us for a few days. It was the first time she had come to us since the Grand Heir's wedding, and she was anxious to see the new Grand Heir Consort in her new residence. The prince was delighted and strangely moved by the prospect of this visit, which filled him with excited anticipation. He went to great lengths to entertain her, and planned every moment of her stay in detail. Did he know that this was to be his last farewell to his mother? Each meal was prepared in the manner of a feast, with all sorts of delicacies, and he composed a poem on her longevity and offered drinks in her honour, urging her again and again to drain her wine cup. Then he took her to the rear garden, where he insisted she ride in a palanquin arranged in the manner of the king's sedan (this was of course a form of lese-majesty) and accompanied by men carrying large military flags, and a band of trumpets and drums.

This was obviously Prince Sado's notion of treating his mother with reverence and filial devotion, but Lady Sonhui, far from appearing gratified, was understandably dismayed by this deranged and disproportionate display of affection. Whenever she saw me, she would take me aside, and shed tears, and whisper fearfully, 'Whatever will happen next? What is this for? What does this mean?' I think until this point she had been unaware of the depths of his dementia. After a few days, she left for the upper palace; at their parting, both of them were in tears, and so

156

was I. I was not at all certain that I would ever see her again in this life.

It was clear that we could not go on as we were, at this unsustainable pitch of misery, madness and destruction, and from that time onwards our fortunes rapidly unravelled. Our enemies were gathering against us. In the fifth month of the *imo* year of 1762, King Yŏngjo was shown — I do not know by whom — a virulent denunciation of Sado, written by a brother of a palace guard, and detailing a list of crimes allegedly committed by Prince Sado. Yŏngjo's outrage was uncontrollable, although he must have suspected something of what was happening. He set up an interrogation committee, on which my father served: my father managed to persuade him that he, my father, should be the one to convey to Sado the nature of these grave allegations.

King Yŏngjo consented, and the usual weary ritual of Prince Sado's filial prostration at the palace gate was followed by a violent confrontation between father and son, during which Yŏngjo charged Sado with beating and killing Lady Pingae, who was now suddenly and retrospectively elevated to the role of 'the mother of royal grandchildren'. How could Sado have done such a thing, Yŏngjo demanded, when he had even jumped into a well and tried to kill himself for love of her? How could he have killed the one he loved? Yŏngjo brought up other accusations, and Sado replied with his usual defence — he was unloved, and perpetually frustrated, and he had been driven to despair

157

and violence by his father's neglect. He lacked advancement, and saw no future for himself. It was his father who had driven him mad.

The informant was executed, and his brother, the palace guard, was interrogated under torture, but he refused or was unable to give any more details about the plot against the throne that King Yŏngjo now seems to have suspected. For the next few days, Prince Sado lived under the threat of royal punishment, prostrating himself daily in public at a designated place — but, during the hours when he was unobserved, he was running wilder than ever, and uttering incoherent threats against those whom he thought were ranged against him. He threatened to kill Lord Yŏngsŏng, the son of the recently appointed President Sin Man, whom Sado loathed. He also appealed by many letters to his sister Madame Chŏng, in the most violent terms, and with some equally shocking and inappropriate endearments, complaining that she was not offering help to him in his extreme troubles. He threatened to make his way unobserved from the lower palace where we lived to the upper palace, through the water conduit, where he said he would murder Lord Yŏngsŏng and others — it is not surprising that many at this time feared for their lives. I know that King Yŏngjo feared for his. And I know that Sado set off, like a madman, through those labyrinthine miles of subterranean water passages, on two successive nights, but he never got very far — either he lost his way or his nerve. On the second occasion he hurt his back, quite badly, and returned in pain as well as humiliation. He was not suited to the role of conspirator or assassin.

Do I believe that Prince Sado intended to murder his father? No, I do not. I think this intention was pinned on him later as an excuse for the father killing the son. But I do think that there were some at court who would have followed Prince Sado rather than his father, mad though Sado was, had it come to open conflict, open choice. He had his loyal followers. The Time-Servers and the Bigots — these were the nicknames of the factions. The Time-Servers were said to support the prince, the Bigots to favour his death. I do not know. I did not understand these matters.

Many officials were paralysed by fear and indecision. They saw danger either way.

'A power struggle for the succession.' 'The tragic story of a succession dispute.' That is how the history books and the *Encyclopœdia Britannica* calmly describe these confused events.

Lady Sŏnhŭi was by now convinced that her first duty lay in protecting not her son, but His Majesty King Yŏngjo. I am not sure when she first arrived at this conclusion — perhaps when she took her leave of Sado after his final bizarre honours to her, perhaps when the fatal denunciation from the palace guard's brother reached King Yŏngjo. She wrote to me when she heard of the episode of the water passage, saying that she had abandoned all hope of her son, and wished only to preserve the life of the king, and the life of the Grand Heir, and the bloodline of

159

the 400-year-old dynasty. While protesting her love for her son, whom she said she loved ten thousand times more than she loved any other, she effectively added her signature to his death sentence. 'I do not know,' she wrote, 'whether I shall be able to meet you again in this life.' Thus she bade me farewell, and consigned me, too, to my death. When I read this letter, I wept unrestrainedly, tears of anger, despair and indignation. I knew that time had run out for us, but I did not wish to give in so easily.

It is my belief that Lady Sŏnhŭi, having written in this manner to me, went to King Yŏngjo and urged on him the death of Sado. She told him that Sado was irrevocably mad, past hope, past cure. 'He cannot be blamed,' she said, 'but he cannot be saved.' Yŏngjo, since the revelation of the extent of Sado's crimes, had been attempting to put right some of the wrongs committed by his son — he had offered compensation to merchants whose goods the prince had appropriated, and to the families of women who claimed they had been raped by the prince or by his rout of drunken followers. (No doubt many false claims were successfully presented at this time, as rumours of compensation spread — how can history keep a reliable account?) Some of those who had offended in the prince's name were executed. But the king had discovered and confronted injuries beyond repair, and wrongs beyond any recompense. He, too, like Lady Sŏnhŭi, was in despair, and he was driven to agree with her verdict. I think he, too, had, by this time, lost all hope. He knew that at last he would have to take action. And so the events that led to the Imo Incident were set in motion.

King Yŏngjo ordered a morning departure the next day for Ch'anggyŏng Palace, and Lady Sŏnhŭi went back to her residence and took to her bed, in great distress.

The news that his father had set off towards us in the lower palace brought panic and alarm to Sado, alarm compounded by the fact that the royal procession chose to make its way through the Kyŏnghwa Gate, a gate which signified misfortune. King Yŏngjo set great store by such symbolic choices. It should also be noted here that all the five royal palaces, as was customary, faced south, towards the fortunate mountain, save for the lower palace, which faced to the east: was this also an ill portent? I do not believe in portents. So why do I take the trouble to record them? It was Sado and his father who believed in portents. There were so many portents. It was on this eve of this day that one of the beams of the hall had given a great groan, as though it were about to break: Sado interpreted this as an omen of his own forthcoming death.

Fearing his father's approach, Prince Sado ordered that all his military equipment be hidden, and he set off, deeper into the compound, concealed in his heavily curtained palanquin, to Tŏksŏng House, where he summoned me to attend him. It was now about noon, on one of the hottest days of the year: it was heavy and still, and not a breath of air stirred the limp wind pennants on their high poles. I ran

161

round to warn my son, the Grand Heir, that something terrible was about to happen. I urged him to keep calm, be brave and watch out for himself. Then I obeyed Sado's orders and went to Tŏksŏng House, where I fully expected some dreadful and enraged attack from him. (On the way, I saw a great flock of magpies gathering and cawing round the pavilion, which even I took to be an ill omen. As you know, I have always had an irrational fear of magpies.) I found Sado not enraged, but subdued, drained and fatalistic, sitting with his back resting against a wall. All that Prince Sado said to me was, 'It looks bad for me, but they will let you live.'

We sat there, together, in silence, for a long while, in the heat of the day, like condemned prisoners, not knowing what to do or to say. Then I think the messenger arrived, telling us that the royal procession and the avenging king had reached the Hwinyŏng Shrine, where he was awaiting his son, who was expected to perform a ceremony there. This, or at least as I remember it, was about three in the afternoon: the official records note a somewhat different time scale for these events. The prince at this news did not rant or rage or plot his escape, as one might have expected. Calmly, he asked for the dragon robe of the crown prince, and for the Grand Heir's winter cap. He said he intended to feign illness. In truth, he had little need to feign. He was ill, ill to death, in mind and in body. As the Grand Heir's winter cap was small, I thought it would be better for him to wear his own cap, and asked a lady-in-waiting to fetch it, but this brought a

162

bitter outburst against me from Sado. He accused me of wanting to live a long life with my son, free of my husband's misfortune, and that this was the reason why I did not wish him to wear our son's cap. He said that I wished to preserve the cap from pollution. He accused me of cruelty and malevolence. I was taken aback by this irrational attack, and immediately pressed the Grand Heir's little cap upon him, but he now refused it, changing his tack and saying, in a reasonable and woefully subdued and resigned tone, 'No, no, why should I wear it when you do not wish me to wear it?'

It was getting late, and from where we sat we could hear the shrill, angry voice of His Majesty at the shrine, and the rapping of his sword. Sado knew he had to go out to meet his fate. He hesitated, but eventually, with some urgings of support from me and from his attendants, he gathered himself together, with one last effort, and stood up, and left the room. I was never to see him alive again. I cannot recall his last words to me, or mine to him. I saw him go to his death, and I did not reach out my hand to stop him.

I will not now attempt to describe my emotions. After a while, I asked one of the attendants to go to the wall and look over it to see if he could see what was happening. He returned to report that the prince had already removed the dragon robe, and was now prostrate upon the ground. I knew that this was the last scene of the last act of the tragic drama of his life. I was too restless and despairing to stay at Tŏksŏng House, waiting passively on the

163

unrolling of events, so I made my stumbling way to the Grand Heir's residence, where we hugged one another desperately, mother and son, and wept. It was hot, and my feet were white with dust, and my face was streaked with tears. We had no notion of what to do next. I have never felt so utterly helpless. My son was distraught. He knew all too well what was happening. The angry voice of his grandfather resounded through the still afternoon air. Maybe I should have stayed away from my son, for my presence was no comfort to him, and I could offer him no protection. But I clung to him, selfishly. At such moments, one cannot endure solitude.

At about four o'clock, I was informed that a eunuch had come to request a rice chest from the kitchens. I could not understand what this request meant, and I was too agitated to let him have what he wanted. Had I known what its purpose would have been, I hope I would have refused it. But the truth is that I did not know what was happening. I was beside myself.

After a while, the Grand Heir, desperately anxious, suddenly stood up, and pulled himself to his full height. His face was full of determination and self-command. Remember, he was not yet ten years of age. He went bravely out through the gate to the shrine, where, I am told, he threw himself to the ground, behind Sado's prostrate body, and begged his grandfather to spare his father's life. Should I have tried to restrain him? Did I have some hope that his intercession might succeed? He was only a child. Whose heart would not have been moved by his tears? Poor child, he feared his father, but he loved him, too, and he was to love him even better after death. King Yŏngjo told him, sternly, in a terrible voice, to get up, and to leave the courtyard. Chŏngjo refused, or was unable to move, and he had to be pulled up and carried away by force. And so he was obliged to leave his dishevelled father lying on the ground in the dirt at his grandfather's feet. He was not brought back to join me, but was taken to the waiting room at his father's residence. To wait for the end. This is all I knew at the time of what happened. I knew that his pleas had been rejected, and that I was alone. I was surrounded by servants, but I was alone.

I knew it was my duty to die. I reached for a knife, but it was taken from me. I knew that it was also my duty to live. Whatever I did would be a crime, a betrayal.

Eventually I, too, unable to bear the passivity of helpless waiting, went out, towards the shrine, but I could see nothing over the wall, and I was not permitted to pass through the gate. My knees were trembling and my breath came fast and shallow. I could hear Prince Sado pleading for his life, and the sound of the terrible rapping of His Majesty's sword, and the wailing of Prince Sado's tutors. The midsummer heat was terrible. The air smelt of death. I could hardly hear the words that Sado was saying, but I could hear the low, defeated tone of his desperation and his humiliation, and I remembered the many times that he had told me that he knew that his father would not permit him to live. He was now, yet

165

again, confessing his faults, and promising eternal obedience. He would study harder, he promised. Like a child, he promised to be good. Was it yet possible that there could be forgiveness? Could the father stretch out his hand, at this last moment, and could the son be restored to favour?

I could see nothing. I could not see over the wall.

I could not see that there was now a rice chest in the courtyard. It did not come from my kitchens. Later, nobody claimed it, nobody accepted responsibility for having provided it, but it was there. It had been brought by the king's command. Somebody had brought it to his presence. I will describe this rice chest.

A rice chest is a large, square wooden box, a domestic object of a nature familiar to all in our country. It is used for the storage of rice or grain. It stands on short legs, and can be locked by a metal clasp. (Some rice chests are objects of considerable value, and are handed down as family heirlooms, as I believe linen chests may be in your country.) The rice chest in question here was a large one, which measured four feet by four feet by four feet. I am told that the first chest to be provided proved unsuitable (presumably it was too small?) and that a second had to be obtained.

Writing down those two harmless words, 'rice chest', is still painful for me, after all these years. During my life, we never used those words. We referred to the rice chest, when we spoke or wrote of it, as 'that thing'.

My own father was later accused of providing the rice chest, but he did not do so. I do not know who provided it. Those who accused my father were malicious detractors.

This is what happened. As the long hot day wore on, Sado's pleas exhausted themselves, and his feeble but repeated attempts to kill himself were repeatedly foiled. King Yŏngjo then ordered his son to climb into the rice chest. And, in the end, he did so. I did not witness this.

We do not know in whose brain the novel idea of the unparalleled cruelty of the death in the rice chest was hatched. Some have complimented King Yŏngjo himself upon it, some Lady Sŏnhŭi, and some, as I have said, have implicated my father. Others have pointed the finger at various ministers. I do not know whose idea it was. It was not known. It is not known.

Sado was young and strong. So why did he climb voluntarily into his own wooden tomb? He sealed his fate. He consented, however reluctantly, to his death.

★   ★   ★

I have tried to give you, from my observations, an accurate, factual description of what happened on that fateful day. It seems that there are two other known contemporary documentary accounts of that day's events and its immediate consequences. My account, of course, is the most trustworthy.

The second account, the most official and the most carefully edited, is in the *Sillok* for the reign of King Yŏngjo. The *Sillok* is the name we give to the official record or gazette of each king's reign. Written in Chinese, these annals were compiled retrospectively, after each monarch's death, but from contemporary sources. They were printed and preserved under rigorous management. The version in the *Sillok* for King Yŏngjo's reign was, in effect, written by a committee — a committee of historians and diarists and editors. The *Sillok*, in all its 2,000 and more volumes, is now preserved as a National Treasure, under carefully controlled conditions. I am told that the *Sillok* for Yŏngjo's reign consists of 137 volumes in eighty-three books, and, although it is full of minute detail, it is reticent about the illness and death of Prince Sado, which are described briefly and somewhat obliquely.

The third account was written by a diarist who was, unlike myself, an eyewitness to what happened in the courtyard by the shrine. He was a recorder in the Royal Secretariat. In my lifetime, I did not know of his account, and I have not yet had an opportunity to study it in full. But I believe there are no major discrepancies between these three accounts.

This third text, unknown to me in my lifetime but thought to be authentic, is said to describe in full, first-hand and distressing detail many of the events of which at the time I knew only by eavesdropping and by hearsay. It was preserved in the Yi royal family private collection, and has only recently come to light. All I can say here is that it is said to confirm my worst fears about the sufferings of the prince, about his futile efforts to strangle himself, about his tutors' determined efforts to thwart his suicide attempts, about his father's persistent fury, and about the confusion that ensued after the prince had been persuaded to climb into the rice chest.

There are many stories about what happened later that night — some say that nails were driven through the chest, and some say that it was padded with straw to stifle the prince's cries. But we all know that eventually the chest was sealed tightly, strapped with ropes, covered with grass, and carried from the lower to the upper palace where it was placed in front of the Office of Diplomatic Correspondence. At midnight, the king issued an edict deposing Prince Sado and demoting him to the status of commoner, but the royal secretaries refused to transcribe and issue it, saying that it was unlawful. The king had to write it out himself, in his own shaking hand.

This may be the moment at which I should try to explain to you, to posterity, the reason — if one may call it a reason — why Prince Sado had to die in the rice chest, and not in some less painful or more dignified manner. Prince Sado had to die like this because it was very important to the state and to the royal succession that he should not die in the manner of a common criminal. It would have been acceptable for him to commit suicide, but this he was not willing or not able to do. He appears to have tried, after a fashion, to kill himself, but was easily prevented. It is not easy to fall on one's sword. (Stronger men than he have quailed at such a moment.

Even that brave warrior Mark Antony bungled it, and had to ask for help.) So Sado had to die in a manner in which no blood was shed, in a royal manner, in a manner in which his body was not disfigured or dismembered. (The consideration that he cannot have looked very pleasant after days of slow, cramped starvation in a rice chest does not seem to have carried much weight with those who devised his death.)

Death by poison would have been acceptable. It had been the custom to present a cup of poison to those members of the upper classes who unfortunately found themselves obliged to remove themselves for the better good of the state. Some, like Socrates, took it willingly, but occasionally coercion followed the presentation, and the poison was forced down the victim's throat. This had happened in the case of Lady Chang, the rival of the virtuous, childless and abandoned Lady Inhyŏn, the queen whose melancholy story had so mysteriously touched Lady Pingae. (Lady Chang, you may recall, was the lowborn mother of the crown prince who later became King Sukchong. King Sukchong was King Yŏngjo's grandfather, and the poisoned Lady Chang was thus after a manner King Yŏngjo's step-great-grandmother.)

The unfortunate manner of Lady Chang's death had cast a lingering cloud over the succession. It was a bad precedent. Perhaps that was why the rice chest seemed to offer a better option than poison. It was certainly cruelly ingenious. The device of the rice chest technically absolved the perpetrators of any guilt.

As Sado was seen to enter the chest unaided, he was deemed to have voluntarily chosen death. I leave it to you to judge whether or not this device was to his father's credit.

I note that some unsubstantiated versions of this day's events claim that Sado was indeed offered a dish of hemlock and refused to drink it. I do not know whether this was true or not. If it was, I did not witness it.

I return, now, to my own actions on that long and dreadful day. I was informed of my son's failed intercession, and of the king's implacable determination to force the death of Sado. I have said that at this point I knew little of the story of the rice chest, but eventually news was brought to me of Prince Sado's incarceration. You can imagine how unreal, how fantastical, how horrible this denouement seemed to me. At last, recovering myself a little for my son's sake, I sat below the gate in the late afternoon shade and wrote a letter to His Majesty, humbly requesting permission to return with my son to my father's home. With difficulty, I managed to find a eunuch and asked him to deliver it to the king. Not long afterwards, First Brother came to me with a royal decree granting that I should be allowed to depart the palace. A palanquin was to be brought for me, and a sedan chair for the Grand Heir. I was unable to walk, but I was carried on someone's back through the Ch'ŏng-hwi Gate, where the palanquin was already waiting for me. A lady-in-waiting rode with me. And so I went home to my father's house, no longer the royal wife of the crown prince, but the wife of a condemned criminal, and a commoner. Despite the slow accumulation of my fears and my sorrows, I had not thought that it would come to this.

I was laid in a room in the inner quarter of my father's house. Soon we were joined by my nine-year-old daughter-in-law, the Grand Heir Consort, who shared our disgrace: her family had sent a palanquin for her, and she came with my oldest daughter Ch'ŏngyŏn. So we were reunited in our humiliation. The shock suffered that day by the Grand Heir Chŏngjo was indescribable, and the horrors of it were not over yet. I do not think Chŏngjo ever recovered. Certainly he never forgot.

It took Prince Sado eight days to die in the rice chest. He was eight days dying. During this period, I remained at my father's house, which was now crowded with many who had fled from the palace, including all the ladies-in-waiting from the Grand Heir's establishment. It was a scene of chaos and displacement and uncertainty. We had to rent the house next door, and to cut a passageway through the fence in order to accommodate everybody. I say 'we', but it was Father and First Brother, I believe, who were obliged to take these practical steps for our family's physical survival. I was, for these first days, beside myself. I was sealed up in the black box of my own grief and horror, and I was of no use or help to anyone. I had always suffered — as I think many of us do — from a mild form of claustrophobia, and the thought of my husband's entombment was appalling to me. I had hated

172

those underground fake coffins he had made for himself, and now he was sealed in a real coffin. My imagination could not abandon him. I died along with him.

Our household, at this time, expanded, as others joined us in our exile. My youngest brother, Fourth Brother, who had always been a close friend of the Grand Heir, came to stay with us; the two boys shared a room in the guest wing for eight or nine days, where Fourth Brother did his best to comfort his young nephew. In strict protocol, the Grand Heir should have done penance for his father's crimes by kneeling in the open air on a straw mat awaiting punishment, and two buffoon officials actually came to suggest that he do this, but we did not pay them any attention. Why should the child suffer more? He was suffering unendurably as it was. We compromised by keeping him in the part of the house with low eaves, as a symbolic gesture of disgrace, a gesture that cost us nothing and which I like to think he, poor child, hardly noticed.

And so we waited for news of the end. Day followed day, and each day my mind was filled with images of death. Of his death, but also of my own. Fasting, drowning, stabbing, self-strangulation: which method should I select? It was my wifely duty to accompany my husband to the Yellow Springs, as his sister Hwasun had followed her husband, and yet it was also my duty to protect the Grand Heir and the future of the dynasty. I prayed to the gods and the spirits for an early death for Sado, and I believe that I hoped he would find some way, inside the rice chest, to hasten his own end. But he did not. Embattled, anguished to the last, he lingered stubbornly on. On the last day, in the afternoon, there was a heavy summer storm, with torrential rain and thunder. The memory of the prince's terror of thunder tormented me, and it is my belief that he died in mortal fear during that storm. I am told he was responding to voices until that storm broke, but that, after it, no sound came ever again from the rice chest.

What were they saying to him in those final hours, those petty warders and pitiless officials who were monitoring his slow decease? Were they taking minutes, attempting to extract confessions?

The *Sillok* records, sparely and bleakly, that the prince was locked in the rice chest, and died there eight days later. It apportions no blame, gives no cause of death. No postmortem was performed.

As soon as his son was safely dead, King Yŏngjo composed a new edict restoring his grandson the Grand Heir to his former title. My son was now allowed to emerge from the shadow of his father's disgrace. King Yŏngjo also renamed the dead prince as Crown Prince Sado, the Prince of Mournful Thoughts. Thus he tried to absolve his conscience, and reshape the past.

I think much about parricides and also about the murders of sons by fathers. I do not think there is a recognized noun in your language for the latter crime. That does not mean that it is a crime that is never committed. Parricide, matricide, infanticide — these are common crimes in myth and in history. But the murder of a grown son by an ageing father? Language hesitates to invent such a word for such a deed. I suppose 'filicide' would serve, but it sounds strangely, and I have yet to find it in any dictionary.

Queen Agave in the *Bacchae* murdered her son Pentheus, but she was deranged at the time, and took him for a lion. The Thracian King Lycurgus killed his son Dryas with an axe, mistaking him for a vine branch. King Yŏngjo was sober when he ordered the death of his son. He knew he was killing his own son.

At least King Yŏngjo does not have the unique distinction of being the only monarch in modern times to have murdered his son. I have recently discovered that Peter the Great of Russia murdered his son Aleksei in July 1718. That, too, was a hot month. Princes die in the dog days. Peter the Great's son had been accused not of madness, but of treason. Some said that Aleksei, having refused to drink the poison his father offered him, was decapitated in his prison cell by a marshal. Some say Peter himself struck off his son's head with an axe. It is then said that one of Peter's mistresses undertook the unpleasant task of stitching the head back on again, so that the appearance of the corpse could substantiate the official view that Aleksei had dropped dead from a stroke on hearing his death sentence pronounced. The Romanovs do not seem to have shared the Yi dynasty's objection to the shedding of blood, but they were devious enough in their

175

own ways. At least Sado had never requested me to do any head-stitching. Body substitution, perhaps, but not body stitching.

After these brutal events, our family embarked upon a period of prolonged mourning. As you can imagine, this was a demanding exercise, full of unknown and unprecedented difficulties. Confucian ritual and court precedent had failed to establish the proper manner of mourning for a royal prince judicially murdered by his own father. Despite the fact that we were a nation unhealthily obsessed by ancestor worship and by protocol, and spent much of our leisure time traipsing around the shrines and monuments of past monarchs and princelings; despite the fact that our history (like all histories) was littered with episodes of treachery and fratricidal and patricidal violence; despite the fact that the tragedy of this particular death had been gathering for years like a slow thundercloud on a distant horizon — despite all these facts, nobody was quite sure what to do, and yet everybody, including, I admit, I myself, was desperately intent upon doing everything 'correctly'.

The simple truth is that never before in our annals had a father so coldly, so brutally, so cruelly and so openly murdered his only son. This horrific crime stands alone in our story, and bears comparison with the most monstrous crimes of the world's story. (As you can see, I read about these crimes, now, obsessively.) So what were we to wear, to placate it, to mourn it, to grieve for it?

The king, immediately after Prince Sado's

death, ordered his residence to be raided. The crypt, the underground chambers, the sleeping apartments were ransacked. The servants discovered military paraphernalia of all kinds — flags, weapons, daggers — and mourning staffs with concealed swords within them. These, in my view, were all evidence of Sado's dementia, but the king seemed to construe them as proof of conspiracy, not of madness. He ordered them all to be burned. I cannot blame him for his horror. I, too, was horrified, had long been horrified by these objects. The king also ordered the execution of many of the prince's associates — a courtesan, a eunuch, a Buddhist nun, several palace servants and craftsmen, and some shamans. I had at the time but little regret over the deaths of these characters, for I thought they had led the prince astray and encouraged him in his lunacies.

I had hoped that the court officials would be allowed to wear mourning costumes appropriate for the mourning of a prince regent, as Prince Sado had served the state as prince regent for fourteen years. But this King Yŏngjo forbade. The attendants and eunuchs had to make do with mourning garments of an unattractive, second-rate pale blue. We were to be sufficiently grateful that Sado's title as crown prince had been restored, for he had died, technically, as a deposed commoner. King Yŏngjo suggested that the coffin be laid at Yongdong Palace, but my father persuaded him to have it carried to the Crown Prince Tutorial Office, which he deemed a more appropriate resting place.

My father, at this time, was in an extraordinarily delicate and dangerous position. He dreaded the consequences of this tragedy for our entire family, but his chief aim was the protection of his grandson the Grand Heir, who was now, in effect, the new crown prince. The king, who had so many times violently dismissed and capriciously reinstated my father, was still in a state of extreme mental volatility, and might have been blown in any direction, but I think, nevertheless, that on one level even at this time he depended on the steadying influence of my father's advice and judgement. My father, by appearing calm, loyal and dutiful, managed to form funeral committees, governed by precedent and law (in so far as there was any precedent), and he undertook to oversee these personally, as president, in every detail.

I know that there are those who believed that my father, rather than Lady Sŏnhŭi, was the prime mover in the death of Prince Sado, and that it was he who suggested the rice chest. Some truly believed this, others found it expedient to say that they believed it. I suppose I cannot wholly dismiss this possibility. He left no account of his actions on earth. Had he arranged Sado's death, he would never have told me: he would have taken the guilt of it upon himself, in order to spare me. It may be that he was implicated, for he had for some years been a witness of the effects of Sado's clothing phobia, and of his violent outbursts. He would have put me, his daughter, and his grandson Chŏngjo first, and preferred our survival to that of his son-in-law. We were his flesh and blood, his stake in futurity. But, whatever his putative involvement, there was no mistaking his distress and grief during these terrible events. At the end of the long last day of Sado's long death, and having arranged for the prince to be laid in his coffin at the Crown Prince Tutorial Office, he came home at dawn to me and, holding my hand, wept bitterly. He wished me a long life — which I have indeed enjoyed, if that be an appropriate word to use — and assured me that, with the Grand Heir at my side, I might yet find peace and happiness in my later years. I thought, at that time, that I was more likely to find sudden death. There were many who wished me dead.

That morning we set off for the palace, the Grand Heir and I, for the formal funerary rites in Simin Hall and Kŭndŏk House. The Grand Heir let down his hair and wailed, and his little girl bride stood at the women's side of the hall with me and his sisters, and we all wailed as we called out for the soul of the departed. I could not bear the sound of my son's cry. It was more than a cry; it was a loud shriek of protest and despair. It was not the sort of noise you expect to hear from a child of nine years.

The body of the Prince of the Rice Chest had been washed with wet towels and laid upon a box of ice upon a coffin table. The nose and mouth, the eyes and the ears had been covered and tied, and he had been clothed in a complete suit of burial garments. I was not able to approach until all these observances had been completed, and although I had been told that the body, despite the heat of the time of year, had suffered little decomposition, I was not able to verify this unlikely assertion with my own eyes. It is very likely that I was told this for my comfort. Nor did I permit my son, his wife or my daughters to see the body before it was enclosed in the coffin. Such sights are not for children. And it was only on that first day of mourning that I allowed them to wail with me. I could not bear to hear a repetition of those terrible cries.

Somehow, we managed to make our way through the days of ritual offerings, each one of which caused new anxieties. Rituals are designed to comfort, but what comfort can be found when each stage of mourning is without a hallowed precedent, and is overshadowed by disgrace? Prince Sado's mother, Lady Sŏnhŭi, who never truly recovered from this disaster — she died two years later of a malignant tumour — came to see me as I sat by the coffin, and could not control her grief. She beat her breast, and banged her head against the coffin, and wailed like a madwoman. She was growing old before my eyes. Perhaps it is worse to lose a son than a husband. I have lost both, and I should know. But yet I cannot say. At least my sons died of natural causes. That is a comfort.

I did not know how to look to the future at this point. No clear path lay before me. I had lost my role and my purpose and my status at court. I had been exhausted by my vain and prolonged efforts to conceal Sado's derangement. My father, always a practical man, seemed to be doing his best to restore favour to and smooth the progress of the Grand Heir, who was formally instated as crown prince in a matter of weeks. I did not think that I could ever look my father-in-law in the face again. How could I ever forgive him his cruelty?

But when King Yŏngjo came in the eighth month to the lower palace for the bimonthly sacrifice at the Ancestral Shrine, I made myself go out to meet him and greet him. It was a strange and emotional encounter. I expressed my humble gratitude for the safety of myself and my son, using conventional phrases that said nothing of the turmoil within me, and the king seemed shaken by my words. Perhaps he was as afraid of me as I was of him. We fear those we have injured, even when we retain power over them. To my surprise, he even thanked me for being so gracious, and said he had dreaded seeing me after what had happened. He told me that it was 'noble' and 'beautiful' of me to put him at his ease. What odd things we can say at these dire moments. Face to face with him like this, with so much suffering behind us, I remembered the well-meant and kindly advice he had given to me when I was a newly betrothed little girl of ten. He had taught me court manners. And look where these court manners had led us both.

The king looked old and shrunken, and so, no doubt, did I. Looking at the king, and contemplating the powerlessness to which I had been reduced, as the widow of a deposed and ruined prince, I suddenly heard myself saying that the king should, if he would, take my son to live with him in the upper palace. I had not premeditated this offer: it came to my lips spontaneously. I think I sensed that my son would be safer if he were under the immediate protection of the king, for, with me, he risked contamination. The king seemed at first surprised by my suggestion, and in a diffident and curiously humble tone asked me if I was sure I could bear to part with him. I think the guilt over Prince Sado's death was a crushing burden to him, and he wished to placate me, as I wished to placate him. I think we both felt inadequate. Even kings can have such feelings. I assured him that my son's well-being and the superior instruction he would receive in the upper palace were of more importance to me than my own happiness. And this was true, in its way.

So the young Crown Prince Chŏngjo went off to live with his paternal grandparents. Lady Sŏnhŭi became devoted to him, in the two years of life that were left to her, and looked after him very tenderly, transferring to him all the affection she had once felt for his poor father. I felt more warmly towards her than I had done in earlier years, when she had seemed to be attacking both Sado and myself, or to be taking sides against me and in his favour. She seemed defeated by the weighty tragedy of her life, and I felt sorry for her. She was growing older — she was now nearing seventy — and she lived in self-reproach, blaming herself for her part in her son's death. She used to say that, when she died, no grass would grow upon her grave. Flies would be her company, in the words of the old song, and heavy rain would fall upon her grave. No turf would cover her; no grass would grow over her. These were her laments.

(Two hundred years later, I sent my ghost to seek her tomb in Seoul. It is in a university campus, near the tennis courts. The young men play tennis near her memorial tablet. The children picnic near the tomb of King Yŏngjo and his queen.)

My son Chŏngjo did not forget me, despite his elevation to the upper palace. Every morning he would write me a note of greeting, and send it down to the lower palace by a messenger before he started the morning study session. I remember how eagerly I would reach for my tortoiseshell glasses to read these affectionate little missives, and how carefully I would store them in one of the drawers of my precious little lacquer writing cabinet. Whenever he could, he would come to meet me and greet me at the postern gate that divided the palaces. He would arrange for physicians and medicines to be sent to me, for I am afraid that during these years I was almost continuously ill. My constitution, although it was naturally strong, had suffered a near-fatal blow. And, in case you are wondering, let me assure you that during these hard middle years my illnesses were not illnesses of convenience: I was on the verge of breakdown, unable to sleep and unable to keep my food down. Lumps of my hair fell out — I wept when I remembered how cleverly Pingae had dressed my hair, and the happy evenings we had spent together talking of ladies' fashions and of poetry. I had not thought myself happy at the time, but I looked back on these evenings with mournful regret. Would I ever be happy again?

And where was Pingae now? Was she reunited with Sado in the other world, and had she forgiven him? In death, did they remember me, or was I banished from their thoughts? Did they suffer after death? Did they make love after death? Was Sado now at rest? I was restless, tormented, and when I slept I had bad dreams. The time hung heavily, in my disgrace, in my long hours in the mourning chamber. I thought of writing an account of my wretched life, but I had not yet the spirit to begin it. I continued to sew and embroider, but I sewed without love. I sewed to stitch my way through time. The needle pierces the cloth; the iron crushes the cloth. I thought of Pingae, safe and dull in the sewing chamber. She should have stayed within, and lived. Ambition killed her.

In those early years after Sado's death, my son missed me sadly, for he was still a child. When he was permitted briefly to come to visit me for a few hours, he could hardly tear himself away to return to his grandparents. Our partings on these occasions were very distressing to both of us. I remember his clinging and his crying. Seeing him weep, I remembered how lonely and frightened I had been at the time of my betrothal and my removal to the palace. I had to harden my heart and behave coldly towards him in order to drive him away. It was difficult. He was too young to be separated for such long periods from his mother. I was afraid that King Yŏngjo would be offended by this all-too-natural and filial partiality for me, and I pretended to Yŏngjo that when my son was with me in the lower palace he longed to be with his grandfather in the upper palace — like a true child, I said, he always said he wanted to be wherever he was not. King Yŏngjo gullibly accepted this explanation, but of course it was not so. At this time, my son still wanted to stay at home with me. I think he may have felt he could be a comfort to me. He was also morbidly anxious to pay proper respects to his dead father, and there was something very disquieting in the way he wailed in the mourning chamber, before Prince Sado's tablet. I wonder how much he knew at that time of his father's crimes, and if such knowledge made him mourn the more. I fancied in my madness that the poor, lonely tablet glowed with light when my son abased himself before it. Was Prince Sado's ghost somewhat appeased by the sight of the Grand Heir's tears?

You would think no worse could happen to us, and in a way the worst was over, but bad consequences continued to flow from that bad act, and some of them were inexpressibly painful to me. I will spare you all the details of my further humiliations, and of my son's estrangement from me, but some I must recount. I had already lost my royal rank and been declared a commoner, but now, two years after Prince Sado's death, I was also declared a non-mother. A royal decree was issued proclaiming Prince Chŏngjo to be the posthumously adopted son of

Sado's brother, that brother who had died as a boy of ten, before Sado's birth. Prince Chŏngjo was no longer to be his father's son; he was now declared to be the son of a long-dead ten-year-old uncle! This was exactly what Sado himself had foreseen. I was demoted, my status as crown princess and legal parent of the future king denied. I was no longer my son's mother. This, surely, was a form of matricide. The decree was made for reasons of state, evidently, in order to secure the succession: there had certainly been doubts raised in some quarters about the propriety of allowing the son of an executed criminal to inherit the throne and the kingdom. I can see that now, but during my lifetime I found it hard to be so calm and so objective. The atmosphere was too thick with suspicion and paranoia for me to see clearly, and I was in much mental distress. I saw insults and danger everywhere. I think I was going through some kind of mental breakdown. But I maintain that I was right to be suspicious. There was much real hostility towards me. Factions were already busily manoeuvring against the Grand Heir and his maternal family: there were other candidates eager to seize or usurp power.

I believe that Prince Sado's sister, Madame Chŏng, was the prime mover behind this royal decree of 1764, the so-called infamous 'kapsin arrangement' that undid me as a mother in the eyes of the world. She was, as I have hinted, an ambitious woman, competitive, jealous and obsessed by power. During Prince Sado's life, she had seen him as her road to power, but, after

186

his disgrace and death, she latched upon the next and most obvious candidate for her own preferment, the Grand Heir. I was often to wonder whether I had been wise to permit, indeed to suggest, Chŏngjo's removal to the upper palace. I had hoped to forestall trouble by meeting it halfway, but maybe, I thought at times, I thought increasingly, I would have done better to keep him close to me for as long as I could.

At first, as I have said, my son was intensely loyal to me, even in separation, and while his grandmother Lady Sŏnhŭi was still alive there was still some natural affection and dutiful respect flowing between the upper and the lower palace. But when Lady Sŏnhŭi died in 1764, Sado's sister Madame Chŏng moved quickly into the space she had vacated.

I must spare a thought here for Lady Sŏnhŭi, my mother-in-law, once known as the Bright Princess. She died an old and sad and defeated woman, who never recovered from the death of her son Sado. King Yŏngjo lamented her death with more than conventional sorrow, I thought, and wrote one of his better verses as a memorial for her, recording the thirty-eight years of their long journey together. He recorded that in the troubles of the *imo* year, it was she that had saved the state.

On the twenty-seventh day of the ninth moon of the year kapsin, she left me and took her long departure. For thirty-eight years we had journeyed together, and now it is all a dream. Who knows what life means? On

187

the last day of the eighth moon I wrote this inscription and got some relief from my sorrow. On the twenty-seventh day of the ninth moon we buried her here by the Yŏnhŭi Palace in a tomb that faces a little west of south.

That is what he wrote, according to one source. Another version gives the twenty-sixth day of the seventh moon as the day of her death, but it makes no great difference. Myself, I was there at the time, and I cannot remember. How can historians be accurate, when even earthly witnesses and immortal ghosts forget?

It did not take long for Madame Chŏng to move into the dead grandmother's shoes. She took over the maternal role, and flattered the Grand Heir Prince Chŏngjo, wooing him with gifts of quilted clothes and fancy shoes and beautifully crafted toy swords. She also played on his suspicions. She abused my family, and managed to alienate him from his wife, the harmless little Grand Heir Consort. In retrospect, I see that she did everything she could to prevent him from producing an heir. Prince Chŏngjo was growing into adolescence now, and his aunt was beguiling and seductive towards him. She was also very possessive: remarks relayed in all innocence to me by Chŏngjo revealed that she seemed to be jealous even of the books he was studying. She flew into a rage on one occasion over a book about the Sung dynasty that he had been reading, and disparaged it, saying it was prejudiced, inaccurate and unsuitable for a boy of his years. She tried to invade his mind. She was one of those women who think the whole world revolves around her: she could take offence at a glance or a gesture. She was perverse and wilful and violent. The king adored her, and, now that Lady Sŏnhŭi was dead, he relied on her more and more.

Madame Chŏng herself had no children, and when her husband died without an heir, she had adopted as her son a nephew from her husband's family, as was the custom. (This child, Chŏng Hugyŏm, you may recall, was the boy whom Prince Sado had taken hostage and locked in a cellar when he was pleading to be allowed to take his trip to the hot springs of Onyang.) She saw this boy as another means of wielding power, and she trained him to ingratiate himself with my son, who was two years younger than he. Chŏng Hugyŏm was a corrupting influence. My father did his best to intervene, and so did Third Brother. Even I tried to court Chŏng Hugyŏm, against my better judgement, and to placate him by finding him safe preferment. This was a disastrous error.

And trouble came not only from that quarter. After the Lady Sŏnhŭi's death, the new young queen, King Yŏngjo's teenage bride, revealed herself openly as our enemy. She had at first displayed due deference to me and I to her. Although I was so much older than she was, never for a moment did I presume to hint that I had been in the palace longer than she and therefore deserved more respect. I did not stand on precedence. Prince Sado had abused her in her absence, but even he had been respectful in her presence. And my father, ever the diplomat, had always taken care to keep on the right side of her and of her father. Open confrontation with her was not a possibility. We had to play a careful game. The young queen's father, once a private scholar but now elevated in rank, had been instructed in court etiquette by my father, but he had picked up too many court tricks, and he began to stir up animosity against us.

In short, we were surrounded by intrigue, and my son's accession to the throne was by no means certain. Under the erratic rule of an ageing king, coterie fought with coterie, and the Hong family continued to arouse much resentment. As I have said, some historians have reduced the whole of this period to this single sentence: 'there was a power struggle between the Hongs and the Kims.' I suppose there may be some truth in that reduction. Hong and Kim, Genji and Heike, York and Lancaster, Montagu and Capulet — that is the way the world goes. In my lifetime, I tried to write true records of this period and its dangers, but it would be wearisome to repeat now all the details of the power struggles and the successive favourites and pretenders that threatened us. It is enough to say that many people, including Madame Chŏng, including even my own daughter's husband, attempted to alienate my son from me, and to gain control of his growing mind. At times they succeeded, and I think I myself erred in judging his adolescent escapades too harshly. I suppose I was afraid that he would inherit his father's weaknesses, and I dreaded any sign of indulgence on his part, or any suggestions from others that he might be open to bad influences. I feared that he was showing signs of a fondness for low life, for the company of courtesans and palace servants, and I reacted angrily to Madame Chŏng's hints that he might be following in his father's footsteps. 'Bad blood will out,' she would mutter. On one occasion, she even dared to say that she feared a repetition of 'that incident' — but even she dared not give the Imo Incident a name. I was frightened and humiliated by her insinuations, and occasionally I reacted rashly, indiscreetly.

For fourteen long years the old man Yŏngjo outlived his murdered son Prince Sado, and these years were packed with every kind of attempted subversion. Madame Chŏng was a clever and devious woman, and she tried many ways of seducing my son. She permanently estranged my son from his wife, the Grand Heir Consort. It is true that the Grand Heir Consort had thus far been unable to produce an heir, but it was not true, as Madame Chŏng hinted, that my son was impotent. Nor is it necessarily true, as she also hinted, that the Grand Heir Consort was infertile.

I felt sorry for my daughter-in-law, the Grand Heir Consort. Never very strong, she had now developed some kind of eating disorder — a kind of disorder that was prevalent in our neurotic society — and she lost much weight. She grew very thin, and seemed to survive on a sparse diet of nuts, mushrooms, and jasmine or ginseng tea.

She ate like a mouse, poor child. And she never, in all her life, spoke a word against her father-in-law, Prince Sado. I think she never recovered from the confused impression of her first night-time encounter with him, when he was so unexpectedly gallant towards her, in such unorthodox circumstances. Sado was a charming man, when he chose to charm. I think the little princess was half in love with him, and she idolized him as a martyr after his death.

It may be that she was the one who was afraid of consummating the marriage. I do not know. She did not confide in me: I think she was afraid of me. I was a daunting figure, wearing my white mourning robes and my widow's crown of tragedy. I suppose I hoped that Prince Chŏngjo would take a secondary consort, in a relationship free of the long shadow of 'that incident' — and this indeed is what happened, though not for some years. Chŏngjo was over thirty before he produced a surviving heir. It seemed for years that he might die without issue.

Madame Chŏng defamed the little princess, and bore herself in an insulting manner towards me. Our enmity deepened. There were unbecoming scenes at court when we chanced to meet. I remember one confrontation, at the time of the death of the little princess's father, which descended into abuse more fit for common people than for women of royal blood. I accused her of being drunk (and she was indeed a heavy drinker), and she accused me of hypocrisy. She even accused me of conniving at Sado's crimes and forcing him into unnatural behaviour. Had I been a better wife to Sado, she said, he would not have taken to murder and debauchery. She blamed the infamous Imo Incident on me. I retaliated, I regret to say, by blaming her for his excesses, and I also accused her of spreading disgraceful slanders about the little princess.

Prince Chŏngjo was horrified by these scenes. And I am now ashamed of them.

I realize that at this stage in my earthly story I run the risk of sounding like a mean-spirited old woman, full of reproaches and laments. How ludicrously petty, in the context of eternity, were my jealous confrontations with Madame Chŏng! My bad relationship with her was unfortunate, I admit it. But it was not wholly my fault. And I was fond, in my way, of the poor little princess.

Prince Chŏngjo survived the machinations of Madame Chŏng and her adopted son, only to fall into the clutches of other predators. He was wooed by flatterers, and I am afraid that he succumbed to the temptations of their company. I dreaded to see him repeat the mistakes of his father, as he began to spend time with drinkers and womanizers. There was no shortage of ambitious young men ready to profit from his friendship. One or two of them even managed to ingratiate themselves with the ageing king, who was by now verging on senility. I watched, helplessly, as gossip spread. One young man in particular, a distant kinsman of ours, Kugyŏng, worked himself into a position of trust, and seemed to think that on the king's death he would move to the centre of the stage, and rule as co-regent with my son — two headstrong young men together, given over to extravagance and self-indulgence.

We were all waiting for the old man to die. And, at last, King Yŏngjo did indeed pass away, in the third month of the year 1776. King Yŏngjo had reigned for more than fifty years, and I myself had known him well, if not intimately, for more than thirty of those years. He had survived many illnesses, and many political crises. He had outlived several of his children, including his son and heir, the guilt of whose death lay on his conscience. He had been failing for years, growing senile and yet more eccentric, and, towards the end of his reign, his eyesight was so bad that he could not see the names on the lists of appointments he had to approve. He turned against his one-time well-born scholarly advisers, and delegated most administrative matters to eunuchs — many of these were able and educated men, and the state seemed to run itself quite smoothly.

King Yŏngjo was keenly aware of the ambitions that surrounded him, and had made it clear that he wanted no obstacle to his grandson Prince Chŏngjo's succession. Nevertheless, he did not let go of life willingly. He struggled against the approach of death. He struggled to hang on to the vestiges of authority. For days he lingered behind the royal death screen, refusing to allow his spirit to depart.

I was surprised that his death moved me, when it came at last. I had never felt entirely easy with him, for I was bowed from the first into an uncomfortable posture of perpetual deference.

194

Yet, despite all the weight of protocol, we had had our moments of human contact, and I think that over the decades he had learned some respect for me. I shall never forget that first meeting after Prince Sado's death, when I found myself comforting him for the unnatural crime he had himself committed. He had feared to find me vengeful and unforgiving, but I was able to indicate to him that I understood the extreme difficulties of his position at that time, and he was able to show me that he was grateful for my understanding. Our lives were unnatural, but we were not devoid of natural feelings. I believe he suffered for Prince Sado's fate, and that he knew in his heart that he bore some guilt for Sado's illness. He knew that he had nagged and hounded his own son to death. That is a hard thing to know.

Yes, I found that I now missed the old king. I missed the familiar irritation of his trivial despotic irascibility. I had grown into womanhood under his influence and protection. Now I was mature, and I was on my own. I was just over forty years of age at the time of King Yŏngjo's death. I had a premonition that I, like him, would enjoy or endure a long life. There would be no easy escape for me.

We prayed much for longevity, in our culture. We surrounded ourselves with its symbols. We celebrated old age, in images of sun and moon, of pine and carp and crane and turtle. Life expectancy was short, and we venerated survivors.

My sense of loss was compounded by my fear

for the future. How would my son succeed as the new king? So many were waiting to bend him to their will — the young queen's powerful faction, and his aunt Madame Chŏng, and innumerable ministers who were jockeying for position in the new regime. And there was the newest favourite, who thought that his hour had come. This new acolyte, Hong Kugyŏng, had managed to ingratiate himself with King Yŏngjo as well as with my son: he was bold and ambitious, and he believed his time would come when the old king died. Those who had fawned on Madame Chŏng's son when he had seemed to be in the ascendant now deserted him for Kugyŏng.

These were dangerous times for my young son. I find I do not wish to describe in detail the mistakes he made, the risks he ran. I have told this story at length, in my second memoir, the memoir written in 1801, and you may find it there. I feared for King Chŏngjo, in his inexperience, and I was right to fear. His enemies were ready to destroy him.

The question of the succession remained unsolved and was becoming ever more urgent. The new king had as yet no son. The queen was now in her mid-twenties, but still childless. King Chŏngjo needed to safeguard his position, and I would have been happy to encourage his taking an appropriate second consort, but, instead of finding a suitable mother for a future heir, Chŏngjo was manipulated by his new favourite, Kugyŏng, into taking Kugyŏng's sister, a pre-pubertal twelve-year-old child, as the royal consort. This girl, to whom he gave the royal title of 'Wŏnbin', was showered with inappropriate honours, and became known as First Consort even though the true queen was still alive and present at court.

This move caused outrage and served no purpose, as the wretched child soon died. She was a little silk grub, killed for her brother's glory in the cocoon of her own silk trappings. When she died, Hong Kugyŏng insisted on extravagant royal mourning for her, with incense-burning more befitting a queen than a nonentity of a child, and, when some right-minded officials refused to participate in these farcical charades, they were dismissed from their posts. Worse than that, Kugyŏng managed to persuade people that the true queen had been implicated in the child's death — he even extracted confessions to this effect, under torture, from some of her ladies-in-waiting. News of these outrages spread out from the palace, and I heard that some shopkeepers in the town became so nervous about the political situation that they shut up their shops and fled.

I will not attempt to describe in detail the tortuous machinations and blatant nepotism that filled the next few years. The court stank of corruption. And I myself was in despair that my son, of whom I had had such high hopes, would bring yet more disgrace upon himself as well as us.

I have to ask myself: was I anxious for myself, or for my son, or for my country? In the four accounts I wrote during my lifetime, I sought to justify my actions, and those of my son, and I argued, I believe convincingly, that my husband Prince Sado had been mad, and was therefore not responsible for his acts. (I would have made a good lawyer.) Correctly, I believe, I exposed in these accounts the crimes of Madame Chŏng and others at our court. But there were some incidents that it was hard to explain away, or to justify. My son King Chŏngjo was, like it or not, responsible for the death of my uncle, having been made to believe that my uncle had conspired against him. Whom should I justify here, the uncle or the son?

Maybe I was a monster mother, and maybe the maternal instinct in me was perverted. My mother love was born in innocence, as I have tried to describe, and it had nothing to do, in those early days, with the indoctrination of Confucian ethics. History has forced me into casuistry.

I find I grow weary of my memories of these confused and tormenting times, and of my own laboured attempts to elucidate them. Which of you will have the patience to follow this sorry tale of machinations and deceptions and expulsions and banishments and executions, in a far-off court, in a foreign land, long ago? Perhaps you have already lost the outline of my story. Maybe you, too, like Henry Savage Landor, that nineteenth-century English traveller to our country, believe that we in Korea 'feel pain less' than Western people because we are 'differently constituted'? Or maybe you believe that we deserved whatever pain we felt. Maybe you, too, feel, as did your intrepid envoy Isabella Bird, that our country was deeply subject to 'the oriental vices of suspicion, cunning and untruthfulness'. Maybe you agree with those historians who described us as a nation ruined by luxury and indolence, by court intrigues and party strife.

Have patience. I will make haste to come to an end. I am moved to proceed to the rest of my agenda, urged on by my obsessed ghost, who leaves me no peace. As I leave her no peace.

The relationship between my ghostwriter and myself is uncanny. We are both rationalists, and we both protest that we have no belief in a supernatural life after death. Yet here we are, harnessed together in a ghostly tale of haunting and obsession. We narrate one another, my ghost and I.

I will attempt to reduce the rest of my long life on earth to a précis, to a few paragraphs, for my ghost is losing patience with me. She wants to sweep through time to tell her own story.

So, as I have described, the reign of my son King Chŏngjo, the twenty-second monarch of the Yi dynasty, began badly, and we feared the worst. But eventually he saw through the wiles of those who flattered and manipulated him, and he became a sound, kind and good ruler. I say it, and it was so. All government slaves were freed under his reign, and he developed generous relief programmes for the poor. Early in his reign, it is true, King Chŏngjo presided over cruel tortures and persecutions, particularly of the Catholics, and several members of his immediate family perished at this time. My uncle Hong Inhan was executed in 1776, the year of King Chǒngjo's accession, accused of disloyalty to his great-nephew the king. My father, a subtle diplomat and a great survivor of many promotions and demotions, was fortunate enough to die a natural death two years later, in 1778. In the same year, Madame Chǒng was stripped of her royal titles and banished to Kanghwa Island, a fate that she had predicted for herself. Four years later, she was allowed to return to live near Seoul, but she had lost her influence, and died in obscurity and disgrace. Her adopted son Chǒng Hugyǒm had been executed in 1776. (Some records say that Chǒngjo poisoned Madame Chǒng, but I cannot believe that this was true.)

In 1782, King Chǒngjo at last produced an heir, to much rejoicing. So much for the tales of his impotence, those tales which Madame Chǒng had maliciously encouraged. But his first-born, like my first-born, died as an infant, and his mother died of grief a few months later. Not long after this, partly through my urging, King Chǒngjo took another secondary consort, the Lady Kasun. She and I were close, as close as mother and daughter, and we had a common aim, which we achieved when she gave birth to you, my grandson Sǒnjo, in 1790. You were born on the eighteenth day of the sixth month, at three o'clock in the afternoon. It was my birthday. I took this to be a good omen.

King Chǒngjo became a good ruler, responsive to the common people: innumerable successful petitions were made to his wisdom and judgement. He always heeded the drum of appeal. He was also a fine artist, a fine scholar and a man of vision. He created a magnificent new library, and encouraged the new scientific discipline of 'Practical Learning'. During his reign, our country began to emerge from the hermit-crab shell which unfortunately but understandably became our image in the succeeding century. We moved into the modern world.

King Chŏngjo was able to rise above the terrors of his childhood. He managed to do this not by forgetting them, but through confronting them. His was a brave spirit. His father Prince Sado had died in dishonour and pain, and Chŏngjo did not turn his back on this disgrace. He met it, as a challenge. He devoted much time to honouring and reinstating the memory of his father. It might be argued, by cynics, that he did this as a means of assuring his own legitimacy; it might also be argued that he was a devout Confucian, who truly believed in the duty of honouring his ancestors. The truth was, I believe, more complicated. *I* believe that what he saw and heard as a ten-year-old child in the hot noonday sun on the day of the Imo Incident affected him so deeply that he felt a deep, unique, personal, filial obligation towards his father's memory. Only by truly reinstating his father could he himself survive as a whole man. He had to dig up the disgraced body, and resurrect it, and rebury it.

I see I have yet again used the word 'filial', which crops up with such monotonous and often meaningless regularity in any discussion of

Confucian behaviour and Confucian ethics — but I think one can forget Confucianism here. Confucianism laid out the cultural means whereby and the manner in which King Chŏngjo chose to celebrate and commemorate his father and me, his mother, but the mainspring of Chŏngjo's actions lay elsewhere. No dictates written in stone guided or impelled him: he was moved from that inner and unique but universal self that is in each of us, which is formed in each of us, which is formed by a pattern which transcends cultural conditioning. I cling to this belief, as the violent storms of disbelief and deconstruction swirl round me, as others try to tell me what I must have said or felt, what Chŏngjo must have said or felt. Little is certain, and with time we pepper into dust. But some angry self remains to protest its identity, its unique enduring life.

The mother cat, the silkworm, the father in the rice chest, the child in the hot dust.

I see now that I am beginning to use words that do not belong to me, words that my appointed ghost has whispered in my ear. Postmodern contextualism, enlightenment universalism, deconstruction, concepts of the self. 'Globalization' seems to be one of the words that goes through the restless dreams of my envoy. I do not even know what it means, or what she means by it. Must I try to find out? Why is she worrying at me like this? What have I done to deserve it? Must I be tormented beyond the grave? Must I go back to school, at my age, and begin again? I am too old and too tired. Even the dead can feel exhaustion, you may be sorry to learn.

And what, I suppose I must ask, has my ghostly envoy done to deserve me? What faults, what crimes, what sympathies, what weaknesses have opened her heart to me? I cannot afford to feel pity for her. I need her services.

King Chŏngjo survived in order to reinstate his father. He disinterred the body of my husband, Prince Sado, and reburied him in a new tomb, in a new city south of Seoul, with new funerary rites. He consulted geomancers, and claimed that the new tomb was more auspiciously placed than the old one, and that his father would rest better there. I do not know what my son Chŏngjo really thought about the auspices, or about the afterlife. Maybe he had a different agenda altogether. Maybe he thought it advantageous to his regime to create a new and better fortified seat of power. Maybe he thought the climate was better to the south. Maybe he wanted to build himself a summer palace, like a Chinese emperor. Maybe he wanted to be remembered as a great patron, as a builder of great monuments. Maybe he hated the memories that haunted the palace where his father was murdered, and where I was condemned to continue to reside. Maybe, like his father, he needed to escape from the stifling past. Many have speculated about these matters. But not even I, who was his earthly mother, know the truth.

What I do know is that he chose to honour my sixtieth birthday in a most lavish and spectacular manner. The sixtieth birthday, known to us as 'hwan-gap', is always a major cause for celebration in our country, partly because our lunar calendar is based on a sixty-year cycle, and partly because in earlier times so few of us lived so long. So I had expected a large celebration, but nothing on the scale that was prepared for me. Songs were written for me; delegations were sent to visit me; prayers were offered for me. There were months of festivity. A banquet was held to which my surviving uncles and vast numbers of cousins and second cousins and third cousins were invited, including some who had been living in exile or disgrace. Even the concubine of my late father was invited, in recognition of her years of service and devotion. I cannot say that I was particularly delighted to see her, as her son and grandsons had proved somewhat too prosperous during my son's reign. But I was pleased by the spirit of amnesty that prevailed.

And I was at last allowed to leave my home. I was permitted to make a triumphal journey, from the lower palace in Seoul where I had been immured for almost all of my adult life, to the new city of Hwaseong, some forty miles to the south. In Hwaseong several days of banquets and feasts and parades and games and presentations had been laid on in my honour, and in honour of my dead husband, who would also have achieved his sixtieth birthday in this year, had he lived. Prince Sado was lying quietly in his new tomb, but I was carried towards him in my palanquin through shouting crowds, and waving pennants, and the sound of music.

This expedition was a shock to all my senses. I had been so long concealed from the larger world, and the world from me. At last I, too, had my journey. I saw the wide river, and the mountains, and the people of my land. I walked by the southern lake, and admired the lofty towers of the fortress, and laid my hand upon the sun-baked wall of the curved battlement. I saw, for the first time, a great view, as from a hilltop. I was sixty years old. I had yearned to see the world when I was younger: could I make any sense of it now that it was revealed to me? Or was it too late? I think I will send my ghost for me to visit Hwaseong, and see what she can make of it. I believe much money has been spent on its restoration. My ghostly envoy is an energetic young woman, full of curiosity. How much of the past, I wonder, lingers in the air? Will she be able to smell the roasted offerings, to see the fluttering of the silk flags, to count the serried ranks of soldiers and courtiers, to admire the horsemanship and the dancing, to walk the fortress battlements?

I was showered with many gifts upon my sixtieth birthday. Tribute was brought to me from all the regions of our land, as though I were an emperor. I was presented with bowls and bottles of fine porcelain, with silks and with jewels, with fans and with screens, with lacquered cabinets. Where are these priceless objects now? Some will have perished, but some were designed to be everlasting, and must surely have been preserved and cherished. Are they for sale in the antique shops of Insadong? Are they on display in the Museum of Ewha Woman's University? Are they to be found in the Museum of the Amorepacific Beauty Company? These gifts displayed the finest craftsmanship of our nation, and I was much honoured in the receipt of them.

But the object that I remember best from all these riches was a strange little curio that had been made in the West. It was given to me by my son, who said that he had bought it through the intermediary of a Chinese trader in Onyang. It was a round, miniature enamelled brooch, less than an inch in diameter, with a gold pin and a gold frame and a split pearl border. It portrayed a solitary Western human eye, an expressive female eye with a light hazel iris, set in a wide brow, and surmounted by a white forehead and curling locks of bright brown hair. I had never seen anything like it. It was rather disconcerting. I have since discovered that such objects, though rare, were briefly fashionable in the West, but how this single eye reached our country remains a mystery. Was it brought by a foreign merchant or an envoy to Canton or Peking, as a reminder of a loved one back home in the West? Had it been sold, lost or stolen? I have a fancy that it may have travelled to Peking three years before it reached me, with the British envoy, George Macartney. I fancy that it belonged to a member of his diplomatic entourage, which received such a muted welcome in the Immobile Empire. Macartney took with him many grand offerings, intended to impress upon the Chinese the superior wealth and technology of the British Empire. This was one of the great transcultural confrontations of history. Maybe my enamelled eye observed it all.

The terrestrial globe, the enamelled eye.

This is only a fancy. I do not know, and I do not know why my beloved son bought this eye for me. He told me that its oddity appealed to him, and it appealed to me also. He said it was a good-luck eye, a long-life eye, an eye to pierce the clouds of the future, an eye with which to see the unseen world. I kept it safe during my lifetime. Where is it now? Has it travelled back to its homeland? And where is the globe that Crown Prince Sohyŏn brought to our country before I was born?

It was in this year, the celebratory year of 1795, that I began to write the story of my life and times. I started this project ostensibly at the request of my nephew, the oldest son of First Brother, and thus the heir to our house. I have said, in this memoir, that it was he that urged me to write, and so he did, but in truth the impulse came also from an inner prompting. The visit to Hwaseong inspired me, and, when I returned to Seoul, I began to write. My memory was awoken, and I was moved to search and re-examine the past. Things were good for me, when I wrote this first draft of my life's events. I had a sense of triumph, and of survival. It was in this mood that I wrote my first account.

Things changed. They did not remain good. My beloved son King Chŏngjo died five years later, suddenly and without warning, in 1800, in his forty-ninth year, after twenty-four years on the throne. He was at the height of his powers and apparently in good health when he died. I believe he suffered a fatal stroke. There was no question, this time, of a dish of poisoned mushrooms, though of course some sensation-mongering historians and fanciful fiction-writers have claimed that he was murdered. This was not a good time for our family, or for me. Again, I faced the agony of the loss of a son, and this time I faced it alone. He had been good to his mother, and I had loved him with all my heart. Widowed for nearly four decades, and distrusted by some of my close family members, I had made him the centre of my life, and I had looked to him for my survival. His death shocked me, and left me full of fear. But I had grown harder with the years. I knew, this time, that I would survive even this blow of fate. I was an old woman when my second son died.

King Chŏngjo is buried in Hwaseong, with his father. They were reunited in death, that terrified boy and that tormented man. I believe that my mortal remains lie there, too, though I have to confess that I am not very interested in their location. My posthumous life and my bid for immortality lie in the spirit world of these memoirs.

My second and third accounts of my life and times were written after my son's unexpected death, in the first and most anxious years of the reign of my grandson King Sunjo, when my grandson was still a child and surrounded, inevitably, by treachery. His stepgrandmother, the young dowager widow of King Yŏngjo, ruled as regent from behind the throne, and her family was in the ascendant. I retreated into obscurity, assuming the role of a harmless widow. But I lived on, to set the record straight, and to defend my father, my murdered uncle, my murdered brother. My memoirs were written in much danger and much bitterness. They became my occupation.

My Third Brother was executed in 1801, the year after King Chŏngjo's death, the year in which I wrote my second memoir. He was accused (I believe falsely) of having converted to Catholicism. There were many purges at this time, many martyrdoms, much hatred of the largely unknown West. Prince Ŭnŏn, the son of Sado's court concubine, was executed on the same religious pretext in the same year. His brother, Prince Ŭnsin, had already been banished and had died in exile. Uncle, brother, stepchildren — all dead and gone.

My fourth and fullest account was written in 1805, when I was seventy years old. I wrote this version for Prince Sado. It is his true memorial. In this version, I tried to tell the truth about his illness.

As I have already mentioned, I believe, now, that Prince Sado was a paranoid schizophrenic. These are the words that are now available to describe his condition.

Does it help to know this?

Yes. It does.

My fifth account is my secret. It is my spirit story. It is the story that will never be fully known, and never wholly completed. It is the story I shall tell to my ghost and to her offspring and to her offspring's offspring. I will whisper in their dreams, and they will wake and wonder what it was that they heard.

Of whom, amongst the living and the dead of history, do I still need to make reckoning? I lived on. My eyesight continued to deteriorate, my ankles ached, and the flowers of the other world began to blossom on the backs of my hands. But I outlasted many of my enemies, and my memory did not falter. I kept my wits about me.

I died in 1815, in the year of the Battle of Waterloo. You, my grandson, outlived me, and reigned until your death in 1834. The Yi dynasty survived until the end of the nineteenth century. The last queen of Korea, Queen Min, died in 1895 in the palace, exactly one hundred years after my visit to Hwaseong. At the age of forty-four, she was brutally murdered by foreign assassins, and her body was incinerated in the garden where I used to watch the ginger dragonflies. Only a finger bone survived the flames.

Queen Min was, like me, a clever woman. The Western envoy and traveller Isabella Bird, from Edinburgh, who held long audiences with her, memorialized her as 'the clever, ambitious, intriguing, fascinating and in many ways loveable Queen of Korea' — a witty and ambiguous epitaph for the last of my country's queens. Queen Min, unlike me, died a violent death, but her weak husband survived, to a life of compromise and shame, under Japanese rule.

But that is another story. (A lavish musical entertainment based on Queen Min's life was ill received in the West in recent times, and perhaps it was not in the best of taste, though I must confess that I enjoyed it, from my immortal vantage point in the Royal Box.)

Our palaces were sacked and burned and deconsecrated, and displays of wild animals debased our royal gardens. That, too, is another story. Other wars followed, in the wake of the wars of the world. The Japanese left; the Americans came. Our country was divided. The Japanese returned as tourists; the Americans stayed on as soldiers. Foreign imports flooded our shops, foreign practices penetrated our culture. We learned new technologies, and our exports increased. We in the south of our kingdom left our chosen form of hermit exile and joined the globe, for better and for worse.

These are posthumous stories. The story is not over yet. The north of our country still attempts to lead a hermit life. It now is labelled 'evil'. It is part of the 'axis of evil', whatever that may be. Evil is not a word for which, at my advanced age, I feel much need.

My writings survived. At first they were known only to a few. The tragedy of Prince Sado has always been a legend in our land, but my writings, which give the true account of one who was both an eyewitness and a chief player in the drama, were not so widely known. But now they have found their way into the wider world, and into other languages. I have watched the process of their dissemination with interest

211

and amazement. My story has seized the imaginations of generations then unborn. Artistic renderings of my life in media then unknown have been projected. My amanuenses and translators discuss and at times misinterpret my affairs in cyberspace. I prompt them, I prompt them. I am not a jealous ghost. I am proud, but I am not jealous. I wish you all to know my story.

It may be that manuscripts describing these events still await discovery. Only last week, a new epitaph on Prince Sado by his father King Yŏngjo was discovered, which is said to cast new light on that tragic death. I found it on the Internet. No story is ever finished. Mine continues.

How could I have foreseen the nature of the world that I have now posthumously entered? I haunt it, and it haunts me. It is an astonishing place, busy and complex and confusing. Its peoples are ever restlessly, needlessly on the move. It attempts improbable syntheses. Its frontiers are porous. There are few hermit kingdoms now.

I come from a time of paper and of silk. Paper lanterns glowed in the night for us, and paper boats with silken sails floated upon the lake for us. Ours was a world of silk and rosewood and hemp and jade and stone and ink and water. Our floors were warm and smooth; our screens were light; our minds were subtle. It was a quiet and violent and brutal and secret country, inside the palace walls.

Outside those walls, ours was a hard land with a harsh climate, a land of gneiss and granite and petrified waterfalls, a kingdom surrounded by water, a country of mountains and of cold peaks and wastes, of banishments and exiles and brambles.

Or so the stories say. I did not see much of it. Maybe it was not like that at all. I did not see the way the common people lived.

It is all changed now. It is a modern country now.

And now I must lead you through the gates of harsh cacophony, through the hideous clamour, through the metallic inferno, through the plastic polymer hell, to the lavish luxuries of the air-conditioned, global, universal third millennium. Stop your nose against the pollution; stop your ears against the uproar. Follow me, to the world of globalization and multiple choice. You may like it there. It is the future. It is your future. Take it. It is yours.

PART TWO

Modern Times

She will arrive too early at the airport. She always arrives early at airports. It is foredoomed that she will arrive early at Heathrow. She tosses and turns, after a late and festive farewell night, alone in her wide and queenly bed, half sleeping and half waking, waiting for the alarm clock (which she does not trust) and the prearranged telephone calls (which she does not trust) and for the morning light of Oxford, which will filter, slowly, through the pale blinds of her high windows, whether she trusts it or not. She must rise at six-thirty. She will rise before six-thirty. She cannot make herself wait patiently for the full light of day, although at this time of year the days are still long, and the dawn still comes early to the city.

We watch her, but she does not know that we watch. She ignores our intrusion. Why are we summoned to her bedside? We are summoned by the book in her hand baggage. It would appear that she intends to read it on the aeroplane. It is already packed, in one of the several easily accessible outer zip compartments of her little dark green case-on-wheels.

The script pulls us towards her, by the magnet of its 200-year-old message. We enter the room, whether we will or no. We flock and throng and cluster near her ceiling, little winged spies, looking down on her restless form. We look

217

around her bedroom, and flow out into her bathroom, her corridors, her apartment. The air is thick with our attention. We are here; we are watching; we will report on what we see.

This restless woman does not have the body of an anxious woman, nor do the furnishings of her room express excessive neurosis. Only the evidence of the methodical nature of her packing betrays her ingrained and perhaps not irrational fear of missing trains and aeroplanes. Those lists on her bedside table, by the water carafe and the bottles of pills, also betray some form of anxiety. But, at the same time, they indicate method. This is an efficient woman, trained in outwitting her weaknesses, in medicating her real or imagined illnesses, in forestalling accidents of forgetting and of oversight.

By the bed, on the floor, a pair of large old-fashioned tortoiseshell-rimmed spectacles lies unashamed and eloquent across the spine of an open book. The book lies face down. The spectacles look like a large winged creature that has alighted there.

Her body seems to be a confident body, not an anxious body. She is tall, and she lies at a diagonal across the large bed, sprawling in restless abandon, filling it from corner to corner with her smooth, large limbs. Her legs protrude from beneath her duvet, and her arms are flung wide. Her large toenails are painted a cracked and peeling garnet-red. The duvet cover is of cotton cloth, with a crisp, bold, blue-and-white Delft design, and the crumpled white pillowcases have borders of broderie anglaise. The woman wears a scarlet nightshift of light, loosely woven muslin, which has ridden high over her round belly. Her pubic hair is thick and curling and tawny chestnut. One of her full breasts is exposed to view: it splays out proudly and firmly beneath her jutting collarbone. It is a breast that has been admired and handled. It is not a lonely breast. It is a voluptuous breast.

Her eyes are shut, although she may not be sleeping. Her lashes are thick. They are slightly clotted and matted with the dissolute remains of the previous day's mascara.

Her hair is thick and curled and tousled. It is tawny brown, with false golden highlights, and it sticks to her high, wide brow in warm tendrils.

This woman is not young, but neither is she old. She is glossy and firm, and she is in her prime. She is a woman who rates herself highly. All this we can read from her recumbent, semi-sleepless form. She hovers between sleep and waking, in that realm where dreams converge with fears and plans and memories.

We can read her destination from the pile of books by her bedside, from the list of contact addresses and dates that she has placed by her carafe of water. Her air ticket and her passport are in the pocket of her well-worn brown-leather shoulder bag, but the computer-printed list tells us that her destination is Seoul, in South Korea, and that she is taking an Air France plane from Heathrow to Paris's Roissy-Charles de Gaulle, where she will change flights for Seoul-Incheon. It seems that she intends to spend several days in South Korea. In Seoul, she will stay in the

Pagoda Hotel. It appears that she has contacts in the British Embassy and the British Council, at a Korean women's hospital, and at a pharmaceutical foundation.

The buzz is that she is flying off to a conference, to deliver a paper. So we whisper as we cluster in the upper air. Has she written her paper? Has she made at least two copies of it? Has she made sure to keep one with her in her hand luggage? Is she planning to take her laptop computer with her? Or has she decided that travelling with such a valued and expensive item would be too much of a worry?

In her little, dark green case-on-wheels, the memoir of the Crown Princess is waiting for her. Its author is waiting to speak to her. Its author, long locked in the silence of death, has found another listener. This fitfully sleeping woman is her new victim. The book is a trap, an infection, a time bomb.

She is well endowed, this living woman. Her bedroom is large and airy and elegantly austere. Our eyes can see clearly now in the first light of the end of the dark, and we can see that the blinds of the bedroom are a pale shade of sky blue with a printed border of clouds, that the walls are a perhaps unfashionable eggshell white and that two white, fleecy sheep-skin rugs lie upon the highly polished wooden floor. Dusky saxe blue cushioned seats line the deep embrasure of the window. There is a bookcase, the contents of which indicate an interest in art and architecture, but we may conjecture that this is but a small and decorative selection from her library, and that her working books are kept elsewhere. A large celadon vase of a delicate pale blue-green, placed on a white painted wooden table in the window bay, holds an arrangement of pale, dried, silvery seed heads of honesty, mixed with orange, papery Chinese lanterns. There is an oval Art Nouveau white wood-framed mirror over the bookcase, in which we may fancy that she frequently admires herself.

It is an uncluttered room. Maybe she has tidied it in anticipation of her imminent departure. Maybe she is a tidy person. Maybe she has a person who tidies this room for her. The only clothes we can see are those that she has carefully laid out for her journey on the back of the blue loose-covered armchair. There is a touch of an institutionalized Walter Pater Oxford about this elegant, lightly inhabited bedroom. Her mark on it is not deep. She is a visitor.

Does she always sleep alone? She has not always slept alone. She wears a golden wedding ring on her left hand, and a gold ring set with pearls on the ring finger of her right hand. For a single person, this is a large bed. She lies in state.

There is one photograph on display, in a slightly tarnished ornate silver Victorian frame. It stands on top of a small table near the window. It shows a very young child of indeterminate sex. The child is propped up against a cushion or a pillow, somewhat far from the camera. A remote, removed child. The child is not smiling at the camera.

There is little evidence so far, here, in this room, of the aggressive electronic age that our

221

first narrator evoked at the end of her section. The digital clock glows red, and a small, red light emanates from the large woman's bedside radio, but there is no television set to be seen. This is not a woman who watches television in bed. Hers is a timeless room, offering less of a shock to the trans-secular senses of the time traveller than might have been expected. The view out of the window, were the woman to rise and look out over the gardens, is more than timeless. It is ancient. It is antiquity itself. The stone of the building is a softly pitted honey yellow, tinged with the greys and rusts and ochres of lichen. A spreading mulberry tree stands in the quad-rangle. It is centuries older than the story that the woman will carry on to the aeroplane in her little green case.

The lower branches of the ancient mulberry tree are supported by wooden props and elaborate metal brackets. The grand herbaceous borders of the walled garden are ripe with the closed green buds of flowers of pink and purple and white. The green nubs of these spikes and spires will begin to open soon, in the searching and sad pale gold of a lowly piercing September English dawn. The striped and neatly mown grass is damp with early autumn English dew.

She is a fortunate woman, to overlook so fine, so finely maintained a view. She must be a princess of her time. What has she done to deserve these riches? Has she inherited them, or married them, or earned them? What is her tenure? Are they hers in perpetuity, or are they on loan to her? What right has she to lie in state?

She has at last fallen into a deep sleep, and is dreaming that she is on an aeroplane heading towards the wrong city. This is not Seoul the Unknown that she approaches, but Denver or Dallas. The airship is flying too low over a tightly clustered crystal forest of fragile skyscrapers, and it is clipping them with its wide wings. At any moment the aeroplane will burst into a ball of flame — but, no, that alarm bell is the ringing of the clock, and simultaneously the telephone by her bed begins to clamour at her, and she awakes, averting the disaster that in dreams may never come.

Dr Babs Halliwell (so that is her name, we are learning fast) answers the prompt college intercom alarm, kicks off her duvet, struggles violently from her bed, switches off the alarm button of her clock before it can scream at her, and waits to answer the preordered double-safe wake-up telephone call before going to the bathroom to run her bath. As she strides across the room, we see that she is even taller than we thought. She has a commanding figure, and she has an air of command. Even alone, unobserved except by the viewless little fluttering denizens of the upper air, she seems to be on show. She performs to herself, a little drama of self-importance, of self-encouragement. She does not speak aloud to herself — it is perhaps too early in the morning for that — but we can guess that at times she may.

Energetically she turns on the bath taps, rescues a thickset, round, short-legged spider from the tub with her face flannel, releases it upon the carpet, brushes her teeth, tests the water, submerges herself, and sponges herself. The aromatic herbal perfumes of her bath gel fill the bathroom air. She raises one foot from the foam, and inspects the chipped and lurid garnet nail varnish with shallow and transitory disapproval. So far, so good, her manner indicates.

Her black academic gown hangs bat-like and severe from a hook on the back of the bathroom door. Her gaze fixes on it, blankly. For a moment she drifts. Is she thinking of abandoning her career?

Dr Halliwell knows she cannot possibly be late, but nevertheless she suddenly begins, nervously, to accelerate. She leaps out of the bath, towels herself, and dresses hastily, while taking sips from a cup of black instant coffee brewed from the kettle in her en-suite kitchen. (Why is she washing down quite so many pills so early in the morning? Is she a health fanatic, a vitamin addict, or is she combating some chronic but invisible malady?) Her undergarments are a healthy and hygienic white, and her knee-high nylon socks are a sunny tan. She assumes a soft cream shirt with cuffs and tortoiseshell cuff links, and, over the shirt, she pulls on a long fawn-and-mauve-checked smock-like dress flowing loosely from a low, round, gathered yoke. Her brown leather shoes are flat-heeled and gold-buckled and new.

She inspects herself, not in the fancy oval Art Nouveau mirror on the wall, but in the full-length functional oblong mirror on the inside of the wardrobe door. She seems to approve of what she sees, and returns to the bathroom where she attends to the application of cosmetics, peering at herself a little myopically in a magnifying mirror. She darkens her eyelashes and her eyebrows, coats most of her face with a smear of foundation and a dab of powder, and wrestles with the recalcitrant cap of a small pot of rouge. It defeats her and she abandons it, pushing it back into her flower-bedizened cosmetics sachet to join its fellow ointments. She bares her large and carefully tended teeth at herself, then stretches her lips to the lipstick. (One of her front teeth is crowned: we suspect a schoolgirl sporting injury.) She paints her wide, curving lips in a dark cinnamon bow. She smiles at herself with a reassuring cinnamon smile. She is ready to face the day and the journey.

She has ordered a taxi to take her the short journey from college to the coach station at Gloucester Green. It is there, waiting for her, at the lodge. The porter is up and attentive. He wishes her a good morning, and helps her into her cab. She has two pieces of baggage, one a medium-sized navy-blue Samsonite suitcase, the other her little green case-on-wheels. Both pieces are clearly and efficiently labelled. 'Have a good journey, Dr Halliwell,' says the porter, politely, as she arranges herself on the cab seat. She smiles, and thanks him. She is on her way.

Her bedroom is empty. It sighs and settles in her absence. Her kitchen is empty. Her rooms are empty. Will somebody come to make up the bed, to clean the bath, to wash the coffee cup? Are there servants yet in England? We will not wait to see. The spies drop like dead flies. We will follow Dr Halliwell to Heathrow.

On the coach, she chides herself for her earliness. She has given herself too much time to spare. She could have ordered the cab for half an hour later. She could have spent at least another half-hour in bed. She need not have worried that the taxi would not arrive, that the coach would be full, that she might have missed a coach by thirty seconds. There is always another coach. They are frequent and reliable. She need not have reflected on the occasion when one of her colleagues had been delayed and missed his flight because of an accident in thick fog on the A40. There is no fog this morning. It is a beautiful, sunny September morning, and the road is clear.

No, she has not forgotten her passport, or her ticket, or her medication. She checks her bag, yet again. All these important objects are still where she has put them. They have not jumped out of her bag of their own accord, or been tweaked away by a hovering host of malevolent bedroom sylphs or coach-station imps. They are inanimate and inert, and they will stay where she put them. She is a rational woman, and she knows that they will stay in their places. Nevertheless, she looks for them once more, before the coach arrives at Heathrow, before she alights to catch the shuttle to her terminal. She has had some unpleasant shocks in her successful and high-achieving life, and is ever well prepared for another. Or so she thinks.

She checks in at the Air France desk,

concealing her foolish relief that her flight seems to exist and that it corresponds with the number on her ticket. (It is not always so. She has, in her time, been booked on nonexistent flights or discovered that what looks like a firm booking is merely notional.) She checks her larger navy-blue Samsonite case through to Seoul, and the receipt is stapled on to her ticket. She watches the case protectively as it moves along on the moving belt, almost confident that she will see it again before too long. Its distinctive purple Pagoda Hotel label, furnished by the travel company that had made the conference book-ings, disappears from sight, like a flag over the horizon. Will it, will she, catch the connection at Charles de Gaulle?

Now she has a mere two hours to fill, to kill. Shall she take breakfast? Shall she buy a newspaper? Shall she sit down in a quiet corner to read one of the books she has brought with her to lighten the sixteen hours of her journey?

She is too restless to read a book. She will be able to read only when she is strapped into her seat, as in a straitjacket of captive attention. She looks forward to this moment with pleasure, but she cannot allow herself or oblige herself to anticipate it. She is a serious reader, this large woman with her deceptively confident manner: she is an academic, and she needs to give the whole of her attention to a text. She is approaching her text, and the text is approaching her, but meanwhile she idles away the time with small distractions.

The departure lounge of Terminal 2, never a

particularly attractive venue, is even more unattractive than usual, as it seems to be undergoing some form of refurbishment. Areas are walled off with amateur panels of hardboard, and sections of roofing gape to reveal unhealthy vistas of pipe and wiring and wadding and cladding. Although it is not raining, water drips from aloft into a bucket. There must be a leak, somewhere up there in the guttering. People from every gene pool of the globe clutter the place, in various stages of exhaustion and expectation, in attitudes of impatience and resignation and despair. Loudspeakers make superfluous announcements about baggage retention and smoking prohibitions. Babies slumber lop-headed in buggies, pale with fatigue. Whole families have set up encampments in corners, on the floor. It is a distressing scene, a scene of refugees in transit rather than of free travellers in a free world. Lucky the few who have a right to wait in the executive airport lounges. Is Dr Halliwell wishing she had been bold enough to insist on an upgrade? Should she have stood on ceremony and status? What *is* her status? Should she have risked putting it to the test? Is she a rising star and a mini-celebrity, as she sometimes believes herself to be? Or has she peaked already, at the age of forty-two? Will she get promotion this year, next year? And if so, promotion to what? It has been a long climb to the midway place where she now finds herself: must she go on climbing for the rest of her life?

At first Dr Barbara Halliwell paces more or less randomly through the Escheresque network of self-duplicating duty-free shops, eyeing perfumes and bottles of liquor and cartons of cigarettes and tins of caviar and Burberry coats and Bally shoes and expensively packaged gift boxes of biscuits and of tea. She returns from time to time to stare at a desirable red silk shirt in an expensive Italian designer-label boutique, but she resists its allure. She likes it, but she has enough shirts, and she may know from past experience that goods bought in boredom in airports frequently prove strangely unsatisfactory, occasionally even defective. When she has walked up and down for half a mile or so, she sits down for a lukewarm cappuccino and a cold wood-wool and kapok croissant, and glances through a couple of broadsheet newspapers which she has purchased.

What does she find in the papers?

She finds home news from the small world of her homeland about cliques and cabals and Underground strikes and errant ministers and defective transport policies. She reads about these matters with a detached interest, and pays grateful tribute to the efficiency of the Oxford Tube and the services of the X70 and the X90. Her gracious Oxford sabbatical has made her loath to return to the chaos and squalor of London traffic and the expense of London life. Living in Oxford is a positional good, a placing beyond price. But she knows she will never get an Oxford job. She has been lucky to have enjoyed a year of Oxford. The cloisters and the mulberry tree and the well-tended herbaceous borders of Japanese anemone and aster and salvia and snapdragon are on loan to her. Her time will soon be up, and she will be obliged to return to the chic and scruffy pavements of North London and Cantor Hill.

She finds new scandals about university admissions and A-grades and rejected students threatening litigation. She sighs. She is glad she is not an admissions tutor, and glad she has no more examinations to take.

She sighs again, and turns to international news, about anti-globalization protests at a summit on another continent. This piece she reads impassively, respectfully. She flips onwards, and in the health section of one of the two papers, she finds an article on a newly developed treatment for multiple sclerosis, and its controversial expense. In the science section of the other, she discovers a précis of an article from *The Lancet* on the efficacy of vitamin treatments for Parkinson's disease. She reads both these pieces with considerable attention, and at one point cross-refers from one to the other. Perhaps, despite her appearance of glowing health, she is a hypochondriac? Or is she a health professional, on her way to a medical conference?

But the stories — and they are stories — which seem to engross her most concern two lurid cases involving the subject of capital punishment. One is the story of an African woman condemned by Islamic *sharia* law to be stoned to death for adultery. An appeal is in progress, and there has been much international condemnation, even from some who in most circumstances describe themselves as multiculturalists. Dr Halliwell reads both accounts of this extreme case, in both papers, with a marked expression of distaste upon her cultured features.

The second story concerns the fate of a condemned prisoner on death row in an American state infamous for its fondness for judicial executions. Convicted of multiple rape and murder while a minor, this no-longer-young man has been appealing against his fate for nearly twenty years. He has twice attempted suicide, and twice been judicially resuscitated. The end of his appeals appears to be nigh. The electric chair or the lethal injection approaches.

This not-so-young man has a British connection, in the form of a British grandmother, which is one of the reasons why his case is receiving some unexpectedly sympathetic coverage in the British broadsheet press. A few British MPs have signed an appeal for clemency on his behalf. It is claimed that new evidence about his state of mind and state of health at the time of the offences has never been presented to the court. It is claimed that his legal defence at the time of the original trial was wholly inadequate, and that any competent undergraduate in the department of journalism at the Northwestern University of Illinois could have obtained a different verdict.

The accounts of this case Dr Halliwell peruses with as much attention and apparent concern as she had devoted to the case of the woman allegedly taken in adultery. Perhaps she is an academic lawyer, on her way to a legal conference? Perhaps she is a human-rights spokesperson?

She has by now finished her coffee, and rejected most of her deadwool croissant. She rises to her feet, and collects her shoulder bag and her little green suitcase-on-wheels. She crosses the thronged arena to stare more closely at the monitor through her large tortoiseshell-rimmed glasses. Her face has a *noli-me-tangere* look of myopic and anxious severity. The number of her gate has just been announced. She returns to the expensive Italian boutique, and inspects once more the desirable red silk shirt. It is of a ravishing shade of clear pure red. She has always been attracted to red. Will she regret it for ever if she leaves it hanging there? There is plenty of time to purchase it, should she choose to do so. Is she running through the items reposing in her checked-in suitcase with its purple Pagoda Hotel label? Is she wondering if she can justify the purchase of this shirt? Is she wondering what functions and dress codes will await her at this grand conference in South Korea? Is she telling herself that silk is an uncertain fabric, not always amenable to travelling or to home laundering, and that the style of the shirt may be too tailored for her taste and her figure and her comfort? Or is she thinking about the woman taken in adultery, and about the man who has spent more than half of his one and only life sentenced to death? Is she wondering if the nineteenth-century concept of social progress retains any validity?

She rejects with some regret the red silk shirt,

and marches herself towards the gate of embarkation.

It is a good while yet before she is finally settled in her window seat. She has already been up for hours, and this is only the first, short leg of her journey. The day is long, and the night and the next flight will be long. She has furnished herself with a wide choice of reading matter, but has considered it not worth her while to unpack much of it yet. On the way to Paris, she makes do with *Multiculturalism: Is It Bad for Women?* and a light second breakfast. She doesn't want a second breakfast, but there it is, on a tray in front of her, and she eats it. She finds *Multiculturalism* surprisingly easy reading. It is a paperback collection of sociological essays, pleasantly packaged. She has nearly finished it by the time she disembarks at Roissy-Charles de Gaulle.

She has to hang around there, too, for she has left herself too much time between flights. Air France flights, she has been told, are often late, often cancelled, and moreover there is, as so often, an Air France strike pending. So she has run no risks, and has therefore left herself with yet more useless hours to kill. Time passes slowly at Roissy. She should have lived more dangerously. At least, she reflects, there will be no chance of her luggage not being transferred, will there? Or has she left *too much* time, and will it precede her, skipping Korea, and go straight to China or Taiwan or Japan?

The Crown Princess is as impatient as Dr Halliwell. She cannot wait to seize this wandering woman's wandering attention.

Eventually, Dr Babs Halliwell finds herself sitting safely in her aisle seat on her way to Seoul, as her plane lumbers noisily and clumsily up into the air, weighed down by its many gallons of heavy fuel. At last, she can begin to relax and to concentrate. She has by now deployed her reading matter efficiently: she has tucked two paperback books into the pocket on the back of the seat in front of her, a third book is on her knee, a fourth in the shoulder bag under the seat in front of her.

She has brought books for various moods and seasons. The two in the seat pocket relate to her travels: one is the slim but classic diary of Lady Murasaki, published by Penguin and translated from the Japanese by Richard Bowring, and the other is a more substantial academic paperback, entitled *A Message from the Crown Princess of Korea, in the form of a Court Memoir of the Eighteenth Century*, translated, edited and annotated by Thea Ŏ. Landry, and published by the Yellow Fields Press. *Multiculturalism: Is It Bad for Women?* lies upon her knee: she has decided she will polish this one off first. (Finally, secreted in her shoulder bag, she has hidden away a detective story set in Venice, in which she will take refuge if the novelty of the Orient and the stress of her conference prove too much for her.)

Her eyes move sternly over the pages, as the aeroplane's pilot tells her in three languages that he has reached a cruising altitude of 36,000 feet. She does not listen to what he says: her altitude in the heavens means nothing to her, and if he told her an outright lie she would not hear him. Her chief aim at this point seems to be to isolate herself in her own space and to insulate herself from her fellow travellers. On her left is an unpromising middle-aged man, unprovided with reading matter, who looks as though he might wish to embark on a conversation. This is not what she wants. So she keeps her eyes firmly on multiculturalism, as she toys with her first lunch. By the time that her tray is cleared, she has finished multiculturalism. She slips multiculturalism into the seat pocket, and she idly takes out the memoirs of the Korean Crown Princess. She starts to read, in an uncommitted manner, as she hurtles eastwards at nearly a thousand kilometres an hour.

Five hours later, she has hardly lifted her eyes from the text. Many thousands of miles she has travelled into darkness through the upper air, but she is unaware of time or space. She is gripped by the eloquent ghost of the lady. The nameless lady of the family of Hong has her in thrall.

It is evident that the story moves and distresses her, for from time to time she lets out little physical signs of a painful mental engagement — an intake of breath, a tugging at her hair, a clicking or clenching of her teeth, a turning down of a page corner, or a rapid consultation of the notes or the index (for the names are confusing, to a Western reader, and far too many of them begin with the letter H). She writes in the margins with fine blue ink; she colours in passages with lurid, glowing pink and green. The childhood and child marriage of the princess, the birth and death of her first-born son, the birth of her second son and of her daughters, the clothing mania of her husband Prince Sado, the slaughter of his concubine Pingae, the prince's thwarted efforts at suicide, the rice chest death of Sado, the death of the old king, the sixtieth birthday state visit to Hwaseong — all these long-ago events enter her consciousness with explosive effect, and detonate there, spreading a fallout of small mental particles through her brain and her body. A lifetime's tragedy erupts suddenly in her head in a puffball cloud of spores. The bodily Dr Barbara Halliwell shifts in her seat, and hitches at the uncomfortably constricting garter tops of her knee-highs, and twists and torments her cuff links, but she reads on, ignoring in-flight movies, patrolling stewardesses and the bored heaving of the large man on her left. She takes a passing glass of water from time to time from the stewardess's tray, but she seems not to notice that she does it. The princess is taking her over, bodily and mentally. Dr Babs Halliwell is no longer herself.

At high altitude, mental particles penetrate and interact with extraordinary velocity, and initiate strange chemical reactions that cannot be quantified. Science has never formally recognized this process, but Dr Halliwell has observed it before, on other flights to other countries, while reading other books. But never has this interchange taken place with such intensity. The princess has entered her, like an alien creature in

236

a science-fiction movie, and she is gestating and growing within her. The pages turn, rapidly, as the princess gains presence and power.

But at last, after several hours, Dr Halliwell is getting tired. She is worn out by so much intensity, and the palace plots and family intrigues after the princess's son's death confuse her. She feels that the princess is not telling her the whole truth about them, and she cannot follow the detail. She tells the princess that she must rest, that she must shut her eyes, that she must go to the lavatory, that she must take a break. The princess, who is herself not at all comfortable at this height, even in her disembodied state, agrees to relinquish her grip for a while: she is sure by now that she has Dr Halliwell at her mercy, and is prepared to grant her a short reprieve.

Dr Halliwell closes the by now well-annotated paperback pages, and places the book in the seat pocket in front of her, looking down with dissatisfaction at her hands as she does so. Her pen has reacted unpleasantly and with hostility to the cabin's air pressure, and has started to leak. Her fingers are blotched blue with its liquefying azure blood. She must go to wash them. It is mid movie, and there is no queue for the toilets. She marches along the aisle on her slightly swollen feet and ankles, and bolts herself into the small prison cubicle. How large is a rice chest, she wonders? The notes on the text have described it and given its dimensions, and there is a helpful photographic illustration of a similar object, housed in a private collection in Paris. It belongs to a family connection of the translator. Nevertheless, she cannot quite visualize the fatal rice chest. Perhaps she does not wish to do so. She has always been mildly claustrophobic, with a not unnatural or indeed uncommon fear of enclosed spaces. Being stuck in a lift between floors is near the top of her list of unpleasant situations, and on planes and coaches she always tries to select an aisle seat. This fear cannot in itself wholly account for the violent nature of her response to this old crime, this ancient tragedy, but it may bear some small part in it.

She stares at herself in the toilet mirror with some horror. She has often noticed that journeys on aeroplanes lend to the skin a particularly unpleasant colouring, and her large, brown, slightly bloodshot eyes now stare back at her from a face which has assumed an unseemly hard, mauve, cracked complexion. Broken veins walk across her cheeks and her nose, and her eyes are rimmed with an unfashionable red, as well as with suave dark brown eyeliner. She looks gross and ugly. Not thus, she hopes, did she appear the night before, in her long, black, silky rayon dress and gold earrings, at the Gladwyn dinner!

The memory of the Gladwyn dinner attempts to cut across and divert the disturbing interpenetrating current of the life of the Crown Princess of Korea, but the powerful ghost of the Crown Princess does not give up so easily. She insists on flowing on, into the bloodstream. She refuses to allow Dr Babs Halliwell to retreat into a comfortable or uncomfortable replay of the previous night's entertainment, into an interior monologue on the petty personal subject of the frustrated amorous attentions of Dr Halliwell's current influential admirer and patron, the notorious philandering historian Robert Treborough. The Crown Princess urges Dr Babs to stick closer to her own royal Korean story, and to dwell on the nature of speeches and ceremonies, hierarchies and protocol, discomfort and ritual, tradition and survival, robes and symbols, power and subjugation. The Crown Princess is not very interested in Dr Halliwell's fleeting earthly loves and losses. Sexual satisfaction had played a very small part in her own life on earth, but protocol and power had loomed heavily over her. Oxford, like eighteenth-century Korea, is a city of ancient proprieties and obsolete customs, of cloisters and cabals, and it is thence, surely, from this common area, that mutual recognition will flow. The Crown Princess believes that it is through the traditions of England and Oxford and the old mulberry tree of the Great Court that she has captivated the attention and colonized and terrorized the imagination of Dr Babs Halliwell.

But she is wrong — well, somewhat wrong. There are connections, but they are not all rooted in Oxford or in mulberries. Dr Halliwell is not herself yet sure what they may prove to be.

Dr Babs Halliwell, having powdered her unsatisfactorily mauve nose with a clumsy dusting of inadequate beige, returns to her seat and opens the text once more. She has nearly finished the last section of the princess's memoirs. She reads on to the end, through the last, fullest and most devastating account of the illness and death of Prince Sado.

Is Dr Halliwell reflecting that her own life, unlike that of the princess, has been of late passed quietly and safely and comfortably, in shady courtyards, by green lawns, in a peaceful and prosperous land, far from primitive and irrational decrees, far from cruel and violent deaths? Is she reflecting on the suburban safety of her childhood, in Orchard View, Banville Road, Orpington, and her happy schooldays at Tonbridge School? Is she casting her mind back to her carefree college days in Sussex, when the world lay all before her?

No, she is not. She is thinking of the true horrors and true sorrows of her own life, sorrows that have been reawakened in her by the memoirs she has been reading. Irrationality, sickness, cruelty and violence may not be relegated to the dark backward and abysm of history. They have not yet been written out of the plot.

Usually Dr Halliwell manages to keep some kind of formal barrier between herself and the most unhappy of her life memories, for she is an academic, an intellectual, and she is accustomed to using her intellect to control and to distance pain. She has used her brain rigorously and in her view righteously in attempts to banish fruitless suffering and vain regret. It is a tribute to the narrative power of the Crown Princess and the skills of her translator that the text on Dr Halliwell's knee has so keenly pierced her intellect and so deeply penetrated her heart.

240

Dr Halliwell's life has been neither unhappy nor unsuccessful, and her public front of cheerful confidence is not unwarranted. But the double negatives in that last sentence have their place in the story, too. Dr Halliwell is partial to double negatives. A colleague, commenting on a draft script of her latest publication, had pointed out this stylistic preference to her. He claimed to have run her electronic text through a grammar analysis program, in order to verify his impression. She had laughed, but she had registered his comment, and checked it, and found that what he said was true. She does indeed tend to espouse the double negative. She has attempted to restrict the proliferation of this grammatical tic in the script of the paper that she is shortly to deliver at the conference in Seoul. She is still doubtful about some of her paper's arguments, but at least they will not now be expressed wholly in double negatives.

Her paper is called 'Dying by Lot: Uncertainty and Fatality'.

She has been neither unhappy nor unsuccessful in her life and in her career, and the freedom of choice and the freedom of movement that she has enjoyed in her forty-two years would have been unimaginable to the Crown Princess or to any of the Crown Princess's female contemporaries. But she, too, has been acquainted with sorrow, loss, fear, restriction, enclosure, premature death. She, too, has tried to live with madness. She, too, feels she has failed to save others from madness. But, unlike the Crown Princess, she has been free to move away from

241

her failures and her sorrows. She has relegated them to her past. She has been free to accept the temporary protection of her Hanbury Foundation Fellowship, in an Oxford haven. She has been free to toy with the idea of a dalliance with Robert Treborough. She has enjoyed many dalliances in her time, for she has a healthy sexual appetite, an appetite condoned and indeed encouraged by late twentieth-century Western culture. But the memories of her earlier womanhood and its sadly doomed accidents and choices continue to inform and to haunt her.

The acuteness of the Crown Princess's comments on Prince Sado's mental state strike Dr Halliwell as implausibly, uncannily, ahistorically perceptive. This woman must have been hundreds of years ahead of her time. Indeed, time has not yet caught up with the Crown Princess. Had she been one of those few rare souls born out of time? Had special pleading sharpened her wits? Does special pleading often sharpen the wits? Has it sharpened Dr Halliwell's own wits? Or has it perverted and diverted them to no good end?

Dr Halliwell knows she ought to try to seize an hour or two of sleep before she arrives in Seoul, for she is flying against the clock and towards the rising sun, and she will lose a whole day (or is it a whole night?) of her life. She needs some beauty sleep, if she is not to arrive looking too utterly hideous. (Although she is an intellectual, she is vain and she is female, and she wants to make a good impression.) She turns off her reading light, and shuts her eyes, but of course she cannot sleep. It is just too damned uncomfortable, crammed into this mean economy seat, next to a large stranger whose elbow has strayed over the armrest into her already inadequate space. Her clothes, chosen though they were for looseness and comfort, are now digging into her and pinching her at various pressure points. Maybe she should have worn tights, instead of knee-highs? No, maybe not. A constriction at the waist is more irritating than a constriction just below the knee.

She should have paid for an upgrade and travelled business class. She should have refused to travel in an economy seat. It is beneath her dignity to travel like this. She has a suspicion that on this very aeroplane there might be more important lecturers than herself travelling to the same conference, but in greater style. Who is there, up front, in the privileged seats? She will be very annoyed if she finds that unworthy speakers have been promoted.

A friend of hers had once travelled back from a film festival in Bangkok on the same aeroplane as the Queen of Thailand. He was travelling first class, at the expense of his publishers, but because of the queen he had been obliged to make do with the business-class toilets. The flight attendants who waited on the queen had crawled obsequiously on their hands and knees to offer her canapés and to serve her drinks and her meals. It seemed that they were not allowed to stand in her presence. Although Babs Halliwell's friend had reported on this experience with some mirth, she could see he had been affected by it. He had never been invited to fly first class before, and probably never would be again, so it was a pity to have this treat buggered up, as he put it, by foreign royalty.

Dr Halliwell does not know much about protocol and decorum in Korea. Presumably things have changed since the days of the Crown Princess, for the country has been through many traumas since the days of Prince Sado and his bride. South Korea is a modern, monarchy-free country now, a modern republic in the grip of a perpetual technological and electronic revolution. There will be no need to kowtow, though there may be a question of chopsticks. Do the Koreans still revere their ancestors, in Confucian style? Or have the old ways and old beliefs been discarded? She knows that in some situations Koreans are still given to removing their shoes and sitting on the floor, and has been warned to select her clothing accordingly. Although she is so large, she is still supple enough to sit on the floor without difficulty.

She thinks fondly of the clothes in her navy-blue Samsonite suitcase, which she hopes has been stowed safely aboard this aeroplane.

The vivid and compulsive story of Crown Prince Sado's clothing phobia has gripped her even more than the account of the hideous manner of his death. She knows a good deal about phobias, but she does not think that she has ever read about this one. It is new to her, and she cannot think of any known parallel. Questions about its origins and meaning, prompted by the revisionist, posthumous thinking of the Crown Princess herself, begin to percolate through the spongy grey masses of her brain and to travel along the unmapped corrugated ridges and wrinkles and valleys of her consciousness. What had Prince Sado been suffering from, and why? Has his affliction yet been named? Was it physical or psychological? Had his torment been rooted in the body or the mind? Would it, in the twenty-first century, have submitted to any form of medication?

The first and only husband of Dr Babs Halliwell, who is still more or less alive though long estranged from her and indeed from himself, suffers from a psychological illness that took (and takes) a physical form. She wonders what he would make of the illness that had seized Prince Sado. Peter Halliwell does not slice off the heads of eunuchs or batter ladies-in-waiting to death, nor does he engage in military games on horseback in his back garden. These anachronistic and extravagant expressions of madness are not available to him, nor is it likely that he would choose them if he could. But he does, like Prince Sado, suffer from a painful and disfiguring skin disease, which intermittently covers his legs and arms and other parts of his body with peeling scabs. This, think Dr Babs and some others more professionally qualified to hold such opinions than she, is an outward expression of his suicidal depressive tendencies. Dr Babs blames Peter's famously charismatic and famously unreliable father for this skin disease, and for the suicidal tendencies. Peter's father had been a hard act to follow. He, or it, had demanded too much of his son. His son had failed, and had gone mad. The father had not been a king, but he had been as cruel and as despotic as a king. His son, like Prince Sado, had never been allowed to succeed.

Peter's father had been caught out cheating. Not at cards, nor at examinations. He had not cheated, it would appear, for financial gain. He had been an abstruse professional cheat, an academic cheat, a falsifier of experiments. Those who wished to condone him called him a fantasist. Those who wished to condemn him called him a liar. He had been notorious, for good reasons and for bad. History has not yet written its final verdict on Peter Halliwell's father. Peter had not waited to hear it. He had pre-empted it.

Dr Babs Halliwell crosses and uncrosses her legs, and glances upwards at the monitor, which is showing a tiny model aircraft jerking and edging and edging and jerking its way across the map towards the Hermit Kingdom, the Land of Morning Calm. Then she shuts her eyes again. Three hours still to go.

She has no inclination to embark on Lady Murasaki or the Venetian detective story, although those are the books that she had selected for this journey. The Crown Princess's memoirs she had not, in any deep sense, selected, for a week ago she had never heard of them. They had been sent to her anonymously, packaged in cardboard, through Amazon.com, by somebody who seemed to have neglected to request the enclosure of a gift message. She recalls now that she had opened the package with suspicion, and looked for some time through the cardboard casing for the name of the sender. Clearly the gift was connected with her forthcoming journey, so it must have come from someone with whom she had discussed her visit to Korea, someone who had been interested enough to remember what she said. Was it from somebody involved in the organization of the conference? Had every participant been sent a copy? This, although possible, seemed unlikely, as the book did not seem to have any evident connection with the conference's theme, which was, ostensibly, 'The New Frontiers of Health: Globalization and Medical Risk'. Dr Halliwell can now think of many ways in which the Crown Princess's work could be made to relate to this topic, but that is because she is clever, and because her mind works that way. She does not believe that these connections would have readily occurred to others.

She had tried without success to discover who had sent her this curious and, as it now proves, explosive gift. First of all she had accused her mother because her mother, a voracious and proselytizing reader, had occasionally sent her gifts through Amazon, and because Babs was always happy to have an excuse to gossip with her mother. But her mother, over the phone from Orpington, had denied any such act of generosity. 'No, not me, darling,' she had protested. 'I don't know the first thing about Korea. Except for the war, of course. I remember the war. Terrible photographs, terrible weather, far too many dead. General Westmoreland, wasn't it? Or was it General MacArthur? And the Thirty-Eighth Parallel? And a lot of Turkish troops? Aren't they talking about reunification these days? The sunshine policy, that's what they call it. When did you say you were off? Do take care, darling, won't you?'

Babs's mother is an intelligent woman, born in a generation that thought it smart to dissimulate intelligence. Her daughter Barbara is an intelligent woman, born in a competitive generation that needs to display and exaggerate intelligence. Her mother's words have prompted Babs to find out what the words 'sunshine policy' mean. She has in consequence become quite a fan of President Kim Dae Jung. She is grateful to her mother for this discreet prompting.

Babs had next approached her current beau, Robert Treborough, about the mysterious memoirs, but he also denied any knowledge of the Crown Princess. Babs Halliwell had not asked him directly whether or not he had sent her the book because she did not wish to suggest the possibility of favours that might not have been offered and would not necessarily have been welcomed. But she had introduced the lady's name into her conversation with Robert, and also the name of the lady's translator, and had drawn a blank on both. Robert Treborough is a smart aleck who hates to deny knowledge of anything, and he would certainly have claimed knowledge, had he had any. So that ruled out

Robert. Robert is a historian, of sorts, but Korea is not his patch, and the eighteenth century is not his period. Nevertheless, he was annoyed with himself for not being able to respond to her oblique references. He is a very competitive man.

Next Babs tried her friend Polly Usher, who seemed a likely suspect. Polly was a keen if random reader, and she and Babs Halliwell had for years enjoyed exchanging recommendations. Polly certainly knew Babs was off to Korea to deliver a paper on 'Dying by Lot: Uncertainty and Fatality' because Polly had been kind enough to read this paper and to comment on its contents. Polly might well have known about the Crown Princess.

Babs Halliwell and Polly Usher had been brought together by a book. They had first met near the Great Ormond Street Hospital for Sick Children, while eating a lunchtime snack in an eighteenth-century public house called The Lamb. Both of them were reading the same paperback novel, part of which was set in the Great Ormond Street Hospital for Sick Children. They had exclaimed over the coincidence, compared notes, and become friends for life. That was a long time ago. Polly's sick child had been less seriously sick than Babs's child, and was now well. Babs's child, who had been very sick, was dead. But that was a long time ago, and Babs tries not to think about it too often. She is so successful at not thinking about it that she occasionally forgets the very evident connection between the field of her academic studies and the death of her child. This is a considerable feat of denial and willed disconnection, and Polly, who is as clever as Babs, does her best to collude in it. Polly has mother's survivor guilt, and the last thing she wishes to do is to upset her less fortunate friend.

Polly, like Babs's mother, pleads innocence and ignorance. She, too, has never heard of the Crown Princess. Could it, she suggests, have been sent by an admiring student? Several of Dr Halliwell's protégés, both male and female, have in the past developed old-fashioned 'crushes' on their good-looking, high-profile and high-bosomed tutor: maybe it is from one of them who is trying to curry favour?

Babs had herself thought of this possibility, but it is not one that she wishes to pursue. So she had let the matter drop. Somebody, in the future, might claim this act of generosity. But for the present, she had been content to accept the gift, and, as we have seen, had also been sufficiently intrigued by it to choose it as her travelling companion.

Her royal escort now lies patient and inert in the seat pocket, waiting to arrive in her much-changed hometown of Seoul. Babs must have dozed, after all, for she is woken by the offer of some small and indeterminate meal. She toys with it, apathetically, and sees that the toy aeroplane on the screen has nearly reached its destination. It is due to arrive mid morning, Korean time. Babs is by now longing for a shower and a change of clothes, and hopes there will be time for these in the Pagoda Hotel before the first official conference event of the day, which is a lunch reception in the Chosŏn Suite. Etiquette does not oblige her to change her clothes as frequently as a Korean prince or princess, but she feels crumpled, even in her crushproof modern fabrics, and she would like to stretch her body and refresh her garments. She is being met at the airport, or so her conference invitation and several e-mails have informed her: with luck, this will expedite matters, and she will have half an hour or so to smarten herself up before she has to face the music and meet her fellow participants.

She is particularly looking forward to meeting Professor Jan van Jost. Jan van Jost is one of the reasons why she has accepted this invitation. An appearance at a conference at which Jan van Jost speaks will stick a glittering golden star on to any ambitious young academic's curriculum vitae — well, perhaps not the CV of any academic, but the CV of any academic who has an interest in sociology, evolutionary biology, medical ethics, or globalization. Jan van Jost is the guru of globalization, risk and dark choices. It would not be correct to say that he is Dr Halliwell's hero because she is too competitive and considers herself too cynical to have a hero, but she does know who he is and where he stands, and she wishes to see him plain.

Cynical though she may be, in some professional respects, she is nevertheless excited by the prospect of arriving in the Far East. She has never been further east than India, and she is expecting to see a land quite different from anywhere she has been before. Her e-mail

251

correspondence with her hosts has been tantalizing. She has been intrigued by the way her own correspondence, when she presses the 'Reply to Sender' button on her laptop, immediately transliterates itself not into incomprehensible Korean *han'gŭl* hieroglyphs, but into the classical Greek alphabet. Luckily she is acquainted with this alphabet, and had at once recognized her own name, ΛΟΓΥΟΣ ΒΑΣΒΑΣΑ. Why her alphabet should thus mutate in midair is a mystery to her, but it is a pleasing one. She is sure that Korea itself will be full of such transcultural surprises.

Through the window, across the bodies of her fellow travellers, she can glimpse what she takes to be a tilting expanse of the Yellow Sea. It is, in effect, of a bruised and yellowish sedimentary tinge. She wonders if the Crown Princess had ever seen the sea. She had seen and crossed the Han River, on her way to Hwaseong: was that the only occasion on which she had ever left the confines of Seoul?

Babs thinks of the Crown Princess, sitting in the shade, sheltering from the blazing sun in the corner of a baking courtyard, as her husband pleaded for his life. She thinks of Prince Sado, trying but failing to kill himself, and being revived at the brink of death by his doctors, to face a worse and lingering death. She thinks of her own husband, Peter Halliwell, marching night after night with remorseless tread around the confines of their tall North London house. Up and down the two steep flights of stairs, and round and round the central stairwell he had marched, and round and round each room, hour after hour, hour after hour, as she lay in bed and listened to him. He paced and paced, and from time to time he would groan like a beast. 'I wish I were dead, I wish I were dead,' he would groan and cry. 'I want, I want, I want,' he would monotonously repeat. She had not been able to help him. Depression had been diagnosed, but such a diagnosis was inadequate. Whatever afflicted Peter was more desperate even than a severe clinical depression. It was more like despair. Violent, rodent despair. He had been violent, but mostly towards himself. At least he had not sought relief in murdering others.

Prince Sado had admitted that he found relief in killing. This, thinks Babs, is astonishing. Astonishing self-knowledge, in such dark ages. What had given him so much access to his own mind?

The plane descends, and Babs Halliwell banishes Peter from her consciousness. She braces herself for landing and for the excitement of social interaction. Who will be there to greet her, and how will she recognize the person? How will the person recognize her? She has been told to select the VIP channel, but she cannot see that there is one, so she goes without difficulty through normal passport control to the baggage-claim area. While she waits for her suitcase to emerge from its lair, she has the foresight to visit the currency exchange desk to acquire some Korean *won*, in case of emergencies. She will receive a handsome per diem, for this is a long and surprisingly well-funded conference, but

253

who knows when she will lay her hands on her discreet brown envelope? She likes to be independent. By the time she returns to the luggage belt, her navy-blue Samsonite suitcase with its purple Pagoda label has already heaved into sight and is about to disappear once more. She grabs it, and marches towards the exit notice, where a smiling young man is waving a large card with her name upon it. He has spotted her, and identified her, and is waving energetically. She waves back, relieved that she is in the right place on the right day. She is tall, and noticeable, and easy to spot. She advances upon the smiling young man, who grasps her hand in greeting, and then grasps the suitcase from her, and tries to appropriate her hand baggage. She lets him have the suitcase, but keeps her other bags. He is smaller than she is, and she is a feminist.

His English is excellent; his smile unfaltering; his manner eager but calming. His name, he says, is Mong Joon. He hands her a card, which she thrusts into her pocket. He ushers her into a taxi, enquiring after her flight, and points out features of interest as they are driven from the airport island of Incheon along a busy motorway towards central Seoul. She notes an expanse of tidal flats and marshland blooming with banks of a soft, grey-blush-pink and grey-green water plant. Then they come to a wide and busy river crossed by many bridges, and plied by many ferries. They pass steep green hills topped by radio masts, and make their way along multilane highways in heavy traffic. She is feeling a little dizzy with the newness of it all, as he hands her a copy of the conference programme and the day's events. She is expected, imminently, at the lunch reception. She begins to suspect that she will not have time for the shower to which she had been looking forward, and she is right. This smiling minder is telling her that she has arrived just in time for the official lunch reception. Although he smiles, he is firm about this. She staggers into the hotel, beginning to feel that it has already been a very long day, and is checked in at reception. Her suitcase is labelled, and immediately vanishes. Her hand baggage is helpfully wrenched from her. Yes, she has time to visit the ladies' room, but he will wait for her right here, to escort her instantly to the Chosŏn Suite. They must not miss the official reception and the heralded arrival of Jan van Jost.

The young man's accent is globalized American. He has studied at Berkeley, as he has already informed her.

In the ladies' room, she does her best to repair her complexion. The lights are more flattering than those of the aeroplane toilet, and the application of a little powder and moist cinnamon lip paint restores her equanimity. She combs her hair, and sniffs at herself: does she smell of overnight transit? Perhaps, but it is too late to do much about that. She sprays herself with a little eau de Cologne, a refreshingly innocent Orpington perfume to which she has been lastingly loyal. She is ready to face the music and Jan van Jost.

The Chosŏn Suite is already full of labelled

people of many nationalities. She registers her name, and takes her badge, and looks around her. Whom does she recognize? As yet, nobody. Cameras flash; drinks are offered. Perhaps unwisely she accepts what she takes to be a glass of wine. Her smooth-faced young minder introduces her to a clutch of Korean professors, and a journalist asks her to pose with one of them. She makes small talk. Soon, she knows, there will be speeches.

But the speeches do not come. More drinks come, and nuts and crisps and varnished rice crackers and pickled radishes also come, but no speeches. Everybody is waiting for the speeches, and for the opportunity to attack the buffet lunch, temptingly displayed on a side table. Babs Halliwell, whose minder is not-so-discreetly watching her every movement, has managed to find an acquaintance in the form of a microbiologist from Australia, whom she had first met three years earlier at a dinner at All Souls in Oxford. She remembers him well, partly because he had at this dinner claimed an earlier acquaintance with her husband Peter, and partly because they have since been in e-mail correspondence on medical matters. He remembers her, and seems pleased to see her. He is billed to give a paper, if she remembers rightly, on fertility rates and gender imbalance in post-industrial societies. He has put on weight since their last meeting, but on this she does not comment. His name (she peers myopically at his label, just to make sure it really is him) is Bob Bryant.

Bob Bryant voices the opinion that they are all having to wait for Jan van Jost, who is too grand to be prompt, and who wishes to make an entrance. He is said to be flying in from a lecture tour of China, but he should have arrived by now. Indeed, he should have arrived the night before. Bob is hungry and wants his lunch. Babs says she is not so hungry, but would like a chance to check out her hotel room and hang up her clothes. Does Bob know van Jost? Well, he wouldn't say he knew him, but he has shared a platform with him, says Bob. 'What is he like?' asks Barbara. 'Dapper,' says Bob, who is not. 'An Armani intellectual,' says Bob. 'Aha,' says Babs, as though she had known this, though in fact she had not.

The proceedings begin without the King of the Conference Circuit. He has been delayed, some whisper. He is resting, others mutter. He is playing hard to get, conclude the journalists. Babs Halliwell is disappointed in him. In her view, the great should condescend. They should not stand on ceremony and make difficulties for the organizers of public events. She is annoyed with him for keeping her from her shower and her deodorant and her change of garments. Bob Bryant looks crumpled and casual, but that's all right for him — he is an Australian, and that's his style. It is not her style. She is from Orpington and Oxford, and she likes to impress.

The delegates are warmly welcomed in several languages, and more photographs are taken. The unfortunate and conspicuous absence of Jan van Jost from these official records will be keenly noted. Maybe somebody will be able to airbrush him in. Babs is not sure if she is hungry or not, but allows herself to be propelled towards the buffet and a plateful of small slivers of this and that. Somebody speaks to her about the Korean national dish of *kimchi*, and she samples it and praises it. She likes it: she likes ferocious foods.

She is beginning to feel very blurred, and is desperate for a siesta before the evening's plenary address and the ceremonial dinner. How will she ever learn to distinguish these polite and grey-suited Korean gentlemen one from another? It will be hard to memorize their unfamiliar names, and she feels she cannot continue to peer down at their chests through her large varifocal glasses. She knows that everybody will find it all too easy to recognize her, for she sticks out in this assembly like a giraffe. There are so few women here, and she is so tall. This is nothing to be proud of. If anything, it is a disadvantage. Everything she does is far too conspicuous. At times, this is useful, but not when one is trying to slip away unobtrusively.

At last, she manages to take her leave, and to make her way to the hotel desk, where she claims her key and enquires after her baggage. It has been taken up to her room, she is told. So she follows it, up to the fifteenth floor. The fifteenth floor appears to be not quite finished: its walls are in the process of being papered by a small army of female paper-hangers wearing combat dress of a pale hospital green. Curling strips of wallpaper cover the carpets and their marbled surround. Paranoia strikes at the proud heart of

258

Babs Halliwell: she is sure that Jan van Jost will not be allocated a room on an unfinished floor. Even Bob Bryant will be better placed than she, for this is a male-dominant culture. (She had learned this from sociologist friends and, more recently, from the Crown Princess.) But she marches on, towards her door, and inserts the electronic key. At first it does not work, but that is because she has put it in the wrong way round. She removes it, squints at it, reverses it, and tries again. This time the little green eye blinks back, and the door gives, and at last she is received into the anonymous safety of Room 1517.

She sits down on one of her twin beds with a sigh of relief, and kicks off her flat-heeled, gold-buckled shoes, which are beginning to pinch. So far, so good. And yes, there is her little green case-on-wheels, and her navy-blue Samsonite suitcase, neatly arranged for her upon the canvas strut of the collapsible luggage holder. This also is a relief. She had been slightly flustered at the airport by the eager welcoming waves of her minder. But all is well. She unpacks from her hand baggage her sponge bag and her hairbrush and her change of underwear and her red nightshirt and her dressing gown and her slippers, and she takes out her reading matter, and she arranges her books and her conference papers and her pills by the bedside of the bed nearer the window that she has decided to favour. She thinks of taking a shower before opening her suitcase, but she decides that it would be better first to unpack the rest of her conference clothes and to let them hang out in the wardrobe.

This is a mistake, as she will now discover.

She approaches her suitcase, and peers at its combination lock. Her magic PIN is 7777. She has been told that it is unwise to have so obvious, so memorable a number, but she is afraid that she will forget anything more complicated, and, anyway, who in the world would want to open her bags and steal her dresses?

The suitcase does not seem to want to open. She fiddles with the combination, readjusts her glasses, and tries again. Again, the lock does not respond. Is it broken? What can have gone wrong with it?

Impatiently, with rising panic, she presses and pushes, to no avail. Then she pulls at the zip on the compartment on the suitcase's top, where she knows she has stored her thin raincoat and her small umbrella. She gropes in the recess, but they are not there. Somebody has stolen them. But the compartment is not empty. From it, she pulls out a copy of *The Economist*, and a crushed wad of Korean newsprint, and a Korean magazine. She stares at these objects in horror. Somebody has broken her lock, stolen her rainwear and stuffed her case with foreign reading matter. Who could have done such a wicked thing?

It takes her what seem like whole minutes to work out what she has done. She cannot believe it. She has taken the suitcase of a stranger from the luggage belt, and left her own suitcase at the airport. She has become one of those fools at whom all those superfluous warnings are directed. 'Many suitcases look alike' — how often has she heard and read that phrase? She has failed to identify her own luggage, and she has seized the suitcase of another.

She tried to breathe calmly, and to look at the international, ubiquitous Samsonite suitcase. It is, indeed, identical to her own, in every way. It is the same shape, the same colour, the same size, and it has been subjected to the same degree of wear. It, too, has a purple Pagoda Hotel tag tied in an identical manner to its identical handle but — and here she has to force herself to gaze directly at the horrifying evidence — *it is labelled with an unknown name.* The owner of this suitcase is not Dr Barbara Halliwell from Oxford, but a Dr Oo Hoi-Chang from Amsterdam. She is still in too deep a state of shock to be grateful that this person has written out his name in her alphabet as well as in his own. These newspapers, this magazine, belong to Dr Oo Hoi-Chang, who, somewhere in this hotel, will be wondering what the hell has happened to his suitcase.

It is clear that he must be booked into this hotel and that he must have been on the same flight, or this confusion could never have taken place. That at least is a small mercy. It is a very small mercy, but it is a mercy and a mitigation.

Dr Babs Halliwell cannot face summoning her smiling boyminder Mong Joon, although he had assured her he would be ready to help in any emergency. She feels too foolish. She sits down, and tries to work out what to do next.

Where will her own suitcase now be reposing? Will it still be at the airport? Has she still got her baggage tag? Yes, she has. Here it is in her handbag. It is stapled on to her air ticket, as it should be. She supposes she could take a taxi back to the airport and try to effect an exchange, but she is not sure if she can manage this, in view of her inability to speak or read a word of the Korean language, in view of her panic and fatigue. She knows she has provided herself with a token supply of Korean money, but God knows how much a taxi to the airport is supposed to cost.

She thinks, hard. She decides to try to throw herself on the mercy of Dr Oo Hoi-Chang, if she can locate him. Maybe he is attending her very own conference on the New Frontiers of Health: Globalization and Medical Risk? If so, would that simplify or complicate her position? She scours through her conference papers, but can find no mention of him. (How does she know he is a man? Because of the magazines. Women do not read magazines like that. They are not pornographic magazines or motoring magazines, but they are inescapably male.) Would he speak English if she could locate him? How could she bring herself to confess to him her stupid, her unforgivable error?

Dr Halliwell decides to be brave. She works out her plan. She rings down to reception, and asks to speak to Dr Oo Hoi-Chang. She is asked to spell out his name, and she does so. She is not sure if she is relieved or appalled when the receptionist says that she will put her through.

She hears the phone ringing in the stranger's room. She hears the voice of the doctor. Naturally, he responds in Korean. 'Do you speak English?' is all that she can find to say, and she says it. 'Yes,' says the doctor, hesitantly. 'I have your suitcase,' says big, bold Babs Halliwell, on the verge of childish tears. 'I have it here, in my room. It is a mistake. You understand? A mistake.'

The doctor understands. Moreover, he sounds mightily relieved, which she had not quite bargained for, though it is a logical response. In fact, he sounds quite excited. Where is she? Here, in this very hotel? Yes, she is in Room 1517. Shall she bring him his suitcase, at once, she asks? No, he will come to collect it. He is on the same floor. He is in Room 1529, just along the corridor, and he will be with her very shortly.

She rushes to the mirror, to dab at her face. Her scratchy eyes are glistening and red-rimmed with shame and anxiety and exhaustion. She hears his feet along the corridor; she hears his discreet tap at the door. She opens it, and there he is, the doctor whose goods she has appropriated. He stares at her, shocked, as she guesses, by her size, and his eyes dart beyond her to his treasure.

Faintly, she waves him in. He is all smiles. Yes, yes, this is his very own case. He checks the combination lock, and it springs open to reveal the lucky man's suits and shirts, neatly pressed and contained beneath their stretching diagonal straps.

'It was identical,' she says, and repeats, and

263

parrots, with pathos. He seems to understand this.

What next?

This is the moment at which Dr Oo reveals himself as a hero. Instead of making off at once with his possessions, and making good his escape from this barbarian madwoman, he stays to enquire after her suitcase and to examine her plight. He is a man of sublime intelligence. He tells her that her case must still be at the airport. He had waited in vain for his, he says — or this is what she thinks he is saying — and he had seen one very like his own, with a Pagoda label, travelling round and round the belt. In the end, he had worked out what might have happened, but by this time the suitcase had disappeared from the belt and must have been taken into storage. So he had reported his loss, and had made his way to the hotel, to wait on events. He says he is very glad to see his things again, and now he will accompany her to the airport in a taxi to retrieve her suitcase for her.

She cannot believe that Dr Oo is such a gentleman. She cannot believe that this is what he is proposing to her: to her, a stupid stranger. But it is. He makes many comforting and conciliatory sounds, as he instructs her to pick up her shoulder bag, and to make sure that she has her room key, and to follow him to Room 1529, where he will deposit his case and pick up his wallet. She trails after him, as he trots briskly along the corridor — a corridor which by now seems, miraculously, to be completely repapered and workwoman-free — and she waits meekly at

264

the threshold of his twin-bed room (a room which is, like his suitcase, identical to hers), as he reorganizes himself. Down in the lift they travel together, as she makes deferential noises and looks humble and grateful. Into a taxi he ushers her, and they find themselves bowling along, back the way she had come that morning, across the wide, flat river, past the posters, past the radio masts, past the bridges and the marshy banks of pink marine sedge, towards her lost bag.

On the way, he asks her what she is doing in Seoul, and she tells him. His English, once he gets his ear attuned to her responses, is good: it is as good, and as American-accented, as the English of the baby-faced, Berkeley-educated Mong Joon. She tells him about her conference, and he tells her that he is in Seoul to attend a different conference, on a different topic. He is not a doctor of sociology or philosophy or economics or even of psychiatry, but a medical doctor, a neurologist. His speciality is the stroke. The conference will discuss new treatments for stroke patients. She finds this reassuring. If she has a stroke, he will resuscitate her. If she faints, he will revive her. Her profession is abstract and frivolous in comparison with his. She is full of admiration for this small, neat, self-possessed and courteous gentleman.

Her one regret, at this stage, is that she had not taken a shower before ringing him. She had been too impulsive, too eager to right her wrong. He has travelled much better than she has. She feels gross and dirty, and she is afraid that she stinks. She knows that it is said that people of the East think that all Westerners stink, and in her case she fears it may be true. She sniffs at herself, surreptitiously, and the result is not reassuring. He must find her disgusting. She is ashamed. How much more the gentleman he, to escort so gallantly so unattractive and so large and so deeply stupid a female! Is there anything that she can do to reclaim her self-respect, to dignify herself a little in his eyes?

Luckily, she finds that the bundle of Korean *won* that she has with her will be more than enough to cover the two-way taxi fare. She had been wise to change some money, although it is her own folly that has made its use so necessary. He protests that he will pay, but of course she insists that she must, and, correctly, he allows her to do so. Once more she trails after him, as he leads the way to baggage enquiries and, after some hassle, successfully extracts her suitcase from a back room. This time she belatedly, superfluously and carefully, before witnesses, checks its label, and her name, and its baggage tag. She is not sure that the young men in baggage enquiries are sniggering at her, but she concedes they would have a right to do so if they so chose. Dr Oo certainly does not snigger; on the contrary, he is at pains to point out that her suitcase is indeed the very same as his own. Anyone, he says, could easily have made such a mistake. This is not true, but it is very politely put.

She could embrace this man. She could kiss him, were she not so repulsive to herself. He has

266

a steel tooth. She has always fancied men with steel teeth.

On the way back to the hotel, along a route with which she is rapidly becoming too familiar, she relaxes enough to tell him that she is simply longing for a nice hot shower, and that she blames the Crown Princess of Korea for her absent-mindedness at the baggage belt. 'I had been reading all day and all night,' she says. 'I have been reading this extraordinary book.'

She cannot tell whether or not he responds to the name of the Crown Princess because he is so very polite that he nods with seeming interest at everything she says.

When they get back to the Pagoda Hotel, he insists on carrying her suitcase for her, up the marble entrance staircase from the street level, and into the lift, and up to the fifteenth floor, and along the corridor to her room. He watches, benevolently, as she fumbles clumsily with her room key to Room 1517. 'You are tired,' he says, kindly. Yet more tears well in her eyes, as she stretches out her hot, large, not-very-clean hand to him in gratitude and farewell.

'Perhaps,' he says, as he (perhaps a little reluctantly) takes this distasteful hand, 'perhaps, if we have some free time, we may meet for a drink? Perhaps I may take you for a tour of the Crown Princess's palace? The garden is beautiful. You may see where she lived, if you would like.'

So he did know of the Crown Princess, this enigmatic foreign doctor man. She so longs to recover herself in his eyes that she perhaps rashly says that she would be delighted to meet him again. She will leave him a note, or he will leave her a note, when they have sorted out their respective schedules. They will make an assignation. Again, profusely, she thanks him. And she retires into her room, at last, and throws herself in exhaustion and disgrace upon her bed. She sees that her red message light is blinking furiously, and, as she begins to peel down her socks from her swollen ankles, her phone begins to ring. Her broad-cheeked, smiling, putto minder, Mong Joon, is after her. He will want to know why she tried to escape. But, she vows, he will never, ever find out. It is all too shaming. She will never tell.

★ ★ ★

It is late afternoon, and Dr Barbara Halliwell sits in the middle of the second row of the Sejong Auditorium, as she inattentively listens through her multilingual headphones to yet more welcoming addresses. On the bench in front of her is her conference pack of papers, her conference ballpoint pen, her conference notepad, her conference map of Seoul, and the by now well-read, dog-eared memoirs of the imperative Crown Princess. As the speeches proceed, Babs begins methodically to draw an egg-and-dart pattern round the edge of the top sheet of her virgin notepad. She appears to be listening, but her mind is scattered into particles and is wandering. Global harmony, global

268

resources, global warming, information inter-change, international cooperation, birth rates, death rates, tuberculosis, malaria, the human genome, genetic patenting, AIDS ... The phrases hover and buzz through the air-conditioned atmosphere, but they do not settle for long in the jet-lagged consciousness of Dr Halliwell. Altitude and the Crown Princess have shattered her perceptions into many little disconnected but perhaps potentially interlock-ing fragments.

She is in other places and in other times. One of her many astral bodies is travelling restlessly, like a shuttle, apologetic, ashamed, backward and forward along an airport highway, clutching a suitcase and smelling of sweat and dirt and pressurized bodily gases. This bodily persona is attempting to charm a kind but inscrutable man with a sexually attractive steel tooth. Another of her bodies is sitting immobile in a hospital in a sterile room, gazing at a small child in drug-controlled pain, a child she can no longer touch or reach, a child behind glass, a child doomed to an early death by her own ignorance and by her protective love and by her defective genes and by the overheating imperfections of medical science. Another persona that seems to have attached itself to her by some form of metempsychosis is cramped in a male body in a rice chest, listening to the punishing god of thunder. Yet another crouches in the shade of a compound wall, hiding from the heat of the noonday sun, penning a letter of urgent appeal for a stay of execution. An offspring of this crouching woman is dialling 999 and the emergency services in the small hours of the morning in Kentish Town in North London.

The Crown Princess sits invisibly at the elbow of Babs, self-summoned from two centuries of sleep, urgent with her messages from the other world. Dr Halliwell cannot yet decode them. They are in an alien language. They are about illness and madness. They are about the abuses of parental power. They are about transmission, and failures of transmission. They are about maternity, and death, and progress. Dr Halliwell is the chosen vessel. Dr Halliwell is feeling a little unwell. It is all too much for her. She is clever, but not *that* clever. She feels overwhelmed and inadequate. What is she doing here in Seoul? She has strayed too far from home. She understands nothing. She has tried to think of herself as a reasonably competent person, but incompetence has now struck her like a whirlwind. She is off course. She has no course. She is lost.

Professor Jan van Jost, however, is found. That is him, sitting at the end of the front row, a few places to her right, in this modern but rather gloomy auditorium. He is somewhat smaller of stature but better looking than she had expected him to be. He is neat, even-featured, lightly tanned, and his hair is a crisp, short-cropped, silvery grey. The back of his head signifies effortless authority. He is also, as her Australian colleague Bob had forewarned her, extremely well dressed, in a well-cut suit of an unusual shade of pale straw-green. A glow seems to emanate from him and to bathe him in its soft

270

warm light. He glows like a royal personage or a film star, discreetly but inescapably positioned in a gathering of subdued and attendant courtiers and peasants. This is surely the quiet, steady glow of fame.

Jan van Jost's keynote address, which he will deliver in mid conference, is entitled 'The Leaden Casket: Meditations on the Apocalypse'. He is known for his colourful literary allusions and what some consider his excessively flamboyant prose. He appears to be intending to lob an explosive into this sober conference. Will it be about AIDS? Will it be a warning of the end of the world? It has occurred to Babs Halliwell that his title may seem to have some connection with her own, though this, if so, is a coincidence. She is to speak on triage and risk assessment in complex experimental choices of medical intervention. Her approach is ethical, rather than medical. His remit appears to be even more comprehensive, as befits a guru of the globe.

She will not speak about the fatal choice that she herself had made for her own child. Will Jan van Jost also have a concealed agenda? Yes, of course. Which of us has not, however abstract our reasoning may claim to be? A scarlet thread runs through all things. But Babs Halliwell has no idea of what that thread might be, for she knows nothing at all of van Jost's personal history.

Bassanio, in *The Merchant of Venice*, paradoxically chooses life and love when he chooses the leaden casket. Gold and silver are the bad choices, the deadly choices, made by bad

271

princes from foreign lands. They are the exotic, multicultural choices, the hostile choices of Africa and Spain. To choose dull lead is to choose real life. The leaden casket is not a coffin for a Coffin King. Lead represents humility, submission, virtue, grace, survival. Is this a universal symbolism? Hemp and cotton and silk; lead and silver and gold; magpies and ravens and birds of doom. These thoughts drift in and out of the well-stocked consciousness of Barbara Halliwell. Her head is too full of matter. She has seen *The Merchant of Venice* several times, and, like most twentieth-century spectators, she finds it a problematic play.

Peter Halliwell persistently refused to take his medication. He had that right. Their son Benedict had had no choice but to submit to his medication. He was an infant, and therefore he had no choice. He could not be informed of his condition, and he did not need to give consent. The medication killed him. It had been intended to offer him a chance of survival, but in fact it killed him. Thus their only child Benedict Halliwell had died. Peter Halliwell had never forgiven Babs Halliwell for this death and for the faulty gene and the false medication that had caused this death. He had accused her, to her face, of being a murderer. He had seized her by the throat and yelled at her that she was a murderer. She had shaken him off quite easily because she is a strong woman, and he had been drunk at the time, and not by nature a killer. And she had forgiven him for it because he was mad. She had tried to move on.

Peter Halliwell had not moved on. He became the Prince of Mournful Thoughts, the Coffin Prince of Kentish Town. It was not the death of his son that drove him to his ultimate despair, Babs now believes, though that was surely a precipitating factor. She is now convinced — or has convinced herself? — that it is the life of his father that destroyed him. These things have long, long fuses. Peter was encouraged and tormented and provoked and ultimately rejected by his father, and that is why he has ended up in such profound, imprisoned, helpless inertia, imprisoned in a well-guarded and expensive Retreat.

She had once, in their early days together, found the intensity of his despair glamorous. It had seemed theatrical and amenable. It had attracted her. But it had not been amenable. She is older, wiser and, on the whole, happier now.

The unmedicated and unassuaged Peter Halliwell had raved around the steep Victorian stairwell of the North London house that they had inhabited. He had threatened to kill himself, on more than one occasion, but when at last he made a serious attempt to do so he had fallen into the common error of not finishing the job properly. To be fair to his intentions, he could not have been said to be guilty of issuing a 'cry for help'. He had been less histrionic, more committed to the act than that phrase would suggest. But he had chosen a bizarre form of self-execution. He had tried to hang himself from the stairwell, with a noose made out of knotted silk ties. He had tied together a motley collection of ties — an old school tie, a college tie, a club tie, a joke Christmas present tie with teddy bears — but he had tied them together very badly, under the influence of half a bottle of vodka and a bottle full of sleeping pills, and the improvised noose had broken. Babs, in bed, had heard the thud.

Maybe she should not have dialled for the emergency services. Maybe she should have let him lie, and let him die.

Is this the message of the Crown Princess? Surely not. There must be some more universal element in her story. She cannot have crossed the centuries simply to tell Babs Halliwell that four years ago Babs ought not to have dialled 999 for an ambulance.

Babs Halliwell shakes her head, as these thoughts buzz round her ears. She cannot concentrate on euthanasia in the Netherlands, even though, in her own country, she is chair of a committee on the right to die.

According to a footnote in Thea Landry's translation, Crown Prince Sado had tried to kill himself, on that fatal day, on his father's orders, by strangling himself with the girdle of his garments. 'Die!' his father had yelled at him, and the son had tried to oblige. But he hadn't tried hard enough, and the doctors had intervened and revived him with pills and potions. And so he had died in the rice chest, some days later. So much for the Hippocratic oath. Though the Korean court doctors probably did not subscribe to the Hippocratic oath, so one couldn't really

274

blame Hippocrates.

She had never understood about the neckties. Peter had always hated to wear a tie. He said they were a ludicrous sartorial item and made him feel strangulated. So why, of all available methods, had he chosen to strangle himself? If he'd left it to the sleeping pills, he might have died a better death.

Crown Prince Sado and Benedict Halliwell and Peter Halliwell had been tormented by doctors. The lives of the crown prince and the baby had been artificially and painfully though unsuccessfully prolonged, and that of Peter Halliwell continues to be so.

Barbara Halliwell is a healthy woman who happens to have an unusual chromosomal abnormality that had caused her son's severe combined immunodeficiency disease. This disease is extremely rare. It afflicts 1 in 100,000. She had been the carrier. The carrier female in these cases is asymptomatic and healthy. It had all been nothing other than genetic bad luck. There had been no guilt attached. Benedict's illness could not have been foreseen. The treatment which might now have saved him was not then available, and is uncertain now. She had been offered the choice between two bad choices.

Benedict Halliwell is long dead, and his ashes are long dispersed on Primrose Hill, but his mother is alive, and she is drawing another pattern, this time of daisy heads, on the second page of her conference notepad.

Benedict had been cremated because Barbara

had refused to allow his unusual body parts to be preserved for medical research. This choice had been illogical on her part, but she has never regretted it. The child had suffered enough. She suspects that the hospital had kept some bits anyway, without telling her. That's all right by her. There are some questions it is better not to be asked, some choices one does not wish to confront.

One day, one day soon, all patterns will be revealed. One day, one day soon, all patterns will be understood, and all ills repaired or prevented. The virus with the corrective gene will be planted back into the system, and the system will be restored. Dementia will die, depression will die, and the dead will rise from their graves and be made whole. The dead will speak. Long before the last trump, the dead will speak. Or so some seem to say. So the Crown Princess believes and hopes.

Jan van Jost has his story to tell, the story of the leaden casket. He will tell it soon. He, too, like Babs Halliwell, is drawing patterns on his conference notepad. He favours Dutch daffodils. A little border of daffodils sprouts gaily from his purple pen. Everyone has a story to tell. The number of stories here is bewildering. The Sejong Auditorium rustles and bristles with competing and conflicting stories, all trying to find a mouth, a voice, a pen, a screen, an outlet. Australian stories, Korean stories, French stories, Japanese stories, English stories, American stories, and stories from the Netherlands and the nether world. They are all here, jostling about in this complex, overwhelming global muddle.

★ ★ ★

The tall woman and the smaller man keep their assignation. Here they are, in the late morning, walking together through the great gateway of Changgyeonggung, also known as Historic Site No. 123, or the Palace of Glorious Blessings. They are armed with tickets and information leaflets. Dr Halliwell may be seen to clutch her leaflet tightly: she can hardly believe that she, here, now, is about to enter the very gardens and see the very buildings where the Crown Princess lived out her life and wrote her remarkable memoirs. She is treading the very ground that sad Prince Sado trod, and her escort Dr Oo Hoi-Chang has assured her that she will see signboards and inscriptions written by the very hands of King Yŏngjo and King Chŏngjo. She is familiar with the glories of Hampton Court and Versailles, but the palace of Changgyeonggung seems to her to be a far more mysterious and portentous survival from the past. Who would have thought that this place could still be here on earth, and that she could in her body enter it? Truly, a paperback book can have much to answer for.

The tall woman and the smaller man walk with measured steps along the white gravel. Both are wearing dark glasses, for the September sun is bright. The ghost of the Crown Princess walks along with them, and a magpie jerks and struts

277

its way before them. There are not many tourists to be seen, though a straggling line of small schoolchildren wanders off to their right, towards the Botany Garden. 'What is your name? What is your name?' they had eagerly pestered Westerner Babs as they passed, and they had mimicked her reply. 'Barbara, Barbara!' they had cried, in chirping happiness. The name of 'Barbara' resounds joyfully round the shrubberies, where in spring the azaleas bloom. On the lawn, a couple of gardeners squat and root for weeds with simple instruments. These gardeners are timeless, ageless, genderless. They could well have been there, unchanging, for two hundred years. It is peaceful and quiet, here in the Land of Morning Calm. Two old men sit companionably upon a bench, with cardboard cups of tea or coffee in their hands. A small, striped squirrel runs along the tiled ridge of a wall. The song of the cicadas is faint but persistent.

Dr Oo and Dr Halliwell are playing truant from the second morning sessions of their respective conferences. She is supposed to be listening to a Japanese sociologist, and he should be listening to an American cognitive scientist talking about aphasia and speech recovery. But they have decided instead to stroll together in the palace gardens. Dr Oo turns out to be very well informed about the lives of the Crown Princess and Prince Sado, and the Yi monarchs of the late eighteenth and early nineteenth centuries. Dr Halliwell had at first found this level of knowledge surprising, in a middle-aged neurologist on the far side of the culture gap (surely not all contemporary expatriate Koreans can have so refined an historical awareness?), but she has now discovered that Dr Oo's interest in the subject and the period is not wholly coincidental. His sister, it appears, works for UNESCO in New York, and has been closely involved with the plans for the restoration of the fortress of Suwon-Hwaseong, which was registered in the UNESCO World Cultural Heritage List in 1997. Hwaseong, says Dr Oo, is Historic Site No. 3, and well deserves its important listing. It is an extraordinary monument, or collection of monuments, says Dr Oo — and, yes, it is indeed the very place where the Crown Princess celebrated her sixtieth birthday in such a spectacular manner in the year 1795. It is a very well-documented event, says Dr Oo. Would Dr Halliwell like to visit the fortress? He would be happy to show it to her.

Babs Halliwell makes non-committal noises. This man is too kind, too kind, and she is touched by his apparently altruistic forgiveness. She is not sure that she can interpret it correctly. In a Western colleague, she would take his politeness as a presage to some kind of sexual overture, for she knows she is considered attractive and usually feels herself to be so, but she cannot escape the conviction that to him she must still appear gross. She is much cleaner than she had been on their first encounter, but she is still large and unwieldy. As a growing girl, as a too rapidly growing girl, she had been self-conscious about her height. (One of the attractions of Peter Halliwell had been his tall stature: he was one of the few men who could look down on her.) It does not take very much to revive that early self-consciousness in her, and she suspects that Dr Oo cannot possibly find her appearance and her person pleasing. Nor can he be lonely in Seoul, for this is his birthplace. He has not lived here for some years, and most of his family has emigrated, but he must have friends here, so he cannot be suffering from conference-isolation. So why is he wasting his time on her? It is a puzzle.

It is a puzzle, but she cannot afford to dwell on it too closely, for her curiosity about the Crown Princess and her need to step in the footsteps of the Crown Princess are powerful, and she needs him as a guide. She would never have found this palace compound by herself, even though it is listed as Historic Site No. 123. She cannot believe that she is gazing at the buildings where the drama of the princess's long life was enacted. True it may be, as Dr Oo explains, that many of the original buildings have been over the years destroyed by storms and fires and invasions, but, nevertheless, some of the fabric is authentic, the layout is as it always was, and the bronze sundial and the astronomical observatory and the heptagonal stone *taeshil* that contains the placenta of King Songjong long predate the tenure of the princess. So, too, do some of the trees. They had been old when the Crown Princess was born in Pansong-bang. Like the mulberry tree of Babs's Oxford courtyard, they have been propped and cherished over hundreds of years. She peers at their inscriptions. Seven hundred and fifty years old is this twisted juniper, with its long, grey, reaching branches and its green, spiked tufts! And here is a tree with foot-roots of stone, a petrified tree, a tree that is neither vegetable nor mineral, a rock tree of nameless age.

The landscaped granite slopes set in grass remind her of somewhere vaguely familiar, but she cannot work out where.

The pavilions and halls of history take shape before her. So that is the writing of King Sunjo, the grandson of the Crown Princess. Those are his bold and flowing Chinese characters, emblazoned over the threshold of this fine banquet hall with its beautifully decorated tile-ends and its aspiring eaves! She gapes like the tourist she has become. And here is the hall called Sungmungdang where Sunjo's grandfather, the temperamental King Yŏngjo, used to receive and test university students in person, and, according to her English-language pamphlet, 'throw parties to encourage them'. And that is the hall where he greeted those who had achieved the highest grades in the civil and military examinations — a formal graduation ceremony, she supposes? Dr Oo is not sure, but agrees with her suggestion that the culture of the period that has so caught her interest was indeed dominated by the examination system. And still is so, in so many ways, he adds. The old-fashioned Confucian examinations had at last disappeared, amidst wars and invasions and modernizations, but a new examination system has replaced them. Students protest — Korean

281

students are good at protesting, they have a fine tradition of protest — but they submit.

What, she enquires, does King Yŏngjo's calligraphy mean, up there over the doorway of Sungmungdang? Those three large Chinese characters, what do they signify? He shakes his head. He cannot read them. He can find out for her, perhaps. They will say something grandiose, he has no doubt.

Dr Oo is proud of her close attention to his nation's cultural treasures, but after half an hour and more earnest perambulation he suggests that maybe they could both now do with a cup of coffee. There is a machine nearby in the gardens that makes excellent Maxwell House, he says: let him show her how to use it, the knowledge may come in useful during her stay, for these machines may be found in many places — on the underground stations, in subway shopping malls, at street corners, in the corridors of universities. 'We live too fast in Seoul now,' says Dr Oo. 'All cities live too fast. We grab our coffee as we go.'

She watches carefully as he puts the coins in the machine. She will never remember the symbol on the button for 'black without sugar'. She has not time to get the hang of the *han'gŭl* alphabet, although he assures her it is much easier than it looks. The shot of coffee is, as he had said it would be, excellent. They sit together on a bench by the lake, and watch the imprisoned fish leap from its still, small waters.

'So,' says Dr Oo, 'you give your paper tomorrow. And so do I. And then, the next day, we can go to Suwon-Hwaseong for a day trip and a walk round the fortress walls.'

He is pushing it a bit, but she does not discourage him. She does not say that the day after tomorrow she thinks she is supposed to attend the long-awaited plenary presentation of Jan van Jost because she is not quite sure if she has got her conference programme straight in her head.

She has tested the name of Jan van Jost on Dr Oo, but cannot tell whether or not he has responded to its full glory. Dr Oo can be inscrutable when he wants, but so, she guesses, can anyone. The truth is that she herself has failed to respond to Jan van Jost's glamour because Jan van Jost has so far failed to notice her existence. She is still annoyed with him for being late in arrival, and does not think he has been sufficiently diligent in turning up to conference events. The general opinion, amongst delegates, is that Professor van Jost thinks too much of himself. He is arrogant and evasive. He is not convivial. He does not mix. She is quite sure that he will not attend her paper tomorrow afternoon, so why should she attend his? Would it not be better to take a day off, with this charming and well-mannered stranger?

She sips the last dregs of her bracingly strong coffee. This well-attended conference is so far doing little for her academic morale. It has made her uneasy about her status and her prospects. She has to vacate her handsome Oxford lodgings by the end of the month, to make room for a new Hanbury Fellow. She must return to the rat race of London, and to her teaching commitments there. She is not sure if she has spent her fellowship year well enough. She is not sure if she wants to go on teaching at all. She has played her cards badly with Robert Treborough, and anyway she does not like him very much. Why is she always attracted to such competitive bastards? Is it because she is so competitive herself?

Would she have been different, if Benedict had lived? Or if she had dared to have another child, with one of her subsequent and saner lovers?

This thought, which rarely visits her, comes to her now like a little bird, and perches in her spirit.

They rise then, the tall woman and the smaller man, and they continue their tour along the pathway that leads them to the royal Jongmyo shrines. They cross a footbridge that takes them over a busy, multilaned city road. They are elevated, this modern couple, high above the traffic of the modern city. They look down from the green past, on to the busy metal bonnets of Hyundai and Daewoo. They are uplifted, on another plane. Time here is on two levels, and old time leads them from the queen's palace, across the gasoline-polluted ravine of the twenty-first century, to a vast, silent, empty, pale, paved courtyard, bisected by a narrow royal pathway of slate blue. The ravine reminds the woman of somewhere that she knows well, but she cannot quite bring it into consciousness. It hovers, this other place, this concept of a place, just out of her reach. It makes some join, some

284

connection, in the intricate pathways of her memory.

A sign outside the courtyard reads 'Solemnity', in large English lettering, but they hardly need its injunction. This space is silent and solemn, like an outdoor cathedral. There are long, low buildings with carved and winged eaves, where dragons march along the rooftops. There are doors in walls leading to mysteries. There is a well, and a purification chamber. In the distance, they hear a strange chanting, to which both listen, intently. It seems to come from another era. Can the voices of the dead reach the living?

Dr Babs Halliwell is beginning to feel exhausted by the strangeness of everything that she sees. She knows nothing of this kind of architecture. The bright, painted colours and patterns of the woodwork are strange to her. She does not know what any of it means. She cannot understand any of its symbols or principles. It seems at once utterly foreign and yet somehow deeply familiar. Can it be that the Crown Princess, who so forcefully took possession of her astral body on the Air France flight, is now forcing and urging her onwards, towards some other denouement in real time? Has the Crown Princess invaded some of her memory, and is she forcing upon her some new agenda?

These thoughts occur to her, but she knows that of course they are complete nonsense. Babs Halliwell scorns the supernatural. She has never liked ghost stories. She does not believe in metempsychosis or the transmigration of souls or reincarnation. She does not think that we may be punitively reborn as worms or dogs or rats or microbes. She does not even believe in the more plausible Buddhist concept of enlightenment along the eightfold path of meditation. She does not believe that the ghost of Marie Antoinette appeared to two respectable English Oxford women academics in the grounds of Versailles in the year 1901. She is not superstitious. She knows that we cannot speak to the dead, nor they to us. Never. They can never speak to us. So why is she feeling so light-headed, so confused, so besieged, so transported?

Jet lag and culture shock and hunger, suggests the wise Dr Oo, as he sits her down at a little table in a spruce and spotless small café on the busy sidewalk just outside the palace gates, and encourages her to order a little light lunch. She has no idea what any of the dishes are, and cannot read a word of the menu, so he orders for her: this will be as useful a tip as the lesson of the Maxwell House machine, he assures her. She must learn the word 'bibimpap'. Bi-Bim-Bap. He makes her say it several times. Bi-Bim-Bap. She will feel much better when she has had some of it, he says. And it arrives, accompanied by various delicious little sushi-style side dishes and pickles, and it is delicious. Bibimpap, or Bi-Bim-Bap, is a heated iron bowl of rice, topped with various vegetables and sauces, and a charming poached egg. A light and innocent dish, a fortifying dish. She can stir it all up together, or pick bits out, as she chooses. She can do whatever she likes with her bibimpap. It is a free and easy dish, and she can get it everywhere, in varying formats. This, he agrees, as he delves into his own, is a fine example. They have been lucky here. He has not been to this café for some years, and he is pleased to find it as good as ever. Seoul is changing rapidly: it is good when the good things do not change.

Over the rice, he responds to her questions. He is willing to tell her more about himself, and his sister and his mother in New York, and his wife in Amsterdam, and his sons at school in Amsterdam. He is working at a research hospital, where he is studying the effect of certain recently developed drugs on those who have suffered from severe strokes. 'Stroke patients,' he tells her, as he moves into didactic professorial mode, 'are much neglected by the medical profession, although the stroke is so common an event and kills and disables so many. It is the commonest cause of death, after heart failure. Mostly they are old people who have strokes, and we do not care for the old. It is not considered exciting work by many. In South Korea, we talk much about longevity. In principle we care for the old, we talk much about respecting the old, but I am afraid we care for them only when they are old and well. We do not like people who are old and ill, people with mobility and communication problems. Like you in Europe, we ignore them somewhat. Sick children, sick young people, people with unpredictable rare diseases in middle age — these are interesting stories, for everyone, everywhere. These are newspaper cases, cases where we have to make dramatic decisions, perhaps dangerous decisions. You tell me that you speak about these decisions in your paper on medical risk. It is an interesting subject.

'But an elderly person with a stroke — this is just what happens to us, we accept it. We do not pay much attention, we do not even try to understand what happens in the brain, we do not bother with re-education programmes or even with much stimulation. In my hospital in Amsterdam, where I work, there is an excellent volunteer service, which brings professional readers of short stories to entertain and interest these stroke patients. Sometimes poems even. We can test the attention span, and the memory span, and the effect of stimulus, the effect of a new face, the impact of a new person in the hospital ward. There is much that can be done. It is not a waste of resources. There are few high risks in my area. There is more to be found of simple neglect.'

Babs chopsticks up a morsel of sea greenery, and asks him why he first became involved in this field? Why did he specialize in stroke patients? She already knows he will have an answer. And he has.

'It is because of my mother,' he says. 'My mother, she suffered a serious stroke while quite a young woman. I was still at medical school, here, at Seoul National University Hospital, just across the road from where we are now. For a while she lost her speech, and she lost permanently use of one arm and one leg. She was wheelchair-bound for some years, but slowly she has recovered. She has been my experiment,

288

my inspiration. She is a fine woman, my mother. She is OK now, in New York. America is good for old people. It has every contrivance. Here, we have been slow with improvements. The World Cup 2002 brought more help for wheelchair users to travel in this city. It is better than it was. You have not been on the underground yet, I think? You must try the underground before you leave. It is easier to use now, after the World Cup. The maps are excellent. Very clear maps. Very good and helpful English-language notices.'

The thought of plunging down into the underground makes Babs Halliwell feel faint with fatigue. This immersion in Korea past and present is challenging. It would have been more restful to have stayed in the Sejong Auditorium to listen passively to the Japanese professor. On the other hand, Dr Oo represents something unique. He is a multicultural opportunity that is not to be passed over. The Crown Princess has sent him to her as a messenger, and she must follow him.

Dr Oo suggests that, while they are in the neighbourhood, they should pay a short visit to the Munmyo shrines at Sung-Kyun-Kwan University. Then he will let her go back to her hotel for afternoon rest and the evening programme. She will never find these shrines without him, and they are worth the visit. This was the university where his brother studied. His brother is now in software, working on Chinese-character transliteration programs. She will like the Munmyo shrines. They are more private, less visited than the royal Jongmyo

289

shrines. Is she up to it?

Babs, who had thought the Jongmyo shrines fairly quiet, is sufficiently intrigued by the thought of the yet more deserted and yet more secret shrines to agree to stagger on. Her feet are painful, but if he can do it so can she, for she is younger than he. (If she agrees to go to Hwaseong with him, she will abandon vanity and wear her trainers.) Mercifully, he hails a taxi, and they take a short ride uphill, and disembark at the beginning of a broad and populous road leading up towards a large, modern campus. The shrines, he says, are to the right: the main royal gateway to them is under restoration, so they will have to go round through the back entrance.

As they approach, on foot, they hear the sound of chanting, perhaps the very same sound that had been airborne towards them over the high wall of the queen's gardens. And when they enter the courtyard, by a side door, they find that they are not alone. There is a faint air of desertion and dereliction, but the far end of the courtyard is filled with rows of people in colourful costume, performing some kind of ancient ritual. These people chant, and a stout man from time to time strikes a vast hanging drum. Nobody could possibly mistake these substantial figures for ghosts, for they are very twenty-first century in figure and deportment, and some of them have false beards and moustaches. Is this a film set, or is it a religious ceremony?

It is neither. It is, says Dr Oo, a rehearsal. It is a preparation for an enactment of ancestral rites by a Confucian Society. He had forgotten it was the season for these events: he should have remembered when he heard the chanting floating over the garden wall. These are not actors, and they may not be true Confucians. They are re-enactors, not actors. Every year they dress up and go through these rituals, to honour Confucius and his ten philosophers and his six sages. So it is religious, she pursues? Not really, he says. Look, there are several women lined up in the ranks in dark green silk dresses. That is quite irreligious and anachronistic. In true Confucian ceremonies no women could ever take part. Your Crown Princess, she would never have been admitted to these observances in this temple. It is true that on her sixtieth birthday she went to Suwon-Hwaseong in royal procession and great pomp, but she had to remain hidden in her palanquin. And here, she would not have been admitted. These green-robed women, they would not have been here. Perhaps the Confucian Society is short of members and now has to accept these women to make up numbers. Anyway, says Dr Oo, Confucianism is not a religion, in the Western sense of the word. It is not supernatural; it does not recognize the soul.

The re-enactors of this pageant do not seem to mind that she and Dr Oo are wandering round their sacred courtyard, gazing at the Hall of Great Accomplishments and the Hall of Illuminating Ethics. Modest paper lanterns of red and blue hang along the wooden eaves of the cloisters, and small children play in the dust. A very large granite turtle with a smoothly rubbed nose rests beneath a mulberry tree. A woman appears carrying a great raw leg of pale meat in a metal basin. It is an offering to the ancestors. Babs and Dr Oo peer into the gloomy interior of the shrine, and see rows of little, dark brown boxes on tables, arranged to receive more food offerings. It is all very odd. It is neither real nor unreal. The scene belongs neither to the past nor to the present. It belongs to no time.

Babs follows Dr Oo in his exploration of the hinterland of the compound, where young people who seem to be students are living in rooms that line one of the courtyard walls. They, unlike the re-enactors, are not at all keen to be seen. They wave away these intruders, and try to repel them, as the rulers of the Hermit Kingdom had for centuries tried to repel earlier visitors from the outside world. Dr Oo mumbles what she takes to be apologies, but the young people understandably continue to look displeased. They do not want this gross and grotesque Western woman to see their washing pegged up to dry and their shoes lined up on the floor and their unscholarly magazines lying on their reed mats. This lack of welcome does not deter the inquisitive and tireless Dr Oo from penetrating yet farther into a homely little labyrinth of cottages and gardens that strays and tumbles off to one side of the main structure. Here golden melon flowers bloom, and pale pink roses clamber, and large gourds lie unharvested and unwanted upon the paths. A glimmer of red gold and pale blue autumn light strikes the turning leaves in the afternoon sun. Familiar-looking weeds flourish in neglected borders: she thinks

292

she identifies the modest meadow yellows and pinks of cow-wheat, mallow, bistort, tormentil. For some reason, this garden reminds her overwhelmingly of her paternal grandparents' garden in Orpington. The sense of mingled recognition and bewilderment is simultaneously both shocking and comforting. She feels on the verge of some immense discovery about human nature and culture. But maybe she is merely tired, and her feet do sadly ache.

'I can't tell you how interesting all that was,' she tells Dr Oo, as they taxi back together towards the Pagoda Hotel. 'I can't thank you enough. I would never have seen such things without your help.'

'Tomorrow morning,' he tells her, 'your conference has a group coach tour round the city and to Cultural Expo 2002. I read of this on the hotel notice board. Your group coach tour will not show you the things that we have seen. I wonder what Professor van Jost will make of Expo 2002.'

'I don't suppose Professor van Jost will bother to come on the group coach tour,' says Babs Halliwell. She cannot quite keep a tone of disappointed pique out of her voice, although she knows it is wholly inappropriate. She hopes that Dr Oo will not notice it because she is ashamed of it. And she wishes to make a good impression on Dr Oo because she stole his suitcase.

★   ★   ★

When Dr Halliwell reaches Room 1517, she finds that her message light is blinking. She would have been surprised and annoyed had it not been. She needs to be needed. She had expected the oblique reprimand from her boy-minder, who wonders where she is and why she hadn't been there to hear the Japanese professor, though he puts it more courteously than that. There is also an invitation from her Australian friend Bob Bryant, suggesting they meet that evening for a drink in the bar, and another, more important message from the National Women's Hospital wanting to set up an appointment to show her its work on gene therapy and cancers of the bone marrow. This is a subject near to what was once her heart, and close to her professional concerns, so she responds at once, rings back, and sets up an early morning meeting for later in the week.

Her programme is filling up. Will she have time to get to Suwon-Hwaseong in the company of Dr Oo, to celebrate the anniversary of the sixtieth birthday of the crown-princess-turned-queen-mother?

She has solved one memory puzzle: it comes to her, suddenly, that the granite boulders of the Palace Gardens remind her of the artificial landscapes of New York's Central Park.

Dr Babs Halliwell knows that she should, at this point in the afternoon, put her feet up and read her Venetian detective story, like a sensible young-middle-aged woman. But she cannot settle. First she washes her Lycra knee-highs with the hotel-provided sachet of detergent and hangs them from the towel rail to dry. Then she places her lecture trousers in the trouser press and switches them on to grill. Then she tries to lie down, and remembers to swallow a few of the pills from the bottles that she has arranged upon her bedside table. She attempts a little deep breathing relaxation exercise, inhaling and exhaling lungs full of the purified and air-conditioned air. Her guardian spirits, who have temporarily assumed the form of one small but rather noisy insect, watch this decorous and regulated behaviour with approval, but they suspect it will not last. They know her too well. And they are right. The hot brightly lit lure of the city and the dark challenge of the underground are too strong for the healthy appetites of Babs Halliwell, and she is too restless to dispose herself quietly upon either of her twin beds. She is overstimulated and overexcited. She has the sense to change her shoes, and to check that she has plenty of *won* in suitably small denominations about her person, and then she plunges recklessly off into modernity.

It is the first time that she has set foot out of doors on her own, without an official group guide or Mong Joon or Dr Oo to guard her, and she finds the street instantly confusing. A tide of people is flowing along it, and traffic is pouring in both directions along the impassably wide roads and round and round a monumental traffic island occupied by a vast and handsome three-storey-high medieval oriental gate. The junction is busier than Hyde Park Corner or

Marble Arch. At first, she takes the line of least resistance, and allows herself to be carried along the pavement by the crowd of shoppers and homeward-bound workers, past little stalls selling gadgets and trinkets and socks and shoes and magazines and bottles of water, past shopfronts displaying stylish garments. It is an orderly and friendly chaos: everyone has told her Seoul is a safe city, and she feels safe, though she has no idea where she is going. She lingers long by a street trader selling an amazing variety of hosiery. She sees on display some highly desirable knee-high, scarlet nylon stockings, with a pretty pattern of butterflies in the weave. She really wants them. Shall she buy them? No, of course not. She really does not need a pair of scarlet socks.

She tears herself away, and glances back, to take her bearings, but her tall hotel, with its conspicuous purple logo, has already vanished from sight. She wonders if she will ever see it again. She is in an expensive downtown shopping neighbourhood of big hotels and big stores and international labels; she knows there are other, more distinctively Korean districts to explore, but how will she ever find them? Somewhere there are famous clothes markets and food markets and herb markets, and a celebrated tourist-favoured place called Insa-dong with traditional handicrafts and antiques and art galleries and tearooms. She longs to see all these things. But where are they? Is it worth trying to find them, or shall she just go with the flow? Can she reach them by subway, and dare she try to do so?

She has various maps, but they show bewildering conflicts and contradictions in scale, in orientation, and in the spelling of place names. The maps of Seoul are not like the maps of London or Manhattan. Plans of the underground, as Dr Oo had hinted, evidence more regularity. She will give the underground a try, if she can find where it is.

She plunges down steps that might or might not lead to a subway line, and is instantly sucked into another subterranean layer of the city. There is a whole new metropolis down here, with a spreading labyrinth of galleries and arcades and tunnels where touts are offering job lots of surprising items. Books, brassieres and packets of biscuits are heaped about in random piles on the pavement in front of bijou boutiques selling jewellery and shirts and sports shoes. It is confusing, chaotic, enticing. Babs's sense of direction has by now vanished, but eventually she sees, in the far distance, a green sign saying, in English, 'TRACKS'. She makes for the tracks.

Three hours later, in the safety of the Pagoda bar, she tries to tell Bob Bryant where she has been, but she does not make a very good job of it. Her account is as baffling to him as her adventures had been to her: the only part of it he latches on to is her confession that she had forgotten the magic word of 'Bi-Bim-Bap', and had ended up by default with a small plateful of the most disgusting cold red noodles covered in chilli sauce. She, who prides herself on being able to devour anything, had been unable to get

297

them down, and now, after all that walking, she declares that she is famished. She is ravenously awaiting the chicken wings with fries that she and Bob have ordered to accompany their beer. Bob has had one or two suppers already, but he is game for another.

Bob has been to Seoul several times, and he is far more interested in conference gossip and catching up on stories of academic life in the United Kingdom and the United States than in Babs's naive impressions of a foreign culture. He can do without the travelogue news, for South-East Asia is not nearly as foreign to him as it is to her. He is no stranger to the many varieties of *bibimpap*. After this conference, he is on his way to another conference in Japan, but he does not want to talk about that either. He wants to tell her about the implications for the nature-nurture debate of the latest findings on a fancy new way of rewiring the brains of laboratory rats, and he wants to share with her the view that Dr Radda's paper on the hereditability of certain forms of resistance to bowel cancer had been substantially lifted from a paper delivered some weeks ago at Stanford and subsequently pasted all over the Internet. It had all been about high salt and low fat, and it had racist implications anyway, says Bob.

Babs picks up a crispy, brown chicken wing and starts to tear at it with unladylike ferocity.

'What doesn't?' she comments, as she swallows the tender white fibres of fowl and gobbles a few fries.

'God,' she says, still chewing vigorously, and in

298

excuse for her poor manners, 'those noodles were the end. Cold and slimy and hot at the same time. I like hot food, but cold-hot food is horrid. Could anyone really like them? Mind you, it was a very cheap, touristy kind of eatery. It wasn't very authentic.'

'Do your students plagiarize?' asks Bob, as he attacks his bowl of high-salt, high-fat fries with similar gusto.

'I haven't had any students for a year. But yes, when I have, they do. And so do I. I plagiarize, and I appropriate. So do we all. Don't we? Nothing comes from nowhere, does it? And with the Internet, you can't always tell, can you? I just copy out these chunks of argument, and then I can't remember who thought of it first. What does it matter who thought of it first, as long as it gets you somewhere interesting?'

'That's a very dangerous attitude, Dr Halliwell.'

'Dangerous for me, perhaps, but I don't suppose it hurts anyone else very much.'

Both fall silent, as they gnaw at the small bird bones. Both are thinking of Peter Halliwell's father, a famous anthropologist who had been accused of falsifying the controversial results of years of remote fieldwork in Africa. The principal accusation had not been substantiated, but he had committed other smaller but more easily verifiable professional offences, and his career and reputation had suffered disastrously. Each knows that the other is thinking of this. It does not need a fancy theory of telepathy or neural interaction to explain it, and Babs is not at all surprised when Bob's next remark is 'And how's your ex, Babs?'

Peter is not Babs's ex, for she is still legally married to him, and still wears her wedding ring, but she is used to this terminology and does not challenge it. She considers it a fair question, for Bob Bryant had known Peter Halliwell in the old days, before Peter lost his mobility and most of his mind. Bob had met Peter long before he met Babs. Bob had met Peter before Babs had met Peter. Bob and Peter had been tennis partners when they had both been postgraduates at Cambridge. This seems unlikely now, for Bob Bryant looks too unfit to play tennis, and Peter Halliwell can hardly walk and rarely leaves his room in the Retreat. But twenty years earlier, they had been contenders, and had together won the Ashley College Cup.

'Oh, God,' says Babs, in initial response.

'Don't say if you don't want,' says Bob, who is kind, though curious.

'I don't mind saying,' says Babs.

And she says. Bob Bryant listens, courteously. It is a sad story. Babs has had a tough time, a raw deal. That's what all her friends say, and it is true. But Peter Halliwell has had a tougher time, and a worse deal.

'What about medication?' asks Bob, when she has finished her update on Peter's condition.

She shrugs.

'When it might have done him some good, he wouldn't take anything. Maybe he was right not to want to, I don't know. Now it's too late, they fill him up with God knows what.'

'Is it really too late?'

'Far too late,' says Babs. 'You should see him. You wouldn't ask.'

'Dying by Lot, eh?' says Bob, and waves at the waiter in hope of another pint of beer.

'I suppose voluntary and involuntary euthanasia will have been adopted worldwide in a hundred years,' says Babs, in indirect response to this. 'But we'll call them something different. I mean, it's inevitable, isn't it? Do you know what it costs, to keep Peter at the Retreat? It doesn't matter to me — financially, it's covered — but it is a lot of money, to keep somebody in such misery. Somebody who would much rather have been dead. No, I won't, thanks, but I wouldn't mind a shot of something. Is there any particular kind of Korean hard liquor I should try?'

She smiles ingratiatingly at the waiter, wondering if she will ever get rid of this overpowering sense of her own physical superfluity. She had hoped that in Bob's large-bellied, barearmed company, she might begin to feel a little more refined, but she still feels too big. Alice in Wonderland must have felt like this, when she went down the rabbit hole. Is there a shrinking potion on sale anywhere, she wonders?

The neat, slim, willowy, androgynous waiter recommends that she try some *soju*. OK, she says, she is game for that.

'You can get this aphrodisiac,' says Bob, 'with a dead snake floating in it.'

'Fair enough,' says Babs.

'Kim Jong Il, the Dear Leader of North Korea,' says Bob, 'is famed to be one of the world's greatest consumers of Hennessy VSOP Cognac.'

'Fair enough,' says Babs, sniffing cautiously at her glass of *soju*.

'Are you going on the trip to the Expo?' asks Bob, as he watches her take her first small sip of the tapioca-based firewater.

'Of course,' says Babs. 'I never miss an outing. I love an outing.'

★ ★ ★

Babs Halliwell had predicted that Jan van Jost would not join the coach tour. She was wrong. She has made various false assumptions about Professor Jan van Jost, and this was one of them.

Professor Jan van Jost does join the coach tour. At ten o'clock the following morning, he ceases to sulk in his suite, emerges from his superior isolation, and joins the party. There he is, in the foyer, waiting to become a tourist, waiting to be handed his Tour Welcome Package and his Guide to the Expo and yet another map of Seoul. He is looking pale and affable: the halo of fame still surrounds him, but it glows a little less brightly, and his skin has a taut and tired transparency, a delicate pallor beneath the tan. It occurs to Babs, who is mollified by his very attendance, that he may be somewhat exhausted. He is in his late sixties, and he has been touring China. China is enough to tire a younger man.

She is further mollified when he follows her on to the coach, and elects to sit beside her. It is true that in her role as the only woman delegate who has signed up for the outing she has been directed to a good window seat at the front, with a good view: no doubt he takes his place next to her in his role of alpha male. Nevertheless, whatever the reasons, here he is, nodding pleasantly at her, and dutifully opening his map upon his knee. 'Good morning,' he says, agreeably. 'And how are you this morning? Have you been enjoying Seoul? Is it your first visit here?'

She is disarmed by the condescension of this fairly elementary politeness, and, as they sit there waiting for something to happen, she tells him a little of her impressions of the city. He listens, with deference. 'You have seen far more than I,' he offers, when she mentions the queen's palace and the stone tomb that houses the king's placenta. 'Do you have a special interest in Korea?'

She demurs. She does not embark on the story of the Crown Princess and Dr Oo because it is too long and too complicated: no, she says, she is here simply because she was invited. Does he know the country? And had he enjoyed his visit to China?

The coach is still stationary, in front of the hotel. What are they waiting for now? Babs can see her putto, Mong Joon, on the hotel steps, keeping his eyes on her until she is safely on her official way to her official destination.

Jan van Jost says that China had been difficult and that, no, he does not know the Korean peninsula, and that is why he is here.

'I used to think,' he says, with an apologetic

303

smile, 'that I would visit every country in the world before I died. Now I know that is not true. But at least I can add South Korea to the list. To tell you truly, I would like to visit North Korea also, but I gather this is not yet possible. I saw the President in the Blue House yesterday, and he tells me in five years I can surely go to North Korea. But that is too far away.'

She wonders why he wants to go to North Korea. He is a man of the left, but not that far left, surely. She is impressed that he has met the President in the Blue House, which she correctly assumes must be the South Korean version of the White House. This is fame. She is sitting next to fame.

'In the hotel foyer,' she says, as he seems to begin to withdraw from her into an inward and melancholy mode of reflection, 'there are leaflets about trips to the Demilitarized Zone. I was a bit surprised. You can visit the Infiltration Tunnel and the Anti-Communism Hall.'

'Really?' He seems to perk up at this bizarre information. 'How extraordinary!'

She is flattered by his interest and digs around in her shoulder bag. Yes, here is the leaflet. Visit the DMZ, the most heavily fortified border on the planet! See the tanks and propaganda! See the Freedom Bridge and the flora and fauna that thrive in this vast deserted region in the absence of all humankind! Peace and tension coexist upon the border! A nature reserve created by conflict! Through a telescope you can watch the North Koreans go about their daily life!

Jan van Jost is fascinated by this brochure

— he is a sociologist, is he not? — and he is pleased when she says he can keep it. There are plenty more, she assures him, on the concierge's desk. She is pleased when he tucks it away carefully in his Armani breast pocket. And the sociologist in him is clearly also taken by the fantastic apparel of the couple of tour guides who now board the bus. These young women are improbably dressed in shiny gold-and-turquoise uniforms, and their oddly cut and strangely draped trouser-skirts are far, far too short. Their brown legs are long and look painfully naked, and they wear peculiar and playful little hats upon their heads. Babs Halliwell is embarrassed for them, and she can see that they are embarrassed for themselves.

Jan van Jost is the soul of courtesy. He speaks gently to these overexposed young women, as they wait by his elbow at the front of the coach for the driver to start the engine. What is this colourful costume? he wishes to know. It is historical costume of Koryo period, says one of the girls. No, no, mutters the other, it is Unified Silla period. Koryo, says the first. Silla, says the second. Koryo, says the first. Not very authentic costume anyway, says the second girl, in conciliation. They both smile, nervously. They are college girls, not courtesans, although they appear to be dressed as courtesans. They seem overawed by van Jost, yet at the same time on the verge of insubordinate laughter. Do they know who he is? Have they read his books? Or does his unmediated aura shine undimmed across all boundaries and all frontiers? He does his best to

305

put them at their ease. They look very charming, whatever their costume is meant to represent, he tells them, gallantly. They blush.

The coach careers round Seoul, and over a bridge towards the Expo. Those seated further back cannot see much because of the darkly tinted windows, but Babs and Jan get a good view of traffic jams, skyscrapers, sculptures, bronze statues, street traders, medieval gates and medieval walls. The girls give a lively commentary through a megaphone on aspects of Seoul ancient and modern, on Korea's success in the World Cup, on the Koreans' passionate love for their football team's coach, the Dutch hero Guus Hiddink who had led their team to such an unexpected victory. We love all Dutch people now, they needlessly assure van Jost, who accepts the compliment gracefully.

Babs Halliwell is not quite sure why they are on the way to visit the Expo, and she is not much clearer when they arrive there and clamber out of their coach. The exhibition, or exposition, appears to be a cross between a theme park and a trade fair. The international and multicultural gaggle of sociologists, evolutionary biologists, evolutionary psychologists, social psychologists, behavioural economists and clinical experts straggles bewildered round its stands and its marquees. They are shown the most modern electronic technology juxtaposed with faithful reconstructions of old tea-shops. They are introduced to displays of traditional weaving and knot making and bamboo pyrography. They watch a craftsman engaged in *dancheong* ornamental painting, using vivid shades of blue, crimson, yellow, white and black. They follow obediently as Miss Silla and Miss Koryo usher them smartly round a big tent displaying upon illustrated panels the long history of Confucianism. The conflicting answers of these two ladies to the questions of their flock spread further confusion. Babs, a compulsive tourist, is fascinated by everything, including the amicable disputes of the guides. She wonders if they know anything about the Crown Princess, and is wondering whether to raise her from the dead when she finds that she is being herded into a darkened auditorium. Anxious not to get lost, she sticks close to her group, and finds herself sitting, once again, next to van Jost.

Side by side, in the darkness, they obediently watch the screen, as it fills with images of temples and parks and palaces and lakes and mountains. It is a three-D, virtual-reality travelogue of exceptional virtuosity. Professor van Jost and Dr Halliwell, side by side in their dark green velvety upholstered armchairs, travel together weightlessly through time and space: they ascend pine-forested peaks, plunge through precipitous waterfalls, abseil up torrents of frozen granite, and swim underwater amongst the roots and beneath the leaves of lotus and lily. They march along ramparts and spirit roads, and creep into underground chambers. Bodiless, they pass through paper screens into inner courtyards and secret lacquered rooms. Armies of bowmen take harmless aim for them, temple bells ring for them, red-bridled high-stepping horses prance for them, painted constellations glimmer in a dark blue vault for them. It is kitsch and yet it is enchanting. Towards the end of the display, in a spectacular grand finale, a host of large multicoloured butterflies flies out from the screen towards them. One of them settles on the shoulder of Dr Babs Halliwell, and Jan van Jost, astonished, reaches out his hand to touch it. His hand passes through it, for it is not there, it is a hologram hallucination, and his hand comes to rest on the real fleshly viscose-clad shoulder of Babs Halliwell. The butterfly departs, but his hand rests there for a moment on the thin fabric and the firm flesh, and she looks at him, and he looks at her, and there, in the darkened cinema, their eyes meet, and they both smile shyly, like lovers in the dark, joint captives of illusion. His eyes seem to hers to be full of film-star tears.

The lights go up, to an appreciative murmuring from the audience and a little naively enthusiastic applause. It had been a wonderful show! Miss Silla and Miss Koryo, now walking hand in hand, smile proudly as they lead their docile scholars back towards their waiting coach. Professor Jan van Jost and Dr Barbara Halliwell walk side by side, not hand in hand, but something has passed between them, and they take their seats for the homeward journey side by side as though they were lovers, as though they were man and wife.

As the coach crosses the broad Han River, from south to north, from new Seoul to old Seoul, Babs Halliwell says to Jan van Jost, 'I came to this conference because I wanted to hear

308

you speak. I wanted to see you, in the flesh.'

This was not true, and it is not true, but it has a truth somewhere in it.

Jan van Jost smiles ruefully, and looks down modestly. Then he looks at her again, eye to eye.

'You come too late,' he says, 'for I have nothing to say.'

She takes this in.

'Then I come to hear you say nothing,' she says. 'Nothing will be enough.'

He is about to speak once more, when Miss Koryo leans over, and taps him anxiously on the shoulder with her megaphone. She and Miss Silla have been whispering feverishly together, and now Miss Koryo says, 'Please, Professor van Jost, we have decided the costume is not Silla or Koryo. It has features from Unified Silla, but it is a fantasy costume. But we want to say, women in the Silla kingdom had very high social status.'

'The Silla kingdom was 57 BC to AD 935,' says Miss Silla helpfully, discreetly consulting a clipboard on her knee. 'Koryo period not so good for women, and the Yi dynasty, worse still. But Silla, this was a good time for women in this land.'

'And now is another good time for you,' says van Jost, generously and genially.

'Please, Professor,' says Miss Koryo, emboldened, 'please sign my programme!'

'And mine, please, if not too much trouble!' says Miss Silla.

Graciously, he signs. Heavily, he sighs. He is the Prince of Mournful Thoughts, the Prince of the Leaden Casket. Babs Halliwell is proud to sit by his side. She does not ask for his signature, although she almost wishes that she could bring herself to do so. For he is very, very famous.

She wonders if he will come to listen to her paper on 'Dying by Lot' at four-thirty that afternoon. She does not think he will. And he does not. Or if he does, she cannot see him. She looks for him, as she takes her place on the platform and adjusts the microphone and pours herself a glass of water, but she does not think that he is there. She can see various supportive and admonitory presences: both Peter Halliwell's ex-tennis partner, Bob Bryant, and her putto minder are conspicuous in the second row, as well as other delegates with whom she has conversed during the conference. She peers beyond them, into the middle distance. The lighting in the main body of the hall is dim: he may be there, perhaps, hidden away at the back? She does not know if she wants him to be there, or not. She has fallen under the spell of Jan van Jost. She has fallen pointlessly and passingly in love with him. She wishes to charm him, as he has charmed her. But then, she wishes to charm any audience. She wishes every member of her audience to fall in love with her. She is vain, and she enjoys displaying herself to the admiration of strangers.

Is the auditorium full enough? Has she been boycotted because she is a woman? This, as she has been so many times warned, and as dear Dr Oo has confirmed, remains a sexist society, where women academics continue to suffer from discrimination, and she is prepared to be insulted by a poor attendance. But the room seems to be respectably full. Although she is an inferior woman, she is also something of a freak and a peep show. On the Western circuit, she is well known as a lively and controversial speaker. She has debated controversial issues on the radio. She has appeared, effectively, on television. Her lofty stature, such a disadvantage in some social situations, is an asset now. She draws herself up to her full height, adjusts her large tortoiseshell-rimmed varifocal glasses, and launches herself upon her discourse.

Her paper goes down well enough. She delivers it professionally, with practised timing. Her material is dramatic. Unlike Dr Oo's stories of patient stroke patients, her case histories deal with the extreme and rare, with the frontiers of experiment, with the philosophical and ethical aspects of moral decisions made in medical uncertainty. Her histories are the stuff of headline news. She has lived through melodrama, and this is her profit from it. She has the right. She is licensed by misfortune. This is not exploitation; it is a legitimate display of scholarship and abstraction.

She does not, of course, mention the death of her own child, Benedict, but there is no doubt in the mind of Bob Bryant that the personal dilemma which had years ago directed the nature of her research has also informed her argument and the intensity of her delivery. She speaks of bone-marrow disorders, of transplants and donor banks and bone-marrow registers, of chemotherapy and gene therapy, and of the possibility that gene therapy may cause more cancers than it cures. She speaks of current research in Paris and London. She discusses the ethical position of parents who choose to have a second child, a 'saviour sibling', in the hope of providing a suitable matching donor for the first. She speaks of the geographical distribution of certain conditions, and of the mismatching geography of available remedies, either traditional or experimental.

Her discourse is learned and informative. As she nears her final written paragraphs, she wonders which of her shock alternative endings she will select. She has two up her sleeve, one or the other of which she will deliver freestyle, without notes, with as much eye contact as she can force upon her audience. Thus, they will remember her and what she has said. She likes to be remembered.

In her first shock ending, she will discuss the placebo dilemma. She will reveal that she herself is at this moment full of a mixture of chemicals which may or may not be a placebo, and which may or may not be affecting her bone density. Dr Babs Halliwell has gone in for medical risk in a big way. She is a volunteer. She has offered her body to a group of colleagues as a laboratory for tests on a drug, which, it is hoped, will help to develop a cure for osteoporosis. The clinical trials are in mid term, and the results are expected in several months' time.

Shall she confide this information? No, it is too risky and too personal. It might be considered bad form. And she cannot locate Jan van Jost in the gloom of the back rows.

She opts for and embarks upon the second story.

Her second ending is the case history of a woman whom she knows personally, a mother of four and a successful lawyer. After some months of suffering from fatigue and mysterious aches and pains, this woman was unexpectedly discovered in early middle age to have a rare bone-marrow disorder. When a name was given to her malady, she immediately contacted her doctor sister in Toronto, who proved not only to be a matching donor, as one might hope, but also, against any calculable odds, to be one of the world authorities on this rare condition. So she received from her sister expert advice and some comfort, as well as a bone-marrow transplant.

(The long-term outcome of the transplant is still nervously awaited, and at the moment does not look good, but Dr Halliwell, in her lecture, does not mention this.)

What, asks Dr Halliwell rhetorically, was the connection between this sister's long-ago-selected field of expertise and this sibling's later excessive production of red blood cells? Was there any? Was it coincidence? It can only have been a coincidence, for nothing in this woman's medical history could have predicted the onset of this rare disease. It is a disease of which the origins are unknown, though it more commonly afflicts males over sixty than middle-aged professional women from Newcastle upon Tyne. So why had the sister been attracted to this field in the first place? And what effect did or should or could this kinship have on the nature of her medical advice to her sick sibling?

She stares at her audience, leaving these interesting questions in the air. She knows they have no answer. Her story is a story of pure chance. It has no meaning. It is very interesting, but it has no meaning. Its lack of meaning is its meaning.

Did her audience hear her? Or are they all fast asleep, worn out by their morning's trudging round the concrete-and-fibreglass acres of the Expo? She bows politely as she gathers her papers together on the lectern, and detaches the heavy microphone box from the waistband of her trouser suit. There is a decent spatter of applause. She leaves the podium, reflecting that most of them had probably stopped listening long ago, despite her heroic efforts to keep them awake. Throughout her paper, on which she had laboured for so long, her audience would have been thinking about its supper or its salary or its sex life. That's the way it goes with academic papers and lectures. Lectures, like examinations, are an anachronism, a quaintly surviving form of a medieval endurance test, and will soon go the way of the eight-legged Chinese Confucian essay. Anyone will be able to read what she has to say on the Internet, anyway, if anyone is interested. Why bother with the labour of bodily attention, of bodily presence? Why bother with the slow and awkward machinery of headphones and simultaneous translation? Why bother to come all the way to Seoul in the first place?

Text, subtext, content, presentation. The

trouser press in Room 1517 has done wonders for the crease in Dr Babs Halliwell's trousers. She looks down, approvingly, as she descends the steps from the platform. At least she *looks* quite smart, she tells herself, as she struggles against a growing and familiarly dreary sense of inadequacy and post-performance depression. It hadn't been a complete disaster, had it?

★   ★   ★

Babs Halliwell knows that she will have to go to Jan van Jost's lecture, even though he had not taken the trouble to attend hers. She is morally committed to this because of the immaterial butterfly that had landed upon her shoulder. She knows her place. So, when the faithful Dr Oo contacts her about their tentative Suwon-Hwaseong project, she explains that she cannot go on the day he had first suggested because she wishes to hear about 'The Leaden Casket: Meditations on the Apocalypse'. What about the day after that? Fine, said Dr Oo, obligingly. Perhaps, says Dr Oo, he would come with her to hear van Jost? It is not every day that one has the opportunity to hear so great a man, and nobody would notice a cross-conference interloper, surely? It has been very gracious of van Jost to spend so long in Seoul, and to attend so much of this extended conference. Van Jost has not regally breezed in and regally breezed out again, as conference stars so often do. Dr Oo agrees with Dr Halliwell that it would be improper not to listen to van Jost. Suwon-Hwaseong can wait.

So Dr Oo and Babs Halliwell sit side by side to hear Jan van Jost address the subject of the leaden casket of death. His performance is at once highly impressive and almost wholly incomprehensible. Is he talking literally, or figuratively? Is he talking sense, or nonsense? Is he talking ecology, or ethics, or epidemiology, or psychology, or philosophy? He ranges widely through the cultures of the West, invoking Epicurus and Lucretius, Freud and Frazer, Lacan and Foucault, Gotthold Lessing and Doris Lessing, Zola and Lévi-Strauss. He speaks of the diseases of the soul and of the universe, and of the approaching end of human life on earth, and of the backward shadow that the end casts upon our earthly endeavours. He speaks of year zero, ground zero and world zero. He speaks of the Casket Letters which hid the secrets of the passions of Mary Queen of Scots, and of the wooden casket in which Princess Diana of Wales tried to hide the squalid secrets of the British Crown and Court. He speaks of AIDS and of the lure of the Gothic vision of death. He quotes from *King Lear* and from Edgar Allen Poe. He speaks of the 'unreturned gaze', and of the 'beseeching eye'. He speaks of the failure of the Enlightenment and of the transcultural tragedy. Babs wonders at first what on earth poor Dr Oo can be making of all this, but decides it is too late to worry about that: Dr Oo is a grown man, and he'd got into this of his own free will. He must have sat through more perplexing discourses in his time.

The lecture emerges from profound obscurity

316

to end with a simple but inexplicable image, an image of living entombment. Van Jost presents man, buried alive in the body, trapped in the coffin-casket, dying a slow and inevitable death, in a darkening planet, alone in the empty sterile universe.

Jan van Jost bows, to tumultuous and uncomprehending applause. What on earth had he been talking about?

Babs Halliwell asks him, directly, that evening, at the reception in the Dutch Embassy that is being given in his honour. She sees him standing at a picture window, momentarily isolated and accessible, staring out from the diplomatic heights of a hilltop over the vast sprawling modern city of Seoul, and she goes up to him and addresses him, boldly. Had his final image referred, she provocatively demands, to the Korean Prince Sado, the Prince of the Rice Chest? The connections, she says, had been too striking to be coincidental.

Van Jost says that he has never heard of Prince Sado or of the rice chest. Who, van Jost asks, was Prince Sado?

Babs Halliwell tells him about Prince Sado. Somewhat to her surprise, he appears to be as gripped by her narrative as she had been by the narrative of the Crown Princess, and, although she fears the story may be losing something in the telling, she can see that she has his entire attention. He ushers her, wine glass in hand, away from the wide expanse of window to a deeply upholstered ambassadorial sofa, and persuades her to sink down upon it by his side.

317

He presses her for more details about the clothing phobia and the death in the rice chest. He is not quite as interested in the princess herself as Babs is, but she supposes that that is just a natural gender difference, and that he is identifying with the male strand of the story. She is gratified by his eagerness to hear more, by his wish that he had known of this story earlier. He picks it up very quickly. The quickness of his mind is a delight to her. 'I could have worked it in so easily,' he says, annoyed with himself for having missed a trick. 'It would have been an excellent point of reference. I suppose all Koreans know about Prince Sado and this Imo Incident?'

Babs has to confess that she doesn't really know how widespread the knowledge of the princess's memoirs is in their native land. She says she longs to find out. She herself as yet knows so little about them, they came her way by accident, she had brought them with her to Seoul more or less by accident, she tells him. She also finds herself telling him about her acquaintance with Dr Oo. (She does not confess to the suitcase incident.) She tells him that she is going to Suwon the next day with Dr Oo, to see Prince Sado's final resting place. Would he like to come too, she enquires? She has had several glasses of wine by now, and is on excellent form. It is always pleasant to be monopolized by the highest-ranking and most famous man in the room. She glows with confidence. She no longer feels herself to be too ugly and too big. She knows that she is handsome, and admirable, and admired.

Jan van Jost says that he will think about it. He says that he admires her for having got to grips with their host country so quickly. He has been too tired to make the best of his visit so far, but today he feels a little better. He says he would like a bibliographical reference for the memoirs: perhaps he can add Prince Sado to his essay on the Leaden Casket before he publishes. Would he like to borrow them, she offers. Well, yes, he admits that he would. Can she spare them? Of course, of course, she assures him. She hates lending books to people, but van Jost does not count as people.

Later that evening, she brings them down to the lobby of the Pagoda Hotel and entrusts them to him. He says he will read them overnight and return them in the morning. He says he needs little sleep. He sleeps badly, and he reads fast.

She can well believe that he reads fast. The evidence of his erudition is overpowering. He must have been reading all night, every night, for decades. How else could he know so much?

In the morning, he rings her in her room at eight and asks if he can join her expedition to Suwon-Hwaseong with Dr Oo. He has read the Crown Princess's story overnight, and longs to follow up his introduction to her, with the chance of a knowledgeable escort like Dr Oo. He would like to see a little bit of the real Korea, while he is here. Would she mind, would Dr Oo mind, would he be an intrusion? Not at all, says Babs. She is excited by his excitement, and slightly relieved not to be spending a whole day

319

tête-à-tête with Dr Oo. A tête-à-tête could have had its awkward moments. She is sure that Dr Oo will be pleased. Well, almost sure. Dr Oo is a happily married man, or so he says. And three is a good number for an outing.

And so it is that the three of them find themselves on a suburban train, which is making a slow stopping journey towards Suwon. Suwon is now a commuter suburb of Seoul, and it is easier to get there by train than by hire car or taxi, says Dr Oo. They are off on a spree, to visit the UNESCO World Heritage Site. They have escaped their guides and minders and fellow delegates, and privatized themselves.

The one-time Crown Princess, reincarnated as the Mother Queen, had travelled to Suwon-Hwaseong for her sixtieth birthday celebrations with great pomp. This was the only grand state progress of her long life. Unlike Queen Elizabeth I of England, or Marie Antoinette of France, or Catherine the Great of Russia, she had led a retired though not a very peaceful life. But on her way to Suwon, an immense retinue of colourful pageantry had attended her. A thousand-strong procession of bowmen and horses and musicians had crossed the great river Han upon a wide and magnificent pontoon, and scores of court artists had documented every inch of the event for posterity. The Mother Queen had peered through the curtains of the heavily draped royal palanquin at the broad river, and at the hills, and at the spreading southern plain, and at the waving and petitioning crowds of her unknown and distant people, and she had looked back on the turbulent times she had so far so unexpectedly and so shrewdly survived. She had wondered that she had lived so long to see so much. Some of these impressions she later recorded; some she did not.

In her memoirs, the Mother Queen had dwelt much on her gratitude to her son King Chŏngjo for this lavish display of filial respect, and pretended to make much of her own humility and unworthiness. But she was a self-serving and unreliable narrator, and a self-confessed diplomat in her family's cause, as well as in her own. How much of the truth, wondered Dr Babs Halliwell, could one deduce from her various accounts? Babs is irrationally convinced that she can read the subtext of much of the Mother Queen's memoirs. Babs has a sense that she is in direct communion with her. She also knows that this sense must be an illusion, for there are as many subtexts as there are readers. She has been brought up in a postmodern relativist world, therefore she cannot believe in direct messages, either from a text or from beyond the grave. Nevertheless, there is some kind of a message, and it is she herself that is receiving it. If she has a self, which is also problematic.

Babs peers out, not through the embroidered and thickly shrouded curtains of a queenly palanquin, but through the train's glassy modern windows. Jan van Jost and Dr Oo are speaking together in Dutch. Babs cannot understand a word that they are saying, which makes her feel slightly paranoid, but her sense of exclusion is offset by her sense of satisfaction in having been the agent for bringing these two unlikely characters together. It is quite a coup. Probably Jan (as she is now allowed to call him) is pleased to find someone with whom he can speak a little in his native tongue. Dr Oo is something of a linguist, it appears. This will be an outing to remember, an outing for the diary that alas she does not keep. She will be able to dine out on it. If ever she is asked to dine in All Souls' again, she will be able to boast about travelling to Suwon with Jan van Jost.

And so it is that the three of them find themselves disembarking from their commuter train and climbing into a taxi at Suwon station. The taxi heads off up through busy nondescript modern streets and then up a winding wooded hill towards the main entrance of the ancient fortress. Dr Oo now sits in front, chatting with the driver, and Babs and Jan sit in the back. Babs Halliwell is in a mood of happy exhilaration and anticipation. She feels that her powers are restored to her. After a disastrous start, this strange visit is turning out well. It is all far more interesting than she could ever have expected. The sheer good luck of meeting Dr Oo fills her with delight. Her whole life seems to have taken a turn for the better. Surely all will be well. Her guardian spirits, who had temporarily abandoned her at Incheon airport, have not deserted her. Perhaps they had not abandoned her at all — perhaps they had planned the whole thing. She can hardly believe that she is going sightseeing with this distinguished and well-mannered man, and that he seems to be content with her company. How lucky she is, to be where she is, and who she is, and to be living at this moment of history!

Dr Oo has a long conversation with the officials in the kiosk at the main gate, and returns to tell them that they do not need tickets, for the visit is free. The tickets for the royal palaces had been very cheap, but this is free. He shows them maps, and explains that it will take about two hours to make the full circuit of the fortress walls — are they game for this? He thinks it is about five kilometres: can they manage that? Yes, of course they can. It is a glorious day, the September sun is shining on them, and they are all wearing sensible shoes. Shall Dr Oo try to find a guide? He has only been here once in his life, he is ashamed to say, and then he hadn't been paying too much attention to what he was looking at. 'I was with my sister,' says Dr Oo, 'and we were talking too much.'

A guide would be a good idea, agree Babs and Jan, and Dr Oo returns to the kiosk to see if he can raise one. Babs, at this point, thinks it would also be a good idea, before embarking on the walk, to visit the ladies' toilet. She can see a pleasant-looking one conveniently placed by the non-ticket booth, clearly labelled in English writing. Like the Queen of England, Babs believes it is always wise to visit the toilet when one can. So in she goes, and finds that the facilities are indeed very modern. If this is also UNESCO money, it is well spent. There is nobody else in the building, and she seems to have a choice of cubicle designs: she enters one of the larger closets, and sits herself down on a fine throne-like ceramic sanitary structure, which calls itself, to her delight, in English, a 'Royal Bidet'. So far, so good: the Queen of England would not have disdained this vessel. It is when Babs comes to an attempt to flush the toilet that she encounters a difficulty. There is no very clear way, as far as she can see, of activating the flush. She buttons up her trousers, and stares down in perplexity and mild transcultural panic at the array of symbols portrayed on a smart flat plasticated touch panel by the lavatory pan. A row of press pads is aligned by a display of what look like waves and dewdrops, in pretty nursery shades of pink and yellow and pale blue. There is also, alarmingly, a simplified picture of what must surely be a plump lady's bottom, at which an energetic jet of water is pointing. This, too, has its own press pad.

The last thing Babs wishes to do is to unleash a jet spray, so she knows she must avoid that one. The coloured dewdrops look milder, but somehow not quite right for her purpose. Perhaps she should leave the toilet unflushed? No, her Orpington training is too strong for that. She knows what is right. She washes her hands in the en-suite washbowl, dries them on a paper towel, and inspects once more the elaborate control panel, and the rest of this queenly cubicle. This time she is pleased to discover a good old-fashioned handle, set in the wall by the cistern. Yes, that must be the one.

Boldly, she pulls it downwards. Immediately, a

cacophony of sound, a great peal of bells, fills the entire building. It is a fire alarum or a distress signal. What on earth will happen now? She feels very guilty, like a schoolgirl who has set off a fire extinguisher by mistake. The bells keep pealing. She feels hysterical laughter rising in her. This is ridiculous. What on earth will Jan and Dr Oo think has happened to her? She had better get out of here quick and face the music.

So out she rushes, straight into the arms of a young Korean woman, who has clearly come to rescue her. 'So sorry!' says Babs, as the young woman deftly pushes a wall switch and brings the hideous clamour to a sudden end. 'Don't worry, don't worry,' says the young Korean woman, in perfect English. 'So many people make this mistake. It is no matter. Are you all right?'

'Yes, of course I am,' says Babs. The young woman is giggling. She thinks it is all very funny, and so do Jan van Jost and Dr Oo, who are waiting for her by the signboard that marks the beginning of the trail. Babs decides that there is no point in being embarrassed. It is too late for that. She gives a vivid account of the Royal Bidet and its mixed messages. Dr Oo gallantly responds with a description of another Korean device called the 'etiquette bell', which his sister tells him is to be found in many women's lavatories in up-market locations in Seoul. 'You press this bell for the sound of running water,' says Dr Oo. 'To disguise the sound of natural functions. We are a very modest nation. It surprises many travellers from Europe, I believe.'

325

Babs remembers that the toilet, after all this excitement, remains unflushed. But she is not going back to deal with that now.

The young woman who had come to her rescue now reveals herself to be an English-speaking volunteer guide who says she is happy to escort them for the beginning of their journey. She wears jeans, and a purple jacket over a bright lemon-yellow top, and she is slim and small and very pretty. She is delighted and surprised by the enthusiasm of her foreign visitors. And she is extremely well informed. She conducts them to what she says is the most scenic route — they must set off first outside the walls, on a rustic grassy path through woodland, in the green belt that surrounds the historic site. Perhaps, she tells them, Hwaseong means 'Fortress of Grass'? Or perhaps it means 'Flower Bud Fortress'? No one is quite sure of the word's derivation. And then they must enter through the secret gate, and walk along the walls, and inspect the stone watchtowers, and the gun embrasures, and the wooden pavilions with their arrow slits and their painted ceilings, and the great gate of Paldalmun. Look, see how beautifully constructed are the walls, with their remarkable combination of large stones and bricks. Seventy thousand workers were mobilized for a year, and they were well paid and well fed by the standards of the day — a whole army of masons, carpenters, plasterers, painters and tilers had worked here. It was a magnificent undertaking, a great memorial to King Chŏngjo and the new technologies. It is all very fully documented, says

326

their charming guide.

Babs wants to ask what their guide knows about Prince Sado and the Crown Princess, but is afraid of revealing herself as a sensationmonger, more interested in human tales of murder and treachery than in architecture. She does not want to be a vulgar tourist. So she keeps quiet, and listens earnestly. It is a pleasant walk, whatever one's interest in it, a fascinating walk. The walls remind Babs a little of the walls of the city of York, of which she had once done the full circuit with Peter Halliwell, in the early days of their courtship. That, too, had been a conference outing, at the University of York. Peter had been giving a paper on kinship patterns in British Columbia. It had been the early spring, of their love and of the year, and the green slopes had been crowded with hopeful daffodils. But of course, the medieval walls of York are much older and more serious than these walls. These eighteenth-century fortifications, says their guide, are said by some historians to be more playful than real. There is an element of theatre and fantasy in this place. It was never besieged, in King Chŏngjo's day. And when the Japanese came again, such defences were obsolete.

By the time they reach the West Gate, Dr Oo has discovered that their guide knows his sister, and indeed at one point had studied under her. This is not very much of a coincidence, but it is sufficiently interesting to both parties to cause them to relapse comfortably into their own language. They forge ahead, chattering of family connections and of the legendary domestic stress

327

of the approaching Harvest Festival of Chusŏk, which seems to distress Koreans as much as Christmas distresses most of Europe. Babs and Jan van Jost follow more slowly. Babs is a little worried that Jan may be getting tired: she feels protective about him, but considers it would be rude to enquire after his health or stamina. So they walk along together in silence, for a few minutes. They pause, to lean on the wall and gaze along the curving battlements towards the bustling modern city. The stone of the wall is warm.

'And how was China?' she asks. 'Was it your first visit to China?'

He does not reply for a moment. He sighs, and shakes his head, but not, she thinks, in answer to her question. Then he reaches into his jacket pocket, and extracts a crumpled packet of cigarettes, and lays it upon the top of the wall, and stares at it, as though it contains some kind of answer to some other question that hangs in the air. Eventually, he says, with what she now recognizes as his habitual politeness, 'Would you mind if I smoked a cigarette?'

'Of course not,' she says.

'Do you think it is acceptable, to smoke in an historic site?' he asks.

'I can't see that anyone would mind. We are in the open air, after all,' she says.

'I haven't seen any signs,' he says, as he extracts a booklet of Pagoda Hotel matches from his breast pocket.

This reminds Babs that she had seen 'No Smoking' signs and designated smoking areas in the gardens of Changgyeonggung, the Palace of Glorious Blessings, otherwise known as Historic Site No. 123. It may be that smoking is indeed prohibited on these city walls, for this is an orderly and regulated country. But she does not see it as her duty to point this out to him. She is not a school prefect or a policewoman. Why should he not enjoy a cigarette? No, she thanks him, she won't have one herself, she doesn't smoke.

'Neither do I,' he says, as he cups his hand carefully round the small flame. 'I gave it up. But I took it up again, in China. I'll quit, when I've finished the pack. It was quite difficult, my time in China. Quite stressful.'

He looks towards her and smiles at her, as he savours the smoke. His nostrils wrinkle at her as he smiles. After two draws, he extinguishes the cigarette neatly, on the underside of a chunk of UNESCO restoration stonework, and carefully replaces the stub in the pack. She admires his consideration.

He looks at her again, and seems to be about to say something important. Their eyes meet again. She rather wishes now that she had accepted a cigarette from him. Smoking together would have been a further form of bonding. The stub from a cigarette offered to her by Jan van Jost would have been a trophy. She could have preserved it, as she had once romantically preserved, unwashed, a glass from which Peter Halliwell had been drinking. She had kept it for months at the back of her kitchen cabinet.

Had van Jost, when younger, been a

womanizer? Had he been a seducer of students? She hopes he cannot read her thoughts, but she rather suspects that he can. She credits him with supernatural and telepathic powers. Moreover, she is increasingly tempted to believe that he is looking at her with some form of heightened interest. Does she want him to make a move, or to say whatever it is that he has to say? No, she thinks not. Her life is complicated enough. It is enough to know that she is once more looking good, that she no longer feels herself to be gross and disgusting. She is not in need of any further affirmation. She smiles at him, in a cheerful public manner, and diverts her gaze to the space beyond him, where Dr Oo and their guide have paused to wait for them. Babs waves, and Babs and Jan van Jost resume the perambulation, hastening their step to catch up with the other couple.

After an hour and a half, they agree that the site is too large and its monuments too scattered to be comprehended in one visit. Babs would have liked to have seen the tombs and memorial tablets of Prince Sado and his queen, but she gathers that they are at some distance, and would require another taxi ride. She will have to return, says Dr Oo, another day, to this fortress, and therefore to this country. Prince Sado and his queen will lure her back again one day for a second visit.

So they take their rest on a sunny bench in the Pavilion of Flowers and Willows, surrounded by a nursery class of very small children clad in dungarees and shorts and jeans and T-shirts with multilingual slogans. The children are supervised by a teenage nursery school teacher and a plump pavilion guard in a pantomime costume of yellow, black, blue and red, with a magnificently tasselled hat and a tasselled wooden sword. Dr Oo takes a photograph. Then he gets out his mobile phone and makes arrangements for a taxi to meet them to take them back into town for lunch. He has conferred with his sister's ex-student, and has been advised of an excellent restaurant in Suwon with good food and good atmosphere. Would Professor Jan van Jost and Dr Halliwell be willing to try sitting on cushions, Korean style? There is a room with Western tables, but the Korean style might be of interest?

The sister's ex-student says she would be delighted to join them for lunch, and they settle down round a low table to a feast of innumerable small dishes of rice and soup and herbs and roots and mushrooms and fishes and thin slivers of meat. A matronly lady hovers around them in a proprietorial manner, and plies them with beer and rice wine, and ladles clear broth into their bowls from a steaming cauldron. A mood of decorous conviviality is engendered, and Babs Halliwell is encouraged to tell against herself the story of her disastrous attempt to order a Korean meal when she was running alone round the city.

'I had forgotten that magic word,' she says. 'What was it, Dr Oo? Bip-Bop-Bap? Bim-Bop-Bap? Bi-Bim-Bap? I just can't keep it in my head. And then I got these nasty cold red noodles.'

'The food in China,' says Jan van Jost, 'was

excellent. But there were too many banquets, too many speeches. And I am too conventional, I did not like the feet.'

What feet, they want to know. The feet of ducks, he thinks they were. They were white and of a gristle texture. They were prized as a great delicacy, he says, but not by him. The black slugs were not so good, either, he volunteers. Snakes, says Dr Oo, are still quite popular in Korea, for rejuvenation purposes. Also, it is true that we eat dog. Bold Babs says that she has nothing against people eating dogs. If people are prepared to eat chickens and cows and ducks, then why not dogs? Dr Oo says that his favourite Dutch dish is mussels, chips and mayonnaise. It is an improbable gastronomic combination, but it is very good, says Dr Oo.

The French cuisine remains the greatest in the world, says van Jost, who reveals that his mother had taught French and English in a Dutch secondary school. Their pretty Korean guide says she is a Buddhist and a vegetarian. Not all Buddhists are vegetarians, but she is a vegetarian. She does not eat chicken or pig or cat or dog, though she does eat a little fish.

Their small talk wanders to stories of the raw and the cooked, of the pure and the impure. Van Jost has met Lévi-Strauss many times, it seems. (Babs had thought Claude Lévi-Strauss had been dead for decades, but it seems that he is still in the land of the living. Peter Halliwell's father had been acquainted with Lévi-Strauss. Had Jan been acquainted, therefore, with Peter Halliwell's father? She does not ask.) They discuss taboos and multicultural eating habits and the things they could not, would not be induced to eat. They speak of that classic work *Green Eggs and Ham*, and the well-deserved global popularity of its author, the American children's writer and educationalist Dr Seuss. Yes, his work is certainly well known in South Korea, says their Buddhist guide. It is used in schools as an English primer with much success. Then they speak of globalization. Jan says his next conference is entitled 'The Risk of Globalization, or the Globalization of Risk'. It is to be held in December on El Hierro, which is, he tells them, the most westerly and least visited of the Canary Islands. 'A little winter sunshine for all of us pale professors,' says van Jost, with a dry white smile. 'I think I can give the same paper as I gave yesterday. It is a multipurpose paper. I can add Prince Sado to my text, perhaps. 'The Leaden Casket and the Rice Chest'.'

'I suppose,' says Babs, 'that if you wanted to, you could spend your entire year going from one conference to another?'

'I could,' he says, 'if I did not feel obliged to finish my next book. But it may be that I will never finish my next book. And what would that matter? There are too many books in the world already.'

Babs does not particularly want to talk about his next book, or indeed about any of his books, because she is uneasily aware that she has never actually read any of them. She has read bits of some of them, and she has read bits of other

333

people's books about them, and she has had many interesting conversations about them, but she has never sat down with one of her new hero's seminal world-famous volumes and read it through from cover to cover. She knows what he stands for, and what he writes about, but her knowledge of his ideas has percolated into her consciousness indirectly, from non-textual sources. It has permeated her by osmosis; it has reached her by convection currents. She is a fraudulent disciple. This makes her feel morally uncomfortable, and anxious to change the subject. Moreover, she is also by now physically uncomfortable: sitting cross-legged for hours has been bad for her circulation, and if she doesn't get up soon she will have an attack of deep-vein thrombosis, and Dr Oo will have to carry her off to hospital. She wriggles, and heaves, and rearranges her long legs. She notes that her trousers are by now looking very crumpled. They were not designed for this kind of usage. Time to get back to the Pagoda Hotel and the twinned bed and the trouser press, thinks Dr Halliwell.

She is beginning to recall that this evening in Seoul there will be a British Council function at which she will be expected to say a few words. Time to get back to modern times.

Dare she ask Jan if he intends to be so gracious as to attend the British Council buffet dinner, to which he will surely have been invited? No, she dare not. She feels humble, and wishes she had read at least one of his books right through. But he is smiling, still, as they stagger to their feet, and revive their blood flow, and smooth down their crumpled garments. She is immensely impressed to discover that there will be no haggling over the bill because Jan van Jost had mysteriously pre-paid it. He is a man of the world, a gentleman. She is suddenly sure that he will be there this evening.

And, indeed, several hours and a couple of conference papers later, there he is, at her elbow, the *chevalier sans peur et sans reproche*. He has attended the British Council reception, and listened respectfully to her few well-chosen public words of gratitude for hospitality received. Babs is beginning to think that perhaps he has an end in view. Babs knows a thing or two about men, and this man is behaving like a man with a purpose. By now, she also knows a few more things about him in particular, though she is not clear whether these facts have reached her through general conference gossip or from Bob Bryant or from other sources. Van Jost, she is by now aware, has been several times married, and his current wife is said to be Spanish. That would figure. He lives in Paris and in Seville — or possibly Barcelona?

And here he is, by her side, as he had been at the Dutch Embassy, ready to escort her to the minibus that awaits to return them to the Pagoda Hotel. He sits himself down by her, and says, in a quietly attentive and intimate tone, 'It has been a long day, but a good day. I am so grateful to you and Dr Oo for this morning. It was a very unusual expedition.'

She assures him that she had enjoyed every minute of it, and was very pleased that he

335

had been able to come.

'I still have your book by the Crown Princess,' he says.

She is keenly aware of this, and badly wants to get it back, but she bides her time and says nothing.

'Perhaps you would like to come up to my room for a nightcap when we get back, and I can return it to you?' he suavely and it would seem tentatively suggests.

'That would be very nice,' says Dr Babs Halliwell, with a decorum that entirely conceals what can only be described as a sense of triumph. *Wow!* is what she is thinking. It is an almost wholly pleasurable thought, with only the slightest tinge of shame attached to it.

'I'm in Room 1712,' he says, discreetly. 'The year that Rousseau was born. The year of the publication of Pope's *Rape of the Lock*. The year before Diderot was born.'

And, to calm her nerves, he proceeds to demonstrate to her the little *Dictionary of Dates* that he keeps in his palmtop. He says he uses it constantly as an aide-mémoire. She tells him that her room number is 1517, and together they discover that this was the year that Magellan sailed on his first voyage, and the year that Martin Luther nailed his theses on the church door at Wittenberg. She agrees with him that his date dictionary is a very amusing bit of software. It is largely Eurocentric, he says, and he has found few Korean dates in it. It has nothing on the Koryo period, and nothing on the Silla. The Imo Incident of 1762 is not recorded in it, though it has one or two entries noting the *kapsin* coup of 1884, the death of the last queen of Korea in 1895, the Japanese annexation in 1910, and the North's invasion of the South in 1950. But nevertheless it is interesting and sometimes useful. He confides that he has selected the date of the great Lisbon earthquake of 1755 as his PIN. She does not tell him about 7777 and her disaster with Dr Oo's suitcase. But maybe, quite soon, she will. She feels all manner of indiscretions mounting up on her.

Dr Oo's room number, which she remembers well, is 1529, which seems to be the year that the Turks had reached the gates of Vienna. She checks this discreetly, but does not divulge it or comment upon it, for fear that Jan van Jost will think she is a scarlet woman, familiar with too many hotel bedrooms. She has not led a chaste life, but she is not a libertine, and does not wish to be taken for one.

They part, politely, in the dimly lit lobby: she says she is off to powder her nose, and will join him in ten minutes. He makes a slight bow: 'Room 1712,' he reminds her. 'The birth of Rousseau,' she responds.

Is that her putto minder, watching her, making sure she goes liftwards to her bed? Or is it some other spy, sitting darkly in the shadows?

In 1517, she does indeed powder her nose, which is looking much less offensive than it had appeared in the aeroplane toilet. She is looking good. As she brushes her bright brown and streaked yellow hair, and adjusts her underwear, and sprays herself with eau de Cologne, she congratulates herself on having drunk very little alcohol at the reception. She had been too nervous about speaking her few words of thanks to accept more than one glass of wine. She never drinks and speaks, or drinks and drives. But now she can accept a nightcap. She wonders what he will offer her? The prospect of a nightcap with the legendary van Jost is almost too exciting. Is he a man, as other men are?

She taps on his door, and he is there, immediately, in wait for her. She had been right about his accommodation. He occupies a suite: he greets her in the hallway of a large room with two large settees, an armchair or two, several occasional tables, a desk with a fax machine and various other unidentifiable executive items upon it, and a large TV set. A folding double door, slightly open, reveals a further room which contains his king-sized bed. There are vases of flowers, and bowls of fruit. And there, on a Victorian-style polished wood cocktail cabinet, is a silver tray, with various half bottles of spirits, and a bottle of champagne in an ice bucket.

'Now,' he says, in a firm and friendly manner, 'you must sit yourself down, and make a decision.'

She wonders what he is about to propose: is he about to be frontal? But no, all that he now says is, somewhat quizzically, 'You have to decide whether you would like champagne, or some other drink. The champagne is there, and it is chilled. But it may well be that you do not like champagne. Or that you think it is too late at night for champagne.'

338

Babs Halliwell, who has seated herself as instructed, is finding this scene immensely enjoyable. It is like being in a movie with a nice old-fashioned script. It is a movie, and she is the heroine.

Now, the fact is that there is nothing Babs wants less, at this point of time, than a glass of champagne. Unless, of course, it be an aphrodisiac with a bottled snake in it. Champagne is glamorous, but it is also fizzy and full of wind. It may be that Jan van Jost is longing for a glass of champagne — had he texted through to room service for it on his palmtop while she was powdering her nose? — but if so, he will have to drink it on his own. She wants something short and straight and stiff. She peers past him, as he hovers by the silver tray, and says, firmly, 'No, I don't think I'd like champagne. I'd like some of that J&B, please.'

He looks pleased with her decision and, indeed, he utters or mutters the words 'Thank God for that!' Would she like ice, or water, or soda? No, she'd like it just as it comes.

He pours her a few fingers of pale Scotch, into a cut-glass tumbler, and hands it to her. She watches with interest to see what he will select for himself. He appears to pause for a moment, then reaches for a bottle of gin. He extracts a few cubes of ice from the ice bucket, and carefully pours over them a large quantity of the transparent slightly viscous liquor. He does not add any mixer. Then he settles himself down, at her elbow. They are sitting on separate items of furniture, she in an armchair, he on the end of a settee, but they are adjacent.

'You see,' he says, as he raises his glass in a gesture towards a salutation, 'in the matters of spirits, I conform to the national stereotype. And so, it seems, do you.'

He takes a sip from his glass, and she takes a sip from hers. They both put their identical glasses down, side by side, on the glass-topped table, next to a fruit bowl.

'It was good of you to reject the champagne,' he says, after a short pause. 'If you had chosen the champagne, I should have felt obliged to drink some myself. And I am very much happier with a glass of Hollands. As it is, maybe we are both suiting ourselves.'

'I hope so,' she says.

They both take another sip.

'Are you always so well mannered?' she enquires.

'I see no virtue in bad manners,' he says. 'I was brought up to behave correctly.'

'Well, it's very pleasant to be with someone so polite,' she says.

'It is very pleasant to be with you,' he says, and again gives a little bow towards her.

'Thank you,' she says.

'I wanted to say to you,' he says, 'but so far have lacked the occasion — I wanted to say to you that I found your paper very interesting.'

This is unexpected.

'I didn't think you heard me,' she says.

'Oh, yes, I came to hear you. Did you not see me? I sat at the back in the shadows. I wished to sit quietly and without people talking to me.'

'I didn't see you,' she says. Then, a little more boldly, 'I looked for you, but I didn't see you.'

'You speak very well,' he says. 'It was a beautiful paper.'

This gives her pause. 'Beautiful' seems a very strange word for him to use in this context. It is true that he is a foreigner, and that possibly he may mean something more everyday, like 'fine' or 'good': but this she doubts, for up to this point his use of the English language has been more deliberate and accurate and refined than her own. So why should he stumble now? She does not believe that he has stumbled: he means something particular by this remark, and he will shortly, no doubt, expand upon it. She takes another sip of her J&B, her mind by now in turmoil. Maybe she has mistaken his agenda? She is, of course, immensely flattered that he had taken the trouble to attend her paper, but at the same time she is confused and disappointed. She is aware that her awareness of disappointment reveals that she had expected this assignation to end in bed, and that she had been looking forward to this denouement. Can it be her mind that he is after, and not her body? Is he intent on a heavy late-night discussion of triage, fatality, uncertainty and bone-marrow disorders? And if so, is she up to it?

'Thank you,' she says, demurely, playing for time.

He, too, takes another deliberate sip from his glass.

'Yes,' he says. 'Beautiful.'

He lets the word linger.

'And so difficult,' he says, 'with the simultaneous translation. Which is so unnecessary, as they have the text.'

Maybe he is referring to something as trivial as her delivery, which she knows to be good. She doesn't need him to tell her that she has a loud and musical voice, and that she speaks clearly.

They seem to be poised, motionless, on the edge of some glassy ridge or slope. It is not a bad place to be, but they cannot stay there for long. It is too exposed and too chilly and too alarming. She tries not to slip or waver.

'So you have no children,' he says, out of this silence.

This is a surprise move. It could lead in any direction.

'No,' she says, looking at him directly.

'You had a child who died,' he says, returning her gaze.

'Yes, I did. How did you know that?'

'I was told,' he says, unhelpfully.

Shall she ask who told him? She does not dare. But speak she must, now.

'And you?' she decides to ask. 'Do you have children?'

'Oh, yes,' he says, in a resigned and despondent manner. 'Oh, yes, I have children. But they are no longer children. They are grown now.'

She does not want to descend into the banality of an explanation of the whereabouts and a recitation of the exploits of these grown children, so she remains silent, and refuses to enquire after them. She is not interested in the grown children

342

of strangers. She is interested in the sick babies of strangers, but that is for other reasons. So she says nothing, and waits for him to continue his discourse. This strategy works well, perhaps too well.

'But my wife,' he says, 'my wife has no children.'

'Oh,' says Babs.

This is new territory. They have abandoned neutral ground. A third party has entered the room to join them, and Babs is not at all sure if she wants her there. But she is not sure how to evict her. She keeps silence, and so does he. He gives way first.

'My wife,' he says, 'is very anxious to have a child. She is very much younger than I am. She is, you know, my third wife. And I am getting old.'

She manages to assume an expression of denial, which he waves away, as though his age is not the issue. She wonders if he is about to leap into another banality, the banality of telling her that his wife does not understand him. She is not sure what she wants by now — bed or exposition, or both? She is certain that she does not want banality. She wants to continue in her admiration for this man, and she wants him to admire her.

She can see that he is bracing himself to make another significant move, and, shortly, he does.

'I want your advice,' he says.

'Yes?'

'My wife wants to adopt a baby. We shall never have a baby. I believe that she will never have a baby. I want your advice on this subject.'

'Why?' is all that she can think of to say.

She could hardly have asked a better question.

'Because,' he says, 'you look so wise and so beautiful. In those large spectacles that you always wear.'

He leans towards her now, across the firmly upholstered arms of the chair and the settee, and puts his right hand gently on the side of her face. He strokes her cheek, and then he removes her glasses, and lays them down on the glass table, between their twin tumblers of cut glass. She gazes at him, mesmerized. It is a very intimate and delicate gesture. Nobody has ever done this to her before. Nobody has ever dared to do this to her before. Does this gesture come from some well-known continental or Hollywood repertoire, written before she was born? She knows that it must, but she does not care if it does. She is entranced.

'You look just as beautiful and as wise without your glasses,' he says. 'You look like Athena.'

'Thank you,' she says.

He takes her hand now, and holds it, and caresses it. She returns the pressure. This is all very good. It cannot go wrong now.

'Tell me about your wife,' she prompts him.

His wife, it seems, is young, and she is infertile. For two or three years, she had attempted to conceive. She submitted to all the tests, and had now given up hope. 'And now,' he says, in a plain way, 'I do not wish to sleep with her anyway. I have had enough of that. That is finished between us.'

Other people have said this sort of thing to Babs Halliwell, and other people, as she has on several occasions subsequently discovered, have been lying when they said it. But nevertheless she feels inclined to believe him. She wishes to believe him. For the short period of their acquaintance, in this foreign demilitarized zone, she might as well believe him.

'My wife wants to adopt a Chinese orphan,' says Jan van Jost. 'She sent me to an orphanage in Beijing, to look at babies, and to negotiate. It is on this subject that I want your advice.'

She knows that seduction may take strange forms, but this is the strangest that she has ever encountered. He approaches her not as a swan or as a shower of golden rain, but as a prospective adoptive father. It seems that he seriously wishes to discuss with her the practicalities of transcultural adoption, and the ethics of the purchasing of an unwanted little Chinese girl.

She asks if he wants to stay married to his wife. Why not, he says. He will not marry again, he is too old, he has been married often enough. And it is easier for his wife to adopt if she is still in a regular marriage. Even in the enlightened Netherlands, he says, it is easier for a married couple to adopt than for a single person. So he will stay married to his wife for her convenience. And of course he will pay for the child, and take an interest in the child, in so far as his interest seems desirable to his wife and useful to the child.

'But what about you?' she asks. 'Do you want

345

to adopt a Chinese baby?'

'It will not matter to me,' he says. 'One way or the other.'

'Why not? What do you want?'

'At this moment,' he says, 'what I want is to be with you, and to listen to what you have to say. And I think we could talk better about this in bed.'

He is still holding her hand, and he is looking intently from his keen blue eyes into her myopic brown eyes. She leans forward towards him, slightly, and places her other hand on top of his.

'Are you sure that would be a good place to talk?' she enquires.

'Yes,' he says. Then he smiles, suddenly, in a different and less grave mode, and says, 'Well, almost sure. It would depend on whether you agreed that it might be a good idea.'

She will have to commit herself now, one way or another. The chance may not come again. Her heart is pounding. He has made it necessary for her to speak. He has cornered her into a verbal response.

'Yes,' she says, carefully following his lead and his syntax. 'Yes, I think it might be a good idea.'

She is thinking that whatever happens to her, in bed with Jan van Jost, cannot be unwelcome to her. If he wants to talk, she will talk. If he wants to make love to her, she will make love to him. If he wants to do both, she will do both. He is a very attractive man, and her hand is burning in his. His mixture of confidence and diffidence is extraordinarily calming. She feels elevated and unreal. Part of her consciousness seems to be

346

floating somewhere near the ceiling, looking down with interest and approval upon this unearthly bodily drama. She watches herself lean further towards him: he releases her hand, and cups her face with both his hands, and kisses her, very lightly but very slowly and carefully, upon the lips.

'Come,' he says, and rises to his feet, and draws her upright. She is only an inch or two taller than he is.

'I will take my glass through with me,' he says, reaching for it. 'My Dutch courage. Shall I take yours?'

But she has already picked up her glass. He leads her to the double door that opens into the spacious and luxurious bedroom: he does not attempt to carry her large person over the threshold, but he does usher her over it, with a certain formality. The bed has already been turned down, she presumes by the room staff, and two white bathrobes with royal purple trim and Pagoda monograms upon their breast pockets are laid upon it in expectant attitudes. She sits down, on what she takes to be her side of the bed, and kicks off her shoes. He takes up his bathrobe, and disappears into the bathroom. She looks around her, covertly, rapidly, taking in the large pile of books and papers and the bottles of pills on his bedside table, the beige canvas slippers neatly placed under the oriental lacquer bureau, and the aggressive television set that is openly staring from its winged mahogany shutters at the king-sized bed. One cannot tell from any of this if he is a tidy man or an untidy man. Then, rapidly, decisively, she undresses, and heaps her outer clothes on the bedside chair, and folds herself into the hotel bathrobe in her underwear, and climbs into the wide bed of Jan van Jost.

He takes his time, and, as she is about to reach for one of his bedside books, she realizes she has left her glasses in the outer room. But she does not want to get out of this bed to go to look for them, in case she is caught in some indeterminate attitude. She needs to stay where she is, looking composed. Shall she switch on the television? No, that would be very vulgar. Instead, she rapidly scans the titles of his bedside reading matter, which she can read quite well without her spectacles. Like most intellectuals, she has a habit of spying on the titles of other people's books, and the habit does not abandon her now. She recognizes the names of Ulrich Beck, Jonathan Spence, Michael Walzer and Pierre Bourdieu, the texts all well marked with Post-It notes. There are one or two Chinese titles, evidence of his recent travels — she is just trying to make out what appear to be the words 'Lu Xun' on the spine of one of these volumes when he reappears from the bathroom, wearing not the white hotel robe, but a rather attractive black Chinese silk dressing gown embroidered with dragons of scarlet and gold.

She immediately averts her eyes from his travelling library, as though caught out in an act of minor espionage, and speaks, to cover herself. 'Help,' she says. 'I've left my glasses through there, on the table.'

348

He does not ask her what she wants her glasses for, but goes off, like a gentleman, to retrieve them for her. He also takes the opportunity to switch off most of the outer lights. Then he gets into bed, by her side, and puts his arm round her shoulder. She settles against him, comfortably. He is the most reassuring, undemanding man she has ever been about to sleep with. She is amazingly happy and light of heart.

'Tell me about the Chinese babies,' she says. 'And tell me about your dressing gown. Is that Chinese, too?'

He looks down at it, somewhat absent-mindedly, as though to remind himself of its appearance and its provenance. 'Yes,' he says. 'It was a gift. People in China kept giving me things. It was very embarrassing. I am afraid it may be rather expensive. It is very much a gift culture, you know. Like Japan. But the babies, those you have to pay for.'

'Tell me more.'

'They cost about $5,000. They are not really orphans, as you know. They are little girls who have been abandoned by their parents. I think you probably know something about this from your friend Bob Bryant?'

She agrees that she does. She knows all about the tens of thousands of female babies abandoned every year, as a result of China's one-child-per-family policy. She knows about gender imbalance and the missing girls. He describes to her the cots in rows, the newborn babies sleeping quietly, the larger children

349

varying from the blank-eyed to the hopefully friendly. Some of them had been taught to utter the word 'Mama', in an attempt to arouse the attention of Western visitors. What should he do, what should he think? His wife Viveca is passionately desirous of having a baby to rear, but he cannot tell if this is a deep impulse, or a vindictive impulse, or a displaced desire, or a biological tic that will pass with time.

His hand has stolen downwards to her breast, and rests warmly upon it. She sighs. She tells him a little of the birth, the few weeks of hope and happiness, the short and isolated months, and the sad death of Baby Benedict. Does she feel deprived, maternally deprived? How can she tell? She tries to answer his unspoken questions. She says that she does not think she will ever attempt to have another baby. It is too high a risk. She has a chromosome hazard. It is getting late, and she is getting older. And she has a full life without a baby. She does not think that a woman has a right to a baby. But, with the Chinese babies, she can see that that is not the only issue. Does a baby have a right to a mother? Would Jan be doing wrong, to aid his wife in this perhaps transient whim? She does not know, she knows she is not wise enough to say.

'They were very appealing, the little ones,' says van Jost. Would she like to see some photographs? He has a wallet of photographs, here, by the bed.

It is clear that he wants her to see the photographs, he needs her to see them. She does not wish to see them, but she knows she must submit. She reaches for her glasses, he reaches for the wallet. She inspects the grave little faces. Each child has an institutional name and a number. Tears gather in her eyes. They brim over.

'It is too sad,' she says. 'It is too sad.'

'Dying by Lot: Uncertainty and Fatality,' he replies, in her own formula. 'Dying by lot, living by lot. It is not often in a lifetime that one confronts these issues. You have been there, and I find myself there now.'

She turns to him, and he takes her in his arms. He reaches out, and dims, but does not wholly extinguish, the bedside light. Then he proceeds to make love to her, slowly, patiently, carefully. She is at once very sad and very happy. He is considerate and efficient, and seems to know exactly what he is doing, and moreover he seems to want to do it, but she does not feel that he is wholly present in the act. Although he is generously and indeed respectfully paying her so much attention in the body, he seems at the same time to be remote and withheld. Is this because he is so old, and has done this kind of thing so often? He is the oldest man with whom she has ever shared a bed. Is he thinking about the Chinese babies, or about his impatient and expensive young wife, or about something altogether different? Something on a higher and a more abstract intellectual plane?

Afterwards, they disengage, and he lies back against his pillows for a while, with his arm round her shoulders. He is breathing evenly and deeply, but seems to be making some effort to do

351

so, as though he were engaged in a postcoital form of yoga or transcendental meditation. Then he sits up, and reaches towards his bedside table, and pours himself a glass of water, and opens one of his pill bottles, and swallows a pill.

'I have to take care not to exert myself too much,' he says, in self-deprecating apology for this unromantic act.

It is a satisfactory explanation. At once she is all womanly concern.

'Would you like me to make you a cup of tea?' she asks, with her best bedside manner. Then, hearing herself, she starts to laugh, and fortunately he, too, seems to find her remark comic. But he agrees that, yes, a cup of tea would be very acceptable at this point in the night, but he will get out of bed and make it for her, she is his guest. No, no, she insists, she will do it, what sort of tea would he like, she thinks that there is green tea, and English tea, and various herbal teas? She leaps out, before he can forestall her, and struggles back into the white and purple bathrobe, and marches into the outer room, whence she calls back to him the names on the various herbal sachets. They both settle for ginseng, on the grounds that it is the most appropriate beverage for their situation, and she brews it up, and carries back a mug for each of them. They sit up side by side, upright against the high pillows, inhaling the rare and much-prized aroma.

'Well?' says Jan van Jost.

'Very well, thank you,' says Babs Halliwell, politely.

352

'I knew you were a wise woman,' he says.

'I'm not sure what evidence you think I've given of that,' she says.

In response, he puts his hand on her knees.

'Now you, of course, are well known to be a wise man,' she says.

'I used to think I was wise,' he says. 'But now I have reached the recommended Socratic stage of knowing that I know nothing. You have not reached that point yet. You are far too young. And it is quite right that you have not reached it yet.'

'I think I'd better get back to Room 1517,' she says, as she drains her ginseng. 'Funny stuff, this, isn't it? Do you think it does any of the things it's meant to do?'

'You could sleep here,' he says. 'It is a big bed.'

'No, I think not,' she says firmly. She has no wish to push her luck.

'No,' she repeats. 'I'd disturb you. I sleep better alone. I'm a very restless sleeper. I toss around a lot.'

She thinks he seems relieved by this, as he has every right to be. At his age, why should he wish to give up bed space to a large, strange Englishwoman? She picks up her heaps of garments from the chair, and visits his bathroom, and reclothes herself, and emerges to bid him goodnight. It is half past two in the morning. It is respectably late, but not recklessly late.

'Anyway,' she says, as she stoops over him to kiss him goodnight, and forbids him to get up to see her out, 'I have to be up early. I've got an

353

early appointment at the National Women's Hospital, as I think I said. To see some Korean babies.'

'But you won't disappear?' he asks.

'I'll be back for Bob Bryant's paper in the afternoon,' she says.

'I've got some press interviews tomorrow,' he says, 'but I, too, hope to get to hear your friend Bob Bryant.'

'I may see you there,' she says.

'I hope so,' says he.

★   ★   ★

The Korean babies lie in orderly, hygienic rows in little white cribs in their long ward. The cribs are decorated with coy international non-denominational Disney-style cartoon figures in pastel shades. In Dr Halliwell's view, these cartoons are regrettable, but they are no doubt well meant. She pushes memories of the sad teddy bears of Great Ormond Street to the back of her mind, as she peers at the wise and enigmatic little faces of the babies, and listens to the details of their treatment. These children are not orphans, even nominally, and they are very well cared for, but the life chances of most of them are not good. Is it better to be a healthy Chinese girl child in an orphanage in Beijing or Shanghai, with a small but growing statistical possibility of being adopted either abroad or at home by an affluent family, or to be a much-loved Korean child suffering from a rare life-threatening illness? Dr Halliwell's interest in these conundrums is professional and abstract and theoretical, but she is a human being and was once a mother, and the sight of these babies cannot fail to touch her. She listens to statistics and prognoses and makes notes in her notebook. She discusses the recent setbacks in the gene therapy trials at the Necker Hospital in France, where some young patients appear to have been producing an abnormal and monoclonal proliferation of T-lymphocytes. The cure may be as fatal as the disease. She nods, and questions, and assents. Her dry white brain has forgotten her night in the arms of Jan van Jost, and it thinks not of him. But her liquid body remembers him.

She returns to her body in the taxi on the way back to the Pagoda Hotel. Her body, as she rejoins it, is at first in a mild state of anxiety, at having been forgotten for so long, but it soon informs her that all is well with it. Indeed, all is exceptionally well with it. It is simultaneously satisfied and aroused. It is a long time since it has felt so satisfied. The positional skirmishes with Robert Treborough after the Gladwyn Dinner had been most unsatisfactory and unsatisfying. All that her body needs now is a little reassurance.

She and it are shortly to receive that reassurance. When she enters Room 1517, she finds a large bunch of flowers waiting for her. That, in itself, might not be very pleasant — indeed, if that were all that were to be awaiting her, it might be classed as inadequate, or even unpleasant. But there is also, on the desk by the side of the vase of flowers, a letter, with her name upon it, in handwriting that is not the handwriting of a hotel functionary, although the envelope bears the hotel's logo. She has a letter. What will it say? She feels young again, and full of hope, as she prises it open.

It is only a note, but it is more than adequate. It sagely avoids any form of address. It is short, but it is clear. It says:

Happily, you forgot to take your book with you, so you must come back again this evening to collect it. Would you like to have dinner with me beforehand? You could leave me a voice message. But perhaps I will see you at Bob Bryant's paper? I have only two more nights in Seoul, so I very much hope you will be free this evening. There are so many questions I want and need to ask you.

Just as there is no opening salutation, so there is no phrase of farewell. He has signed himself, simply, and she thinks rather modestly, *Jan van J.*

So this, she reflects, as she stares at this wonderfully clearly expressed billet-doux, is the hand and signature of Jan van Jost. He seems to write with old-fashioned blue ink. She wonders if his letters are worth a lot of money: how do sociologists rate in book collecting and bibliographical terms? Not very highly, she suspects. What a mean thought! She banishes it at once. She is a little flustered and very full of what feels like uncomplicated happiness. Shall she leave him a voice message, saying yes to everything?

356

Shall she count on seeing him at Bob's paper? Shall she accept dinner? What shall she do? What would be the most elegant, the most acceptably appreciative response? He is a busy man and at any point during the day he may be waylaid by the press or by the television or by another invitation to the Blue House. She does not think he will be waylaid by a *femme fatale*, as there are not many of them around at this serious conference or in this respectable hotel, but there are doubtless other uncertainties abroad, waiting to entrap him. How can she secure him? He seems to wish to be secured, he seems to wish to secure her, or he wouldn't have gone to so much trouble with his prose style, would he?

She is still wondering what to do when her bedroom phone starts to ring. She picks it up, and it is he, on a very bad line. 'Dr Halliwell? Is that you? You are back?' Is he about to cancel everything? No, he simply wants to tell her that he'll be back from the television station in an hour, and will see her in the auditorium in the afternoon. Did she get his note? Yes? She doesn't have to have dinner with him, but, if she would like to, he will book a table. 'Yes, please,' she hears herself say, across the crackling airwaves.

So that is all settled, then. She is in a high good humour, as she takes her seat towards the back of the Sejong Auditorium. And here he comes, as arranged, prompt upon his cue. He takes his place beside her, and leans towards her to give her a friendly professorial peck upon the cheek, as though they were the oldest of friends instead of the newest of lovers. She cannot help

357

smiling a little too much, and neither can he. She wonders if their new relationship is visible to the entire audience. Are they lit up, as by a spotlight? Do they glow? He is the most desirable man in the world, even though she has never been able to finish any of his books. Surely they must be radiating their luminous mutual delight! People stare at him anyway because he is famous, and she cannot be sure if they are staring at him with any new intensity. Is she captured like the moon in the reflection of his brightness? She settles, expectantly, and they both listen respectfully as Bob Bryant speaks to them on the unexpectedly relevant topic of fertility rates and gender imbalance in post-industrial societies. As Bob speaks, Jan, beneath the bench, lays a secret and confirming hand upon her knee. They are in the public eye, but they are alone, and they are alone together, his hand tells her.

She is completely in love with him, and knows she will remain so for the whole of the next two days. She had forgotten what it was like to feel so innocently in love. The past recedes and vanishes; the distant future stands still. She is here, in the present.

He has booked a table for them in one of the restaurants of another de luxe hotel, two minutes' walk away and just round the corner from the Pagoda: 'I'm sorry,' he says, as they settle themselves in their discreet alcove, 'it is not very imaginative to come here, but without our friend Dr Oo I cannot cope with the Korean menu, and Dr Oo says the food here is good.'

She is glad that they seem to have the blessing

of Dr Oo, her guardian angel. And the food is good, though they do not pay very close attention to it. They are too busy talking.

Three days, they agree over dinner, is a good length of time for a modern romance, though perhaps it may not be quite long enough for them to exchange all the information that seems to pour from each of them, as they begin to exchange their life stories.

He tells her about his childhood. He speaks of his father, who was a miner in the black coalfields of Limburg, and his mother, who was a schoolteacher. He comes from a hard-working, upwardly mobile and self-respecting family. A classic background for a sociologist, he says. His parents were determined that their sons should not go down the mine. An uncle had died underground, trapped in the famous pit disaster of 1948. He remembers well the drama of this death. He himself had been down that mine but once, quite recently, on an anniversary occasion, with a group of journalists. In 1988, he thinks it was. It had been an alarming experience. 'I have this tendency to claustrophobia,' he says. 'Perhaps caused by these events, and by having been reared in the Low Countries. I do not like it below the earth. I have never liked the Channel Tunnel. I make myself travel under the Channel, but I do not like it.'

His parents, he says, had sacrificed much for their children. They had lived frugally for their sake, and the children had studied hard for their parents' sake. He had risen steadily through the excellent state system of the Netherlands to higher degrees in Paris and the United States. Yes, he is happy to say that his parents did live to enjoy his success, and to retire in comfort. But sometimes he wonders if he was not obliged, as a boy, to work too hard and to aspire too much. School examinations, on which his career and his family's fortunes depended. Examinations, followed by degrees, then yet more degrees. Competition, competition. Well, as she will know, he has written much about this. Climbing, climbing, always climbing. It is stressful. It does harm.

He needs to tell her these things because he knows she will listen with indulgence. And so she does.

'Now you need climb no more,' she says. 'You are at the very top.'

He shrugs his shoulders at that, and smiles his wry smile.

'And you?' he asks. 'You, too, have worked hard, it appears.'

She disclaims unusual effort. She declares herself to be an archetypal middle-class grammar-school girl from Orpington, the daughter of a family doctor and a schoolteacher from the West Country. Her parents had met, conventionally, at university, and were still married. She had taken her first degree at the University of Sussex, her second at Oxford. She tells him of her average happy childhood, of her average hard-working happy parents, of her lawyer sister and her journalist brother. She was expected to do well at school, to go to college, to have a career, and she had been aspiring and ambitious. But nothing had been staked upon her. The family fortunes did not depend on her. Examinations had not been a threat to her. 'I was free,' she says, 'to choose my own mistakes. I was fortunate.'

As she says this, she wonders, not for the first time, if this can be wholly true. She wonders why she is so anxious to present herself as a normal person. She thinks of Orchard View, in suburban Orpington, and of the swing in the garden, and of the goldfish pond. She thinks of her paternal grandmother's Orpington garden, with its orchard and its vegetable patch and its gooseberry bushes. She thinks of her maternal grandmother's house in Devon, with its sloping lawn and its grey-barked mauve-blossomed tree, the tree she had loved so much. It is true that she had been a happy child.

'I am a very English person,' she says. 'As far as I know, all my genes are English. This will become more rare, I think.'

He agrees that the nations of the world are merging. They comment on the faces of Seoul, the capital of what was once called the 'Hermit Kingdom'. It, too, is changing. Seoul and South Korea are now open to the world. China, he tells her, is still very Chinese. And North Korea still lives in isolation and in fantasy.

They do not, at this point, discuss the ethics of multicultural adoption, but the subject is present to both of them.

'You are English,' he says, as the waiter removes the soup bowls, 'but you are well travelled.'

'Who, these days, is not?' she replies.

'And perhaps, also, you are not typical,' he says.

'I think types also are changing,' she says. 'They, too, are not what they were. Types, archetypes. Even an archetype can mutate.'

He smiles at her, and half raises his glass to her.

'You are the first and last and only Englishwoman I have known,' he says.

She feels herself, astonishingly, to be blushing, for she knows that he is using the verb 'to know' in a carnal sense. She hides her rare blush behind her napkin, as the waiter approaches with the duck.

Having dealt with their parents over soup, they move on to the subject of their spouses with the duck.

Jan is forthcoming about his wives. She is flattered by his confidence. Either he trusts her not to kiss and tell, or he does not care if she does. His first wife was American, he says, his second French. His first wife was modest, and so were her two sons. They are still on good terms. His second wife is extortionate, both on her own behalf and on behalf of her two daughters. His French wife, he says ruefully, is a paradox. She has adopted the alimony culture, although she says she despises America, and he has had to pay the price. His third and current wife is different. She is crazy. She is a wild card. She is half Spanish, half Swedish. Jan says it is a lethal combination, a disastrous and dangerous genetic mix. Too much merging, too sudden a conjunction of cultures. He should never have married her, but she had been very insistent.

'She followed me round,' says Jan, plaintively, as he dabs at his pale lips with the damask napkin. 'She pursued me. From country to country, from university to university, from conference to conference. What is that word for what people do when they follow celebrities?'

'Stalk?' suggests Babs.

'Yes, 'stalk'. That is the word. She stalked me. She would not let me go. So I married her.'

'You must have fancied her,' says Babs.

'Oh, yes, I did 'fancy' her, as you say. I was in love with her. I loved her. I was vain, and I was pleased that she followed me. She is very clever and very beautiful. But she is also mad. And she is manipulative. I knew this, all along. I should not have allowed myself to be captivated. She is not at all a stable person. She wanted to have a baby with me, a 'genius baby' as she used to say, and look what has happened to that bad plan. It is a very good thing that she cannot have a baby. I am not at all sure if she is capable of looking after a Chinese baby. It is all very sad. In fact, it is a tragedy.'

He looks more ironic than tragic as he says this. He seems to have become resigned to the situation.

'What does your wife do?' asks Babs, as the plates are cleared.

'Do? She does nothing. She writes letters — she writes crazy letters to the press and to my colleagues. She takes singing lessons. She has a good voice, mezzo-soprano. Once she wanted to

363

sing in opera. She is very *maniaque*. She says she believes in horoscopes and messages from the spirit world. She says she can invoke god of thunder, and god of water, and god of underworld, and god of riches, and god of health. This is not true, as I do not need to say. And she does not think that it is true. She plays games. She buys clothes; all the time. She is a shopper. She runs up bills at couture houses. I have had to cancel her accounts with some of the houses and stores. But maybe if she acquires this baby on which she has set her heart, she will become a normal person again. However, this is a big risk.'

Babs agrees that it would be a big risk. But Babs is a kind-hearted person, and she feels secretly sorry for this unknown mad woman, the last wife of Mr Rochester. Also, she thinks that Jan himself is not entirely alienated from this wife, for he speaks of her extravagances with a rueful pride. His own clothes, moreover, are not cheap. He is no stranger to *haute couture*. He may have set his crazy wife a bad example.

She volunteers, sympathetically, that her own husband, to whom she is still legally married, is not wholly sane. But he is not therefore to be wholly written off and abandoned, she says.

Jan van Jost seems to know a good deal about Peter Halliwell. And, as she had half suspected, he does indeed seem to have been acquainted at some point in the past with Peter's father, the charismatic and delinquent anthropologist. She cannot decide whether he has known what he knows for a long time, or whether he has been secretly interrogating Bob Bryant in the bar of the Pagoda Hotel. Perhaps in the privacy of his suite he has been curious enough about her past to press prying questions into his globally connected palmtop. The Internet has a fair amount of information about Halliwell *père et fils*, though Babs does not spend much time looking for it. There is too much there that she does not want to know.

Babs is not sure if she wants to talk to Jan about Peter, although it was she that brought him up. She hopes that Jan's interest in her is not in any way connected with her late father-in-law. She is pleased when, over coffee, they move to more present topics.

Over coffee Jan reverts to the memoirs of the Crown Princess, and thanks her, yet again, for introducing him to them. They had been full of fascination for him, he repeats, although he is not yet sure why. The oedipal conflict, the state examination stress, the palace intrigues, the arcane Confucian system, the clothing phobia, the claustrophobic death in the rice chest? (Interestingly, he does not mention the nature of the unique voice of the female narrator: this does not seem to have struck him as forcibly as it has struck her.) He embarks on a brilliant and well-illustrated digression on the nature of claustrophobia and enclosure: it is so brilliant and it makes her mind race so fast that she can hardly bear to listen to it, though she knows she ought to be trying to concentrate on this privileged discourse. He is the best talker she has ever stared at across a dining table, and there have been some strong competitors. Will his words lodge, somewhere, in some part of her cerebral cortex, whence she will be able to hook them out at some calmer, less erotically charged moment?

He tells her that although he does not know why he has been so interested in the story of the Crown Princess, which had brought them together so strangely and in his view so happily, he does know that he has her to thank for their most enjoyable and interesting visit to Suwon. Suwon will always be one of his happiest and most surprising travel memories. 'It has been a great pleasure to me,' he says, formally, 'to make your acquaintance here. I was not expecting to find any happiness here. I was so very tired, when I flew in from China. I was so very, very tired. You have given me a new lease of life, for these few days.'

He raises his glass to her, and salutes her. She likes his oblique and old-fashioned language and his manners very much. They gaze at one another, intently, over the heavily starched white tablecloth, blue eye to brown eye, as lovers gaze, attempting to read the soul. Despite the rapid telepathic exchanges and short cuts of their long conversation, he has some secret that she cannot read. Whatever it is, it draws her. She gazes into the depths of its enigma. He is at once so present and so absent. She can see many reasons why a woman might want to stalk this man. He is famous; he is handsome; he is urbane. He is well dressed and in every way well presented, and presumably, despite the alimony and the

366

high-spending Viveca, he is rich. He is also very quick and very clever. (Well, he would be, wouldn't he?) But there is more to it than that. There is some other attraction in him that calls to her. Will she have time to discover what it is, in the next two short days they will have together? Or will she, too, be compelled to stalk him? Will she find herself tracking him down at the globalization conference on El Hierro? Will she turn up on his doorstep there, to the music of the wild Atlantic surges, like the lady from the sea?

She knows that she will not stalk him to El Hierro, or to any other place. Unlike Viveca, she is not at all mad. She is sane and she is healthy, and she has a busy life of her own. This is a mantra that she repeats to herself frequently, and for years, whether she believes it or not, it has served her well. She knows and she thinks he knows that he has nothing to fear from her. She will not demand improbable gifts from him or set him impossible tasks. She will not strike dangerous bargains with him. She will not commission him to purchase jewels or Chinese babies for her. She will make no demands on him. What harm can there be, for either of them, in an affair of three days?

They walk back together, arm in arm, to the Pagoda Hotel, down the hot brightly lit street, past the street traders with their busy stalls. The city is glamorous, and its aroma is exotic: odours of gasoline and spices and pickle and burnt sugar and fish mingle in the night air. They are in no hurry; there is a whole night before them. A large yellow Chusŏk harvest moon, almost at the full, floats in the thick and hazy sky. They pass a row of twelve policemen sitting neatly on the pavement on their helmets, by their police bus. It is a strange and curiously orderly sight. Babs reflects, as she walks, that she is lucky to live in modern times, in peaceful, prosperous times. Jan and Babs observe, move on, and linger, gazing at fast food and heaps of merchandise. They pass the stall selling hosiery, and Babs's eyes fall once more upon the scarlet butterfly-patterned knee-high socks. She does not think that Jan has seen her eyeing them, but he has. He is very quick, on her behalf. He has seen her yearning backward glances as they move on. He cross-questions her, she confesses, and he returns to buy her a pair. They cost a few pence. She is not as expensive as the second wife, or the third, he tells her. They are not a very handsome gift. He is ashamed to offer them to her, they are so cheap.

'But I love them,' she says. 'They'll probably be far too small for me. Everyone here is so petite. But they are so pretty. And I do so like red.'

They are not too small for her. They stretch to accommodate her large feet. Later, in bed, they both admire the butterflies. She keeps the socks on, at his request, while they make love, this time more energetically, more confidently, and for a little longer. She knows the routine by now: afterwards, he will reach for his pills, and she will make him a mug of tea.

The supply of ginseng has not been replenished. He selects jasmine; she camomile.

This second selection process has acquired a pleasantly domestic intimacy.

As they drink their teas, he switches on the television, and they sit there, sedately, side by side, watching an oriental operatic spectacular with the sound turned very low. It seems to be coming from some special Chinese commercial satellite channel, beamed towards Korea. He tells her about the bizarre Chinese opera he had seen in Beijing, with its startling libretto, and he describes the rows of underground terracotta warriors entombed in Xian. She tells him about the rehearsals for the Confucian ancestral rites that she had seen with Dr Oo in the gardens of the Munmyo shrines. She tells him about the pale and awful haunch of sacrificial meat. They speak, a little, of the marriage of Prince Sado and the Crown Princess, and Babs's eyes flit covertly towards the heap of books on his bedside table. She can't see the orange and carmine Yellow Fields Press spine of the memoirs, amidst the tower of volumes of philosophy and sociology and linguistics and biography that she had inspected the night before, and she really doesn't want to leave without them. It would be an honour to have a book stolen from her by Jan van Jost, but she'd rather have the book than the honour. It may be out of print. The mysterious donor from Amazon may have sent her the last available copy. She has never heard of the press or the imprint, and suspects they might prove elusive.

Again, he reads her mind. 'You can have it back tonight,' he says, 'but only if you agree now

369

to come back tomorrow night.'

'You may not want me to come back tomorrow night,' she says.

'No,' he says. 'It is you that may not want to. But I am asking you to come back to me tomorrow night. This is important for me. Three nights is correct. It is a magic number. Two is inartistic. And I am a very superstitious person. I shall always be unhappy about you and always regret you, if you do not return to me for the last night. Also, tomorrow night, you must give me your wise and beautiful advice.'

Of course, she agrees to return. How could she resist? There is nothing she wants more than to spend one more night with him. She would have been mortified had he wished otherwise. They make a pact. Now, she will return to Room 1517, with the memoirs. But they will agree to meet the next day. The next day will be his last and her penultimate day in Seoul: he is scheduled to speak at the National University; she at Ewha Woman's University. They both have lunch engagements. In the afternoon, there is free time. In the evening, there will be the official conference banquet, where they will see each other from a distance. After the banquet and the speeches, they will repair to Suite 1712, and spend their final night together, and exchange their final confidences.

'So, it is agreed,' says the miner's son.

'Yes, it is agreed,' says the doctor's daughter.

This time, she remembers to take the book, but, when she gets back to her room, she finds she has left her glasses by Jan van Jost's bed. Oh, well, never mind. She has lots of pairs of glasses. She is always losing her glasses. He will keep them safely for her, until their last tryst.

★ ★ ★

The miner's son and the doctor's daughter do not see one another again until the final banquet. Babs Halliwell, in happy anticipation of their reunion, shamelessly enjoys her day. The campus of Ewha Woman's University is spacious and finely landscaped. It occupies a hillside with trees and statues and buildings ancient and modern. The members of staff are charming; the students seem courteously interested in what she has to say. Babs admires the valuable collection of ancient ceramics and the rich display of textiles in the University Museum. She feels that her eye for things Korean is improving a little: objects that had at first seemed formless are beginning to take on form. She is gaining perspective, and seeing better. She cannot yet care for dragons, but maybe in time she will learn to like them, too.

She lunches on the Pear Blossom Campus with her hosts, and they talk of the changing lives of women in Korea: they all agree with her that they are fortunate to live in modern times. This is the largest women's university in the world, claim her hosts, with 17,000 students, at least some of whom will move on into careers and professions. A whole army of fashion vendors is encamped in the shopping street just outside the university gates, ready to waylay the young scholars and to divert them from their higher purposes, tempting them with heaped emporia of shoes and jeans and cosmetics and evening gowns and wedding dresses. But some will surely make their way safely through the consumer gauntlet. It is a shame that the wedding-dress industry thrives so well in Seoul, and that such fortunes are wasted upon weddings, says Professor Pak, shaking her well-groomed head in mild pedagogic censure. It is not the custom to spend so much in Europe, she believes?

It depends on your social class, says Babs, who had married Peter Halliwell in midsummer in a register office in Bromley, clad in a full-length, bright-red cotton dress made in Morocco. Those had been the days.

Babs thinks, with guilty affection, of her cheap and frivolous red socks, and of the little red skirt of the Crown Princess. She thinks of mentioning the Crown Princess, but the conversation strays elsewhere, and she does not do so. This is perhaps a pity, for had Babs mentioned her, she would have learned that a professor attached to this very campus had recently published a bestselling historical detective story involving the princess and her son, King Chŏngjo. She will discover this one day, but not yet.

Boldly, after accepting a soothing cup of tea in a traditional tearoom, she insists on returning alone by the subway to her hotel. Her hosts bow to her desire to test herself in this manner. She survives the journey triumphantly, without making a false move. She is pleased with herself.

She has conquered the subways of Seoul. Back at the hotel, she finds a message on her machine from Dr Oo. He says he is leaving for Amsterdam the next day; will she be able to find time to say goodbye? She rings him back in his room, but he is out. She leaves a message suggesting that they could take breakfast together the next day in the Jade Coffee Shop, if he is not leaving at dawn. At eight-thirty, perhaps?

She takes a slow bath, and dresses carefully for the final banquet. She is feeling ridiculously happy. Her stay here, after its inauspicious opening, perhaps because of its inauspicious opening, has been glorious to her. She feels purged of old regrets and sorrows, charged with a new energy. Dr Oo and Professor Jan van Jost have done wonders for her morale. Between them, through their differing kindnesses, they have transformed her from a gross and stupid woman into a wise and beautiful woman. She feels power crackling through her hair, as she brushes it and ties it back with a golden ribbon. She clips a pair of dangling golden earrings to her ears, and fastens a golden necklace around her throat. She is in the prime of life, she tells herself, as she admires herself in the mirror in her long black silky crushproof rayon dress.

Her jewellery is not made of real gold. She would not travel with articles of real gold, even if she had any. The pieces that she wears are what shops used to call 'costume jewellery', and now call 'travel jewellery'. The pieces are made of what the police call 'yellow metal'. But the metal shines brightly. It glitters. She glitters.

Her guardian sylphs and spirits watch benignly. They approve of her appearance. They frequently urge her to pay more attention to her toilette. They deplore her intermittent moods of negligence and indifference. She may be an academic, but she is also a woman, as they often attempt to remind her, in their old-fashioned way. This anonymous and well-lit hotel room has been conducive to neatness and good grooming. At one point they had thought of urging her to book an appointment with the hotel hairdresser, but they had relented. In a few years, as they will be sure to advise her, she will be obliged to alter her hairstyle to one of greater gravitas. But, for the moment, this informal, beribboned mode will suffice. They circle round her, checking her from all angles, inspecting her hemline and her shoulder pads and her neckline, and they decide that she will do. She is ready to descend. They usher her out, towards the lift, and gaze after her as she goes to join the throng. Mong Joon, they know, will take over the task of surveillance on the floors below.

The banqueting hall is laid with many tables. At one end of the room there is a platform. There will be speeches and photographs. Dr Halliwell launches herself bravely upon the social sea, and floats from shoal to shoal. She chatters and laughs and utters compliments; she peers at labels and congratulates herself on the fact that during these five days she has correctly registered and recalled the names of a fair proportion of her colleagues. Most of them, modestly, are still wearing their labels. Most of these people are polite and unassuming. She is still wearing her own label, pinned high at a jaunty angle on her left shoulder.

Dr Barbara Halliwell does her tour of the stateroom floor, closely watched by the supervisory gaze of Mong Joon, who, towards the end of her perambulation, approaches her, ostensibly to steer her towards her table, but also to utter what she takes to be a remonstrance. It will be his last chance to control her: his official supervision of her ends with this banquet, for tomorrow she moves, for her last day, to the protection of the pharmaceutical company. But she somehow knows he will pop up again at the airport, just to make sure she leaves the country on time and as arranged.

'You have been very busy during your visit,' says Mong Joon. 'I hear that you went two days ago to Suwon with two gentlemen?' He does not quite wag his finger at her, but his intonation implies that he might well have done so.

'Yes, indeed I did,' she says, primly. 'It was a very interesting outing.'

She can see that a smile is hovering somewhere behind his smoothly dimpled, diplomatic features. She hopes to God he has not heard about the fiasco with the royal bidet and the emergency alarum. If so, she blames that pretty Buddhist in her blue jeans and lemon-yellow top. She is probably Mong Joon's sister or his cousin or his aunt.

'This is your table,' he says, and he firmly pulls out her chair. There, indeed, is her place, and her name card. She sits herself down, obediently.

As the meal and the speeches proceed, she manages to locate her brand-new three-day lover. He is sitting two tables away from her, between the president of the foundation and a handsome Korean woman wearing a stylish emerald-green, gold-trimmed, short-cut satin jacket and a tight long skirt. Maybe she is the president's wife? Jan seems to be paying her a great deal of attention. He is inclining his head towards her, and listening to her with an attitude of studied concentration. Jan is too far away from Babs for Babs to be able to read his features. She is amused to find that she experiences a mixture of jealousy and possessiveness, as she watches him from afar. She knows that she has no right to either of these emotions. And they do not go very deep, which is why she is able to find them so pleasurable. For she is certain that he cannot be talking to the president's wife about Chinese babies. Well, almost certain. Surely the Chinese babies are a bedtime secret that he shares with her alone?

She takes her cue from Jan van Jost, and applies herself to the entertainment of the neighbour sitting on her left, who proves to be the chair of a committee on medical ethics in Kyoto. He asks her if she has been to Japan, and she says no. She asks him if he has been to London, and he says that he has. As they engage in shallow tourist talk, her mind wanders round the room, overhearing words from other people's conversations as they mingle in the common air. Has the conference been a success, she wonders?

Has it achieved anything? Will it have improved the quality or provision or distribution of useful medication? Will it have enabled exciting exchanges of ideas to take place? Will it have enhanced the careers of any of its delegates, or brought more trade or higher status to its pharmaceutical sponsors? Will the new frontiers of health have been shifted to any perceptible or useful degree by the formal presentation of academic papers, by the generous press coverage, by the informal international gatherings in the hotel bar, by the eccentric group outing to the Expo, or by this grand assembly of sober-suited gentlemen and gaily clad ladies? Or has the whole thing simply been an elaborate corporate tax break?

There is a lot of soft money floating around in the ethically dubious sea of medical and pharmaceutical research, and some of it has drifted in the direction of the clever and well-connected Dr Barbara Halliwell. She has had a lucky year. Next year, she will have to work harder, and teach longer hours. Dr Barbara Halliwell thinks, briefly, of Dr Oo and his underfunded stroke patients. She wonders if he got her message about meeting for breakfast in the coffee shop.

For the first hour or so of the banquet, she savours the agreeable suspense and anticipation of waiting for her amorous assignation in Suite 1712. But eventually she begins to grow restless, and she is relieved when the formal proceedings seem to be drawing to an end. Thanks are given; toasts are drunk; applause is rendered. It is during one of the bouts of applause that she notes that Jan van Jost is rising to his feet and making his farewells. He has had enough. He is off to his bed. Is he abandoning her? What shall she do? She is wondering whether he intends that she should follow him, and, if so, how soon she may discreetly do so, when she sees that he is not leaving the room directly, but making his way towards her table. Is he about to cancel their last night together? Is he ill, or exhausted, or disaffected? It will break her heart if he cancels. She half rises, in anticipation of some rebuff. But no, a rebuff is not his intention. He has come not to reject her, but to claim her. He bends towards her, whispers, 'Please, let us go now.' He offers his arm, to help her to her feet. She rises, smiles her excuses vaguely round and about her table, and follows him, as he makes for the exit.

Do many spies turn to watch them as they leave the Grand Saloon together? Is their departure noted? They do not look back to see, but walk onwards, through the high portals, and into the wide and richly carpeted foyer of the mezzanine floor. They make their way towards the lift, and Jan van Jost presses the button to ascend. In the lift, he presses the button for Executive Floor 17. He looks at her now, and she can see that his world-weary face is suffused with a strange glitter. His eyes have a bright and visionary look, as though he has seen something strange. She almost asks him if he is feeling all right, but, as she hesitates, he speaks first.

'I had to get out of there,' he says. 'Suddenly, I

could not breathe in there. I am sorry. To make you leave like this.'

Is he speaking literally or figuratively about his breathing problem? She cannot tell. Quickly, she assures him that she, too, had had quite enough of the banquet, and she watches, a little anxiously, as he fumbles with his electronic key. Has he been drinking? She thinks not. Unlike Peter Halliwell and Robert Treborough and others she has known, he is not, she thinks, a hard-drinking man. The green eye blinks, and they enter Suite 1712, which welcomes them as though it had been expecting them. Babs sinks on to the settee, in a casually premeditated manner, and kicks off her high party heels, to show that she is at home. He sits by her, and takes her hand in his, and compels her to turn her head towards him, to meet his gaze. They look at one another, and, once more, he removes her glasses, and kisses her. It is an attentive but not an impassioned kiss. Then he says:

'Last night, you left a pair of your glasses here. I have kept them safely for you. They are on the bedside table, where you left them. You must remember to take them, this time, because tomorrow morning I go home with all my problems to my wife in Barcelona. You must take all your possessions with you, tonight.'

She promises him that she will check carefully before she leaves. She will leave no incriminating evidence.

She has no idea what will happen, on this last evening. His mood and his manner are strange. She does not know him well enough to guess what they might signify. What does he want of her? Had he been serious in his request for her advice? For her 'wise and beautiful' advice? Or does he want a third night in bed with her? Or both? She finds that she does not mind much what he wants. It is enough that he wants to be with her, for whatever reason. She finds his company extraordinarily delightful, and she would like to be with him for ever, during this last night.

He nurses her hand for a few moments, then kisses it before he relinquishes it.

'I have a gift for you,' he says. 'It is a small gift, but I did purchase it for you myself. I would not like you to think that it was given to me in China, and that I am passing it on to you in a second-hand manner. I purchased it expressly for you here this afternoon. It is a proper gift for a scholar to give a scholar. I will give it to you now, and you must put it in a safe place so that you do not forget it.'

The gift is standing on top of the fax machine on the executive desk by the curtained window. He goes to get it for her, and he presents it to her. It is about eight inches high, and it is square, and it is elaborately wrapped in many layers. Does he want her to open it now? He does. She has always hated opening presents in front of their donors, but he is so calm and confident about his gift that she embarks upon its unveiling with an almost equal confidence. She detaches the envelope containing a card with her name upon it, lays it to one side, unties the first bow of string, removes the outer bag of stiff brown paper, then makes her way through various differently and subtly coloured and textured layers of what he assures her is handmade mulberry paper. Finally, she comes to the object itself. It is a little lacquered cabinet, with many tiny drawers. Its every surface is covered with a different pattern in different colours. It is exquisitely made. Is it a priceless antique? She hopes and fears that it is. 'Open the drawers,' he urges her, and she opens them, one after the other. The drawers are also lined with coloured paper, each in a different and intricate pattern, and they are full of tiny scholarly implements — coloured pencils, brushes, charcoals, miniature scrolls of paper tied with ribbon, a magnifying eyeglass, a paper knife, a little ruler, a bookmark made of embroidered silk. It is a diminutive treasure house. She is delighted with it.

'It is the most beautiful present I have ever received in my entire life!' she says, sincerely. She knows that she has said this before, to others, on several occasions, but this time, each time, she has been sincere.

He is pleased with her pleasure. But he tells her that she must also admire the card that he bought to go with it.

She opens the large dark red envelope, which she had discarded in the excitement of opening the many wrappings. Her name is written upon it in large letters and in golden ink. Inside is a card showing a reproduction of an eighteenth-century Korean paper screen, with a still life displaying just such a little box of drawers as she now possesses. The box is accompanied by other boxes, by a vase of peonies and an inkwell and a bowl of fruit and a peacock feather. But what charms them both the most is the depiction of a pair of tortoiseshell-framed glasses which lies open, in the middle of the composition, upon an open book of *han'gŭl* script. 'You see?' says Jan. Babs sees. She puts her own glasses back on again to inspect them more closely.

'How can I thank you?' she says.

'I am so glad you like it,' he says. 'The name of this kind of composition in this painting is called *chae'kori*. It means 'screens-with-books'. It is a characteristic motif of the Chosŏn period. You see, I, too, have learned something about this country. Not as much as you, but a little. The gift box is my casket of lacquer. As you know, I am fond of the casket theme. This casket does not have many secrets in it, but what it holds, it is all for you. You may look more carefully, when you are home in England.'

In the card, he has written: 'For Athena the wise and beautiful, in gratitude.' She finds this an acceptable message, though she is not quite sure in what way he considers that she has deserved or is about to deserve his gratitude. As she studies it, she senses that he is about to initiate a new phase of the encounter. And she is right. His homage duly paid and his tribute accepted, he now wishes to return to the subject of his crazy wife.

He has not bought his wife a doll's study, or a paper screen, or a jade duck, or an amethyst pendant, but he has, as he now tells Babs, put a

382

deposit on a Chinese baby. This has caused him, as he now reveals, a deep disquiet. He cannot believe that he has committed such a gross, such a reckless, such an inappropriate act. How can he have become a trader in human flesh? What shall he do? Shall he forfeit his deposit, or cancel his transaction? 'I have entered into the territory of dangerous exchanges,' he says, 'on which so much has been written. Both by your friends, and by mine. I have offered money for what money cannot and should not buy. This is not a hypothesis in a book. I have done it in the real world. I do not know what to do. I do not know what I have done.'

He is on his feet now, and is pacing up and down, in a manner that reminds her of her father, who was given to pacing the drawing room overlooking the orchard in Orpington when contemplating hard choices or sick patients. Maybe she loves Jan because he resembles her father. Her father is a scrupulous and well-mannered medical man, a family doctor of the old school.

She tells Jan that, if he is uneasy, he need do nothing. He has made no commitment, surely? Surely it takes many months to arrange for such an adoption? Surely there are many legal obstacles to be raised, in both countries? If he does nothing, the arrangement will surely lapse? He'll have lost a thousand dollars, but that won't matter much, will it?

'There is already paperwork,' he says. 'And maybe not so much time.'

'May I see the paperwork?' she asks, ignoring

383

for the moment the second half of his statement. She knows that he wants her to see the paperwork. He had introduced her, two nights ago, to the photographs, and now he wants her to see the paperwork.

He repeats the formula of their first evening.

'If you do not mind,' he says, 'I think we could talk about this better in bed. It would be easier to talk in bed. Also, I am very tired. I have had a long and tiring day, and tomorrow I have an early start and a long flight. Would you mind lying beside me in bed, just this once more? It is already too late to have an early night, but we could lie comfortably together.'

Of course she does not mind. Perhaps he is telling her that he is proposing bed rest, rather than sexual intercourse? If so, she does not mind that either. She does not mind what he suggests, provided that it does not exclude her. Maybe a night without sexual intercourse suggests a greater intimacy than the sexual act itself could offer?

So, once more, she finds herself sitting by his side, under the crisp king-sized sheets, in her Pagoda Hotel bathrobe, propped up against a heap of pillows, with a dossier of papers spread upon her knees, and a tumbler of J&B by her side. He is drinking a glass of water, but he has urged her to accept the hospitality of his whisky. 'I am a tired old man,' he says, 'but you are young, and I can tell that you have an excellent constitution. It would please me if you would drink on my behalf a glass of hotel whisky.'

Some of the papers are in English, and some

384

are in Chinese. It is true that he appears to have paid a deposit on a baby, for here is a receipt for a registration fee of $1,000. Clipped to the corner of one of the documents is a small passport-sized photograph of a little girl with large eyes and black hair. Babs Halliwell stares at her.

'Is this the child?' she asks. It is now all a little too real for comfort. 'Did you actually see her? Is this an actual child?'

'Yes,' says Jan. 'I saw her. And that is her name. Her name is Chen Jianyi. She is about eighteen months old. Her date of birth is notional, but they tell me she will soon be two years old. She was discovered in a bus station. She had been brought from the countryside, they tell me. She had been abandoned, at the bus station. In a plastic bag.'

'I think you feel committed to this child,' says Babs, in her role as wise woman. 'But you know that there is no real commitment. There are so many other things to consider. As you know. Such an adoption is not to be undertaken lightly.'

He sighs, very heavily.

'There is a commitment,' he says, after a long pause. 'There is a commitment to my wife. And now there is also a commitment to this child.'

'But you do not know this child,' says Babs. 'You saw her once, at a distance, in an orphanage. She was one of many. That is not a commitment.'

'The child looked at me,' says Jan van Jost.

This is an extraordinary thing for a man to

say. It silences Babs. She does not want to say anything foolish. It is very important not to be foolish now.

'She looked at me,' repeats Jan van Jost. 'She looked at me, and she held my gaze. Look at me, Barbara.'

Her ridiculous and unfashionable name rolls strangely and solemnly from his lips. She looks at him. Their eyes interlock. He looks into her brain. He takes her head in his hands, and gazes into her. She is the first to break contact and to look away.

'You see,' he says. 'It is not easy.'

'No,' she says, 'it is not easy.'

'So, I think that perhaps I should take this large risk,' he says. 'For the child's sake, for Viveca's sake, for my own sake. It was a brave child, the way it looked at me. Its eyes were like a well of ink. Like an unwritten book. Like the blank page of an unwritten book. You think I am mad, perhaps. And maybe I am. What do you say?'

'I don't know why you are asking me,' she says. She is alarmed by the strange intensity of his manner. She, who is accustomed to dissimulating her own intensity, has more than met her match.

'I am asking you,' he says, 'because you know about uncertainty and fatality.'

'But I don't!' she cries. 'I know nothing! That was only a lecture. A string of not very new ideas. A passport to this conference. Two weeks abroad. It meant nothing. Well, very little. In life, I made all the wrong choices. You must not ask me for advice on such serious matters. It is unfair.'

He sees that he has distressed her, and at once he retreats. He takes both her hands in his, and rubs them between his own. His hands are cold, despite the humming steady even temperature of the air-conditioned bedroom.

'Of course it is unfair. I apologize. I do not truly ask you to play the oracle. It is a ridiculous conundrum, this conundrum of the baby and the crazy wife. There is no right answer to it. But I needed to talk. I needed to speak. And it was you that I selected as my confidante. It was because you were kind, and because you were there. You have been very kind to me. I apologize for my intrusion.'

'No need, no need,' she says. 'It is an honour.'

She starts to put the papers back in the folder, tidily. He watches her.

'You must do what you think is right,' she says, as she lowers the folder to the floor.

She is suddenly feeling extremely exhausted. She, too, has had a long day, at the end of a long week. This strange conversation has been unaccountably and incalculably stressful and distressing. She feels as though she has been submitted to a lengthy oral examination, which she may well have failed. She feels as though she has herself been asked to shoulder the burden of an unknown child from a foreign land. Which, of course, is not what is on the cards at all. She lies back against the high white hotel pillows, and shuts her eyes. She must not stay long, as he has said that he has to get up early to catch a plane

387

to Frankfurt and then a connecting flight to Barcelona, and she has a breakfast appointment in the coffee shop with Dr Oo. He gathers her gently towards him, and settles her head upon his shoulder, and folds his arms around her. He seems to want to hold on to her. This is very reassuring. The skin of his body is smooth and dry, and he smells pleasantly and expensively of aftershave. Armani, Gucci, Dior — one of those smart, modern male perfumes.

Why should he not adopt a Chinese baby as a diversion for his wife, if that is what he wants? He is a rich man, and rich men have succumbed to far worse foibles than this. It is a generous impulse on his part. She is glad that he does not seem to be disappointed with her or angry with her. His arms are friendly and loving to her. It would not be a good idea to fall asleep, she tells herself, as she begins to drift peacefully away. As soon as he has fallen asleep, she tells herself, she will collect her treasures and creep out, and return to her single twin bed two floors below, and leave him sleeping, and the next morning it will all be as though it had never been.

She is woken suddenly, she knows not how much later, by an unexpected and frightening sound. One moment she is asleep and dreaming, and the next moment she is listening to Jan van Jost fighting for his life. He is having some kind of attack. He is breathing hoarsely and loudly, and he is struggling, and his torso is rearing up from the bed in a spasm of sudden and brief agony.

388

Afterwards, she will look back on the rapidity and fortitude of her instant response with disbelief. She is, when all will have been said, a doctor's daughter. First, she leaps from the bed and reaches for his pills, and attempts to make him swallow one. But this is not possible, for he is choking and she cannot get the pill into his twisting mouth. Then she leans across his body, and reaches for the telephone, and dials Room 1529 for Dr Oo.

By the time Dr Oo arrives, Jan van Jost is dead. She knows this, as she opens the door to Dr Oo. It has taken only a matter of minutes for Dr Oo to arrive on the scene, but Jan van Jost is already dead.

So, just as suddenly, there is no hurry any more. There are only consequences.

Dr Oo, neat in his grey pyjamas and his European paisley-patterned dressing gown, sits on the bedside, by the body of Jan van Jost, and composes his limbs, and closes his staring eyes. Babs, sitting on a chair by the bed, on top of the heap of her clothes, has buried her face in her hands, to avoid those staring eyes, but now she looks up. She is in a state of profound shock. She is also naked, under the bathrobe. Van Jost is wholly naked. It is an impossible situation. Dr Oo pulls the sheets discreetly up, over the professor's corpse. Dr Oo and Babs Halliwell confront one another, like guilty accomplices, though neither of them has as yet done anything wrong.

'I am sorry,' says Dr Oo, encompassing the entire deathbed drama.

'I am sorry,' she says. 'I should not have called you.'

'You did right to call me,' he says. 'I might have been able to help. I can still help.'

Jan van Jost, lying pale beneath the white sheet, looks like a dead emperor. He looks like the noblest Roman of them all. Dr Babs Halliwell stares at him. She has not seen so many dead people in her life, despite her professional interest in death. He assumes, second by second, an extraordinary and growing dignity. Time passes, slowly.

'We must think about how to inform the hotel authorities,' says Dr Oo, gently, after a while.

'Perhaps I should get dressed,' says Babs.

Dr Oo does not contradict her, so she stands up to collect her clothes, with the intention of taking refuge in Jan van Jost's bathroom. But, as she gets to her feet, she starts to tremble. She is overcome with dizziness, a sharp pain shoots through her left leg, and something seems to have gone wrong with her breathing. She collapses back on to the bedside chair, as waves of heat and icy chill pour through her entire living, corporeal body. She gasps for breath. She knows she, too, is, absurdly, inappropriately, inconveniently, about to die.

That is Dr Oo, by her side, forcing her head down towards a brown paper bag that he has somehow managed to produce. Is he trying to suffocate her? 'Breathe,' says Dr Oo, urgently. 'Breathe. Breathe deeply into the bag. Deep breaths. One, two, three . . . '

She tries to obey him, and gradually the

trembling subsides, and the flushes of prickly heat abate.

'It was a panic attack,' says Dr Oo, when she is sufficiently recovered. 'It is natural. You are in shock. It is a question of carbon dioxide.'

'Whatever shall we do?' says Babs.

'You must go back to your room,' says Dr Oo. 'Leave it to me. I will ring the hotel doctor.'

'I think I should stay,' says Babs.

Dr Oo also thinks she should stay, though he does not like to say so. He would clearly have been willing to cover for her, but he is relieved that she does not expect this of him, for he is a law-abiding and respectable medical man. He advises her to get dressed, if she is ready to do so, and she disappears into the bathroom with her inappropriate silky black party dress and her frivolous high-heeled shoes. When she returns to the bedside, she is collected enough to say, 'Please, Dr Oo, I think it is better if I stay to explain to them exactly what happened. But I would very much like you to be with me when they come. And I would be most grateful if you would make the telephone call.'

He agrees that this would be a sensible procedure.

'These big hotels,' he says, in an attempt at reassurance, 'they must be accustomed to . . . ' — he hesitates, searching for a word — ' . . . to incidents.'

He goes into the other room to make the call, leaving her alone for the last time with Jan van Jost. She is by now engaged in replaying every moment of their last night together, and she can

391

see that he had been busy dying all the time. All night, all week, he had been busy with the business of dying.

She can hear Dr Oo, speaking in his birth language in a hushed tone. She sits on the bed by Jan, and takes his hand in hers. It is still warm and malleable. His fingers move in hers, as she kneads them, but his marble face has by now taken on an engraved and immemorial calm. She lays her lips against his cheek, and as she does so she recognizes that all the cool kisses he had so generously and thoughtfully bestowed upon her had been the kisses of a man on the edge of immortality. She speaks to him, although he cannot hear her. She bids him farewell. She bows her head and rests it for a moment upon his handsome and by now ungiving chest.

The hotel doctor arrives very promptly. If he is astonished to find a group composed of one large Englishwoman in a long, black evening dress, one Korean gentleman in grey pyjamas and a paisley dressing gown, and one naked dead Dutch professor, he conceals it well. He examines the body, while Babs retires into the other room. He and Dr Oo converse, in low, urgent tones. Dr Oo, she surmises, must be explaining the identities of the parties involved in the incident. After a while, both of them come to join her, shutting the double doors discreetly behind them. The hotel doctor says, in English, that he has a few questions to put to her. May he ask her these questions now, or would she prefer to wait until the morning?

'Now, please,' says Babs, casting a glance of

appeal at Dr Oo, her friend and her ally.

She is able to describe most of the events of the evening with admirable clarity. Professor van Jost had requested her to accompany him to his suite, as he had purchased a small gift for her, and wished to present it to her. They had left the banquet a little early, at his suggestion, as he was feeling tired. It was just before eleven-thirty. She had noted the time. They had conversed, for an hour or so, and then, again at his suggestion, they had put themselves to bed. At this point in the narrative, she stumbles, very slightly, but the encouraging expression of Dr Oo urges her onwards, and she is able to say that in bed, they had talked for a little, and then they had both fallen asleep. She had been woken by the sound of his distress. She had attempted to make him swallow one of his heart pills (she assumed they were heart pills?), but had failed, and then she had telephoned Dr Oo because he was a medical doctor and a friend of the professor. While waiting for Dr Oo, the professor had died.

'He died in my arms,' she says.

She is warming to her tragic situation. What choice has she but to warm to it? She has no other role to play.

'He died in my arms,' she says, with melancholy pride. Then, to her own surprise, she bursts into tears, moved by the sound of the words of her own epitaph.

The hotel doctor and Dr Oo are very kind to her. She has behaved admirably, they assure her. The professor could have died at any moment. He was fortunate not to be alone when he died.

Nobody likes to die alone in a strange hotel room in a foreign city. She had done the best that she could do.

She tells herself that this may be true. Van Jost had seemed to be comforted by her presence, except during the last brief moments of desperate struggle. He had wanted to keep her there. He had fallen peacefully asleep by her side. And she had done her best. She had done better than most others could have done. In death, she had not abandoned him. She need not feel ashamed of herself.

Dr Oo urges her to go to her bed now, to get some sleep. There will be more questions, in the morning. He will see if he can alter his flight, so that he can fly out from Seoul a little later. He will try to see her through this crisis.

Light-headed and giddy with weariness, she prepares to take her leave. She does not wish to see Jan again, for she has already taken her leave of him, but she is careful, this time, to follow his injunction, and to collect all her possessions. She gathers up her little lacquer cabinet, and her chae'kori card, and her evening bag, and her spare pair of glasses. Dr Oo accompanies her into the lift, and down to her corridor. He makes sure that she gets safely into her room. In the privacy of Room 1517, she sinks on to her bed, and tries to look ahead, at all the complications that she sees banking up in the clouds of the future.

Will there be an autopsy? A postmortem? What will it reveal?

Room 1517 is buzzing with indignation.

Where had Mong Joon been, in Dr Halliwell's hour of need? She should never have been let out on her own. She is not fit to look after herself, in these dangerous and immoral and godless times. It is high time she was sent back to England, where she can try to salvage her compromised reputation. She must put this disgraceful episode behind her, and get on with her real life.

★   ★   ★

The news of the death of Jan van Jost is greeted with the mixture of delighted horror and informed sadness that greets all such small sensations. It speeds westwards on the couriers of the dawn, reaching Europe in time for the next morning's headlines. 'VAN JOST EST MORT,' declares the front page of *Le Monde*. The Netherlands, Portugal, Spain and Germany pay similar tribute. 'VAN JOST IST OVERLEDEN,' 'VAN JOST ESTA MUERTO,' 'MORRE JAN VAN JOST,' 'VAN JOST TOT,' read the multilingual messages. During the day the news feeds back eastwards to Korea and China and Japan through the Internet, disseminating itself into other languages and into other scripts. Even Britain, preoccupied as so often with some antique minor royal scandal, finds space on the inside pages of a broadsheet or two for a small foreign-news item announcing the sudden decease of this celebrated international intellectual. Quite a lot of people in Britain have heard of Jan van Jost, and some of them, unlike Babs Halliwell, have read his books. But they are not the kind of people who count for very much in terms of column inches. There will be decent obituaries in the broadsheets, in the days to come. But nobody in Britain will assume deep mourning for the unexpected and premature death of Jan van Jost.

Dr Barbara Halliwell, in mourning and in shock in Seoul, finds herself in a fantastic, implausible and anomalous position. She knows that she is the last person to have seen van Jost alive, and that she has a story to tell. If she were a different kind of person, she might even have a story to sell. But to whom can she speak? And what is it that she wants to say? She needs to speak. She cannot keep her secrets to herself. She wishes, posthumously, to claim van Jost as her own. Fleetingly her own, but nevertheless her own. Too late, yet not too late, she realizes the significance of his insistence on the third night. One night may be dismissed as a one-night stand, and could be said to lack dignity, even in modern times. One-night stands with famous men are for star-fuckers. Two nights with famous men are inelegant and inconclusive. But three nights constitute a romance and a relationship. Van Jost has protected her reputation from beyond the grave. Three nights have given her the right to own him and confess him. Three nights have given her a stake in the magnanimous heart of Jan van Jost.

It was his heart that had failed him, although, it will be revealed, he had also been suffering from an endemic form of environmental pit-country lung cancer. He had died of natural causes. Although he had died suddenly and on foreign soil, there will be no need for any kind of inquest. His remains will be repatriated. No forensic evidence will be required to link his death with or to detach it from any form of sexual activity. He had been a dying man, with a full knowledge of his mortal condition, and with bottles of pills and inhalers and prescriptions to prove it. The lung cancer will be found to date back to the black fields of his childhood, not to the modest nicotine consumption of his college days. Death had been unavoidable. Why he had chosen to spend what had proved to be the last weeks of his life on a gruelling and ill-paid lecture tour of China and South Korea is a mystery to many, but not to Babs Halliwell. He had wanted to see all the countries of the world before he died. He had told her so, in the early autumn sunshine on the walls of the fortress at Suwon. And he had wished to cheat death by bringing home a little orphan child. He had told her so, in Suite 1712 in the Pagoda Hotel. These were the caprices of his greatness. They seem to her the caprices of a mighty prince.

Her day's appointments are cancelled, as she is interviewed by various concerned parties about the details of Jan van Jost's last hours. It occurs to her, very early in this long day, that she could have avoided all of this, had she so chosen. It would in theory have been easy for her to have abandoned Jan van Jost in his death throes and crept away and disowned him and returned to her own room. She could have left him dead in his bed, and her presence in his suite and his bed would never have been detected. Why would anyone have been looking for her fingerprints? She remembers the tumbler of J&B by the bed, which she had not thought to remove. But it is not a crime to take a drink in a man's hotel room, is it? In this modern day and modern age?

She knows, however, that abandoning him had never been an option. She is a law-abiding doctor's daughter from Orpington. She had done the right thing. She had rung Dr Oo in order to try to save Jan, and she knows that she had been right to do so. And even if Jan had died instantly, before she had time to pick up the phone, she would still have rung for Dr Oo because she would not have trusted herself to be absolutely certain of Jan's death. Although she is entitled to call herself a doctor, she is not a medical doctor, and has never been called upon to certify a death. She has never before been present at the act of death. (Benedict had died while she was trying to find a meter to park her car in Queen Square near the hospital — not that her presence would have made any difference to anything, least of all to him, as she sometimes bitterly tells herself and others.) She has heard of trances and comas and corpses who have breathed again. She has heard of those who have been buried alive. (Jan van Jost had mentioned rather a lot of them in his final farewell lecture, and even more over the table at their last dinner.) How could she have left him, entombed in his leaden casket, in his king-sized hotel bed, and coldly quit the scene? The arrival of Dr Oo had provided a witness not only to Jan's death, but also to her presence at his death.

And this, of course, had been what she had wanted. She had not wanted her role to go unrecognized. She wants the whole world to know that it was she who had been there, at the end. She wants to go down in history, as the last love, as the last fling, of Jan van Jost. This is not a dignified desire, but it is a deep one. Fortunately, correctitude of behaviour and shamefulness of desire have coincided. She has not even done the right thing for the wrong reason. She did the right thing, spontaneously and instinctively, for the right reason. Her conscience is clear. Chopping logic is her profession, and she now acquits herself of any impropriety.

She tries to replay everything Jan has ever said to her, during their brief acquaintance, as she talks her way through the day. The British Embassy contacts her, offering support, should she need it. She takes coffee in the Dutch Embassy, and receives the condolences of the ambassador himself, as though she were a bona fide widow. She remembers that it is there, a hundred years ago, in that very building, sitting on a sea-green plush settee, that she had told van Jost the 200-year-old story of Prince Sado and the Crown Princess. The Crown Princess had been to blame for all these subsequent events. If van Jost had not listened so eagerly to the story, she would never have ended up in his bed. He might have died at the same hour of the same day, but he might have died alone.

Everybody treats her, at least to her face, with

399

great courtesy. She cannot tell what is being said behind her back. She wonders how much of the true story has leaked out, and how many people and countries it has reached. Gossip knows no frontiers. There is no way of telling. Dr Oo keeps company with her during the morning, acting as interpreter and counsellor, but in the afternoon he has to depart. He has managed to transfer from his Lufthansa flight via Frankfurt to a later Korean Airline flight via Heathrow, but he cannot delay any longer. His hospital and his family need him, he says. They part, in the foyer of the Pagoda Hotel. She protests her undying gratitude. She watches him, as he goes off to his taxi, with his all-too-familiar navy-blue Samsonite suitcase, to take the high road to the airport island and the airy silver-spun buildings of Incheon. They have exchanged their e-mail addresses. They will keep in touch.

Most of the delegates of both the conferences have left by now for other conferences, other destinations. The hotel has absorbed a new intake of transients. New notices for new events are posted up on the notice boards. Another visit to the Expo is announced, this time for members of an international dental association. Babs stares at this notice, forlornly, morbidly, as she remembers the virtual butterfly, which had come like a dream and gone like a dream. She is beginning to feel, at last, after all this excitement, unbearably sad. What will have happened to her friend Jan's Armani suits, to his expensive ties, to his socks and his shoes and his presentation Chinese dressing gown? Are they still lying where they were, in Suite 1712? Is his Braun battery-operated toothbrush still in his bathroom, with his Philips razor and his striped sponge bag? And what about his books and his papers and his palmtop? If she were his true widow, instead of a virtual widow, she could go up there now, and pack them for him. But as it is, she has no right. She is a ghost, on the edge of his finished life. How will she get through the long evening alone? She is far too tired to go to bed. Shall she walk the night streets, alone in her scarlet socks?

She walks, and walks, and walks.

Postmodern Times

She is even more tired, as she flies homewards. She is too tired to read, and she is too tired to sleep. She has been transferred to a Korean Airline flight, and upgraded to a business-class window seat, but she cannot sleep in it. She shuts her eyes, and tries to think of the future, but she is ensnared by the events of the past week, of the past two hundred years. She searches for meaning, and finds none. How had these things come to pass? She retraces every word, every gesture of her brief acquaintance with van Jost. She examines and re-examines the script. It was the mystery book that had brought them together. The memoirs of the Crown Princess had initiated their romance. The book is packed safely away now in the dark blue Samsonite suitcase in the hold of the aeroplane, where it can do no harm. It is hygienically isolated in a plastic bag, but its interleaved and intertextual marginalia, written in red and blue, remain proof of and witness to what has passed.

The Crown Princess watches her drowsy envoy with some suspicion. Perhaps this envoy was ill chosen. She has become distracted from her mission. Maybe the Red Queen had been wrong to select a vain, ambitious and flirtatious academic, who is at an age when she still seems to think she has so many free choices to make. Will Dr Halliwell pursue the message of the memoirs when she gets back to her homeland, or will she be distracted by subplots and secondary issues? By Chinese babies, by mad widows, and by the obituaries of that low-born Dutch professor, whose irrelevant demise seems to have caused such a stir? Maybe Dr Halliwell will simply return to work and pick up her life where she left it, before the infection took. Maybe the Crown Princess has wasted her missionary efforts. Maybe Dr Halliwell will neglect her task, which is to perpetuate the enigma of the Crown Princess's life, and to urge on the unearthly reading of her sufferings.

But Dr Halliwell does not forget. She does, it is true, take some time to readjust to her busy urban life. We watch her from afar, as she moves her remaining possessions from Oxford, and says her farewells, and re-engages with London and her large second-floor apartment. Her apartment, on the edge of Adelaide Park, overlooks the city from the newly fashionable heights of Cantor Hill. We recognize now that when we first observed her asleep in Oxford, on the eve of her departure for Seoul, we had received a false impression of her habits. For we had seen her in a controlled, a well-maintained environment, where she had been tended by hosts of helpful minions, and sheltered by regular hours and manageable distances, by centuries of protocol and routine. The mulberry tree in the courtyard and the ancient lichen on the ancient walls had been a protection to her, and the college porter had taken thought for her. In London, she is left more to her own devices, and she is forced to improvise her daily life.

She is teaching several hours a week in two different venues, she sits on a couple of committees, she has articles to write and papers to read and grade, and getting about London is a job in itself. She has a car, but she is very bad at parking it, after the trauma of Queen Square and the Hospital for Sick Children, so she usually leaves it standing safely by the kerb in Cantor Hill, where she hopes it will come to no harm. (It has been vandalized only twice in three years, which is not bad for London: Cantor Hill is not yet a high-risk area.) She is supposed to be writing a book on triage in the National Health Service for an academic press, but it is making slow progress. She visits her husband in the retreat in Northampstonshire once a week, at the weekend, like a dutiful wife, to make sure he is not being deliberately or casually neglected or tormented. These are not pleasant visits, for he tends to stare at her, wordlessly, perhaps reproachfully. Just as their son Benedict had stared at her, from his sterile bubble. But at least the visits help to calm her conscience and to exercise her car.

She takes him gifts from Seoul: a straw-yellow pair of woven hempen slippers, a large wooden box of ginseng tea. She had bought the slippers for him herself, in a street market, but the ginseng had been presented to her by Mong Joon, her minder. He had followed her to the airport with it. He had tracked her to the last, despite the alteration of her departure flight.

Peter puts the slippers on his feet, and he

drinks a cup of the ginseng tea. Does he know where she has been? She cannot tell. She gets into her car, and drives home down the soothing M40, beneath the circling fork-tailed birds of prey, then round the North Circular, and back to Cantor Hill.

She is a busy woman. How will she find time to mourn for van Jost, and to commemorate the Crown Princess?

The manner of her mourning and her commemoration are evident from the leaning towers of books that begin to fill her study. Her Edwardian stained-glass-enhanced windows look out from Cantor Hill towards the south-east, over a great falling vista of London, but the view from her desk is partially obscured by books, which are heaped up on her desk and strewn round it upon the floor. Amongst them we can see not only the crumpled, well-travelled and doubly annotated text of Thea Landry's translation of the Crown Princess's memoirs, with its wedded commentaries, but also a variant earlier version, translated and edited by Yang-Hi Choe-Wall under the title of *Memoirs of a Korean Queen*, by Lady Hong, and what is generally regarded as the authoritative version, translated and annotated by Professor JaHyun Kim Haboush and published in 1996 by the University of California Press under the title *The Memoirs of Lady Hyegyŏng: The Autobiographical Writings of a Crown Princess of Eighteenth-Century Korea*. Babs has been attempting to compare and collate the three translations, and to wrest further meaning from their stories. Both the Choe-Wall and the Haboush provide gripping narratives. The Yellow Fields Press version remains a highly enigmatic text: it lacks an ISBN, and there is no copy of it in the British Library. On closer inspection, the name of its translator is unconvincing.

There is a fourth translation, published in 1980, which she has on order in the library, but she has not yet read it.

Dr Halliwell has been reading widely round the subject of her new obsession, for we can also see on her desk many related works of travel and scholarship. We can see a library copy of Isabella Bird's classic and recently reprinted book about her travels in Korea and her meetings with the intriguing Queen Min, the last queen of Korea. We can see pencilled notes on Henry Savage Landor's lesser known and shockingly incorrect views on Orientalism and the oriental mind, and a paperback copy of Edward Said's master text on Orientalism. (Alas, she can find no reference to Korea in Edward Said.) We can see books on *Culture and the State in Late Chosŏn Korea*, on shamanism, on Confucianism, on early Korean literature, on women in Korean ritual life, on Korean true view painting, on Korean screens and *chae'kori* painting, on Jesuit art in China and Japan. There are catalogues from the Musée Guimet in Paris, and a glossy art collectors' magazine called *Orientations*, full of reproductions of eighteenth-century images of flowers and birds and other so-called 'auspicious objects', painted by Giuseppe Castiglione. (Castiglione is described as 'a Jesuit painter at the court of the Chinese emperors', and we gather that in this transcultural and transitional world he commands strangely high prices. He has become a good transcultural investment: we prize the displaced border artist these days.) There are even some books written mainly in *han'gŭl*, which we know Barbara Halliwell cannot read, and has neither the time nor the patience to learn. Why has she invested in these? The Crown Princess is an exacting mistress.

The robust London magpie that struts upon her windowsill regards these foreign books with an evil and an inauspicious eye. The sun glints on the wicked gloss of its stiff, purple-black feathers.

Magpies breed well and multiply in Cantor Hill. Those species that thrive on urban density enjoy this north-eastern district of London. It is a youthful and multicultural neighbourhood, much favoured by young professionals and by magpies. Magpies and babies in buggies thrive here. Dr Halliwell does not like either the magpies or the babies, and she sometimes wonders why she moved to nouveau-chic Cantor Hill from cut-throat Kentish Town.

On Dr Halliwell's desk, we can also see books by Professor Jan van Jost. She has purchased several volumes of his large *oeuvre* and attempted to penetrate them. But she makes heavy work of them. The indexing is not adequate, and she cannot take short cuts to matters of potential mutual interest, such as the death penalty, euthanasia, transcultural adoption, monoculturalism and global denationalization.

410

(The word 'triage' does not appear anywhere in his works, as far as she can see, which is a pity, as she would have liked to have added a footnote leading to van Jost.) She consoles herself for her lack of perseverance by telling herself that he was an amorous gentleman scholar who had invited her into his bed, not his library, but nevertheless, her stupidity in the face of his prolix continental bravura depresses her combative spirit. We can see her distract herself from her intellectual shortcomings by opening and shutting the drawers of the little lacquer cabinet that he gave to her. In one of them, she has found a message from beyond the grave. It is neither very intimate nor very secret, but it is without doubt a message. It is a visiting card, with his earthly addresses and telephone numbers in Paris and Barcelona, and his personal e-mail address. He has circled the e-mail address in bright blue ink, just for her. This is — or was — very trusting of him.

Shall she try it? At first she thinks not, for she is afraid of an interception by the widowed Viveca van Jost, or by a secretarial custodian. But late one night, she cannot resist trying to reach the cyber body of her late admirer, and she attempts a brief message. 'I wonder where you are now,' she writes. 'I think of you, and I send you my love.' She clicks on Send/Receive, and waits. She is not surprised to get her message back again, almost immediately, with a note saying, 'Returned Mail: User Unknown: Permanent Delivery Errors.'

This is not surprising, but it is not satisfactory.

411

She would really like to know where he is. Are his mortal remains reduced to ashes and, like her grandfather's in Orpington, stored in one of those ugly bronze-finish Thermos-flask-style plastic capsules? (Her grandmother cannot get round to disposing of them because she cannot make up her mind about where they should lie.) Have they been scattered beneath some branching academic tree, or do they await interment in the Pantheon, behind a marble slab? Will the Dutch claim them from the French? Or perhaps the flamboyantly grieving and appropriative Viveca has drunk them down in a glass of wine, as the widowed Artemisia drank the ashes of her husband Mausolus?

Babs Halliwell regrets now that the mildly sensational death of her professor had been handled with such exemplary diplomatic discretion. Her vain spirit would like to boast about him. She would like to lay claim to him, now, but she is not sure how she can do this in a dignified manner. Again and again, she reads the little note that he wrote to her in the Pagoda Hotel, after their first night together. She would like to show it to the world. She would like to publish it in the *Times Literary Supplement*, or in *Sociology Today*, or in the *Proceedings of the Conference on the New Frontiers of Health*. She would like to write an epitaph or an obituary for this man. She would like her relationship to him to be known in the present, and recorded for posterity. She would like to attend a memorial service, in St Germain des Prés or Ste-Geneviève, robed in black, the mystery mistress.

The cameras would question her presence, admiringly.

Or she could perhaps show up in the parador at the conference on El Hierro, in the wild mid Atlantic, and speak to his last paper? She could volunteer to supplement this paper with a postscripted account of the Prince of the Rice Chest? Would this have been what he wanted? He cannot have had time to write it himself, fast worker though he was.

Sometimes she wonders if he had written any more messages for her in those books she had seen lying by his bedside in the Pagoda Hotel in Seoul. When his library is sold, will his marginalia reveal her cryptic name? The name of the first and last and only Englishwoman he had ever known?

While she is waiting for the rest of her books to turn up in the British Library one morning, she idly extends her research to examining a copy of the *Selected Stories of Lu Xun* and is surprised and a little alarmed to find that she discovers Jan's most likely connection with this bedside book is to be found with unexpected ease in its first five pages. She has looked for a needle in a haystack, and found it. Lu Xun presents an image of an iron house without windows, with many people fast asleep inside. These sleepers will soon die painlessly of suffocation. Should the observer cry aloud to try to wake the lighter sleepers, and let them suffer the knowing agony of irrevocable death? Or is there hope for the future, even at the last? This image is connected with the author's boyhood terror of his dying father's terminal illness, pointlessly prolonged by useless and expensive medication. The boy Lu Xun had been obliged to go twice daily to the pawnshop to procure useless and expensive folk remedies — aloe root dug up in winter, sugar cane three years exposed to frost, twin crickets, *ardisia* . . . The father, thought the boy, should have been allowed to die in peace, as he was a hopeless case. His death throes had been cruel and unnecessary. So why should the man try to rouse the hopeless case of China into painful life from its deep and final slumber?

Yes, she can see why this *locus classicus* of inertia, pessimism and despair would have appealed to van Jost. She can imagine his vivid red commentary, his notes, his queries.

Her mind runs on her days and nights with van Jost. She manages to retrieve snatches of his conversation, but much of it is gone for ever. She thinks about his widow, Viveca, and the Chinese baby Viveca had so crazily wished to adopt. She even thinks about the thousand dollars of deposit that van Jost had said he had paid to the adoption agency.

She remembers that van Jost had said that the child had looked at him. This is the most unlikely thing that any man has ever said to her. How can she forget it?

Her son Benedict had looked at her, when he was newborn. His eyes had gazed into hers. He had gazed at her and she at him during the first months of his life, before she had known that she had given birth to a doomed child, before he had

414

been banished from her contaminating care. But after his banishment, he had slowly but steadily withdrawn his gaze from her. He had begun to forget her. He had retreated from her, into his short institutional life. He had ceased to appeal to her for rescue. He had given up all hope of her. She wished she had spoken of this to Jan van Jost. Had they had more time, she might have told him. But, had they had more time, he would not have offered himself to her, would he?

Barbara Halliwell has not mentioned her brief affair to anybody except her friend Polly Usher, and Polly Usher had not received the news in a gratifying manner. Polly had even seemed to doubt her word. Babs had told the story over supper in Polly's cramped and poky little house in Gospel Oak, expecting a better audience. Polly, serving a homely meal of beans and bacon in a thick garlic and tomato stew, had seemed at times to be frankly disbelieving. As a result, Babs has come to feel a coolness about her old friend Polly. Polly had overstepped the mark of friendship. Moreover, for the first time Babs had perceived Polly's house not as comfortingly cosy, but as stifling. Even Polly's food had seemed a little gross and coarse. The Red Queen, watching over Babs's shoulder, had not thought much of the peasant bean stew and the stinking deliquescent French cheese that had followed it. The Red Queen finds London in many ways unpleasant. Babs, who had suffered from culture shock in Seoul, is now suffering culture shock at one remove in her

415

homeland. She feels displaced.

Polly Usher had not exactly cross-questioned her friend about her alleged three-night romance, but she had from time to time put in an innocent-seeming query, as though seeking circumstantial evidence for it. Of course, it was clear to both of them that any woman can say anything she likes about the last hours of a dead man, provided there is no witness and no medical evidence to contradict the narrator's self-seeking version of events. In the circumstances, Babs can invent extravagant claims without any fear of contradiction. She does not do so. She tries to tell it as it was, though she does not tell it all.

Eventually, what with the detailed recitation citing the pills and the cups of ginseng tea and the J&B and the Dutch gin and the Chinese dressing gown and the striped sponge bag and the battery-operated toothbrush and the arrival of the saintly Dr Oo, and with Polly's knowledge of her old friend's track record, Polly did come to believe that Barbara had spent at least one night in the hotel room of Jan van Jost. (Barbara made a better job of summoning up these intimate bedroom particulars than she did of providing an abstract of van Jost's lecture on the leaden casket.)

The story of the proposed purchase of the Chinese baby, however, was unacceptable to Polly Usher. She was so dismissive about it that Barbara regretted having divulged it.

'You seem to be trying to argue that he as good as left you this baby in his will,' said Polly,

416

who had by this stage in the evening drunk several glasses of red French wine.

'No,' said Barbara, 'I didn't say that at all. I didn't say anything of the sort. I said that I felt that perhaps it was my moral obligation to do something about this baby. That's why he told me about it. It was his last wish, even if it wasn't exactly written down in his last will and testament. He did make a point of it, I promise you. I can see that there's nothing I can do about it now, but I can't help feeling that's unsatisfactory. I don't like having to abandon that child.'

Polly continued to look dubious, and after a while risked a remark about Bab's biological clock, and her unacknowledged wish that she herself had had another child, to replace Benedict. Although Babs listened submissively to these suggestions, she did not take them well. She sat there quietly, while Polly accused her of mid-life sexual hallucinations, and of feeling distress and irritation when forced to contemplate her own childlessness.

'You're always complaining,' said Polly, 'that Cantor Hill is too full of babies. You should hear yourself.'

'You're saying that I invented the Chinese baby?' said Babs.

'Not quite,' said Polly, though she was.

'I think that's just vulgar psychological claptrap,' said Babs, looking at her old friend and ally through new and distanced eyes. She had been thinking of asking Polly to share a Korean meal of *bibimpap* with her in New Malden one

417

day, at a family-run restaurant called You-Me recommended by Dr Oo, but she was now reconsidering her invitation.

Polly's ex-husband Solomon Usher is a society analyst. He is said to have royal clients on his books. Perhaps he would be able to produce an interesting interpretation of Prince Sado's clothing phobia? Psychoanalysts are rarely at a loss for an interpretation. Would he have found words for Sado's affliction? The Oedipus complex? Paranoid schizophrenia? Or perhaps autism, which apparently causes some afflicted children to rend and tear their clothing? 'Himatiophobia', the word used by one of the Crown Princess's translators, does not seem to have caught on, but Solomon Usher may have heard of it. And would Solomon Usher have been able to cure Prince Sado? How can one know, thinks Babs to herself. Solomon Usher's view of Peter Halliwell's affliction had been interesting, but not useful. Solomon Usher had left Polly some years ago, to marry another analyst, and Polly had subsequently married a largely invisible medieval historian, but she had kept her first husband's name, and phrases from Solomon's professional vocabulary jargon had stuck with her, and still enter her conversation from time to time. Babs had once found this amusing, but suddenly she finds it irritating, although she had quite liked Solomon, in the old days. She has not seen him for years. Now she wonders if she wants to see much more of Polly Usher. Polly is prim, and she thinks she knows everything. Her face is tight and small and censorious, and her greying hair is cramped. Babs has had enough of Polly Usher. She has had enough of her old life. A novel restlessness consumes her.

Since her visit to Seoul, Barbara Halliwell's life seems to have changed its course. One does not expect a run-of-the-mill academic conference to have such a far-reaching effect. The synapses of Barbara's brain have been mysteriously rewired, and messages are running backward and forward through them in unfamiliar directions.

Babs has lost faith in the wisdom of Polly Usher, and she has lost what little interest she had in Robert Treborough. She does not respond to his telephone calls. She lets his voice speak from Oxford into her London space. Her silence at first seems to stimulate him, for he rings quite frequently, but gradually his attentions wither and die. She knows he will forget all about her soon. She has cast him off, with the rest of her Oxford sabbatical year.

Babs's attentions continue to hover around van Jost, Korea and the Crown Princess. She searches for signs and symbols and correspondences. She reads of funerary rites in ancient Seoul. She reads of the annual mowing of the ancestral lawns around the ancestral shrines, before the feasts of the ancestors, and she remembers Dr Oo and the fake Confucians in the ancient courtyard. She reads of the mourning robes of undyed hemp, and of the mourning staffs cut from the wood of a tree called *Paulownia tomentosa*. She finds those

Latin words '*Paulownia tomentosa*' so inexplicably distressing on the page that she is obliged to look for an alternative English name for this tree in her childhood tree book. Here, she finds it is none other than her old friend, the foxglove tree. This handsome tree, she reads, is a member of the ill-sounding Scrophulariaceae, or figwort family, and its natal home is China. She knows this tree well because a fine example of it grows in what was once her grandmother's garden in Devon. It likes the south-west, as it likes the gardens of Korea. As a child, she and her sister had tried to catch its large and tender mauve and purple blooms, with their deep cream spotted throats, as they fell in the May breeze from its pale grey leafless branches to the grassy slope below.

She remembers the garden near the Munmyo shrines, which had reminded her so unexpectedly of her paternal grandparents' garden in Orpington. She remembers the footpath over the ravine, bridging time past and time present. She remembers the trees in the princess's garden, the ancient trees with petrified feet, the trees with feet of stone.

The Crown Princess trails Barbara Halliwell, as she makes a pilgrimage to the Great Ormond Street Hospital for Sick Children. We follow in their wake. The Crown Princess hesitates at the main entrance, as Dr Halliwell hesitates. The entrance is much obscured by scaffolding and rebuilding, for the historic hospital is in Phase 1B of a major redevelopment, but this does not deter them. Together, they pause to observe the

420

faun-like statue of Peter Pan, erected in honour of J. M. Barrie and his patronage. They peer closely, through their large glasses, at the name of the sculptor, one D. Byron O'Connor, and Dr Halliwell cannot prevent a slight wrinkle of distaste from passing over her features. We note that she does not care for the sculpture. The Crown Princess also regards it with aristocratic disapproval. We observe and they observe that the plants in the shallow earth around the statue are in need of water, but they pass on, for these plants are not their responsibility. They enter, and observe the notice boards with childish drawings pinned upon them, and the signs directing them to the Cardiac Wing and the Maxillofacial Unit and the Craniofacial Unit. There are wards named after the wild animals of the world. Life-sized fibreglass cows graze in a courtyard, and cheerful murals portray idealized scenes of London transport. A playbus stands empty.

They walk past a work of art entitled 'The Beginning of Fairies'. Dr Halliwell does not seem to care much for this either.

They walk past a cabinet displaying a small Japanese military headdress. What is that doing here? The Crown Princess gives it a passing glance of surprised recognition, but Dr Halliwell ignores it and marches on.

The air of this building is thick with grief and pain and prayer. We can hardly make our way through it, disembodied though we be. Dr Barbara Halliwell averts her eyes as a small child with a lolling head is wheeled by on a trolley

421

attached to an accompanying drip stand. Then she turns to her left along a corridor and follows the signs to a small and highly ornate and brightly coloured Byzantine chapel, enclosed like a jewel within the modern, functional twentieth-century structure. The chapel declares that it was completed in 1875, and it is named for St Christopher, who must, we suppose, be the patron saint of children. Its floor is of mosaic, its columns of richly veined marble, and its domes are studded with painted stars. *Alleluia*, declares the chapel. *Pax*, beseeches the chapel. Icons of the sacrificial lamb and the self-sacrificing maternal pelican preside over images of the Infant Samuel and the Infant Jesus. *Feed My Lambs, Feed My Sheep*, its texts exhort us. Truth, Patience, Purity, Obedience and Charity are the names of the winged ministers that rise and keep watch behind its altar.

We watch Dr Halliwell as she sits down for a while, on a dark wooden pew in the church's elaborate golden interior. Is she praying? We do not think she can believe in the efficacy of prayer, at this point in history. Nor have we seen any evidence that she is a Christian. So what is she doing here?

The chapel is not in its original location. During an earlier phase of rebuilding and refurbishment, it had been hermetically sealed on a concrete block in a waterproof casket, and stored away for years. Then it was moved on greased slides by hydraulic rams to its new position, and opened once more to those who wish to pray for the sick and the dead. Unlike those whom it commemorates, it was resurrected intact, after its brief burial.

We watch Dr Halliwell as she leaves the chapel, and pauses before an open Book of Remembrance, in which are written the names of children, and their ages on the dates of their death. 'Lucia Andrews, aged four days.' 'Adewale Manawe, aged five months.' 'Tariq Malhotra, aged six years.' And there is the name of Benedict Halliwell, inscribed in beautiful, anonymous copperplate script. For it is the day of the anniversary of his death. We watch her as she picks up and reads the messages written in the cards left by other parents, other families, who have lost a child on this day. 'It is hard to be apart from you.' 'You are ever in our thoughts.' 'We shall never forget you.' 'May you sleep well, our dearest one.' 'Sue sent the yellow rose, and the other one is from our garden.' 'Patrick still asks for you every night.'

Babs Halliwell has not brought a card. Nor has she brought a flower, to add to those few roses and carnations placed humbly on the small shrine. We cannot tell if she comes every year on this day, or if she has been prompted to do so by some incident, some urgent memory. Maybe we should not have intruded upon her grief. She would not wish Polly Usher to know about this observance, so why should we? She is ill placed in this building. Her name is not on the scroll of the Guardian Angels who watch over it and sponsor it.

Benedict's father, Peter Halliwell, does not know the days of the week, or the months of the year.

Babs, on the way home on the top of the 91 bus, thinks about her 'Three Dead Men' — Peter Halliwell, Benedict Halliwell and Jan van Jost. She chastises herself for this hysterical, this histrionic phrase, which had sprung uninvited, unbidden, unwanted to her mind.

She has tried so hard to rationalize and to control and to conceal the melodrama of her life, but nonetheless, from time to time, it swoops over her and possesses her. She despises it. She does not wish to live hysterically, like Viveca van Jost, on fantasies and dreams. She wishes to be a serious person.

Jan had dignified her with the words 'wise' and 'beautiful'. She believes herself, at times, on her good days, to have a little beauty, but she knows she is not wise. She is grateful to him, nevertheless, for bestowing this quality briefly upon her. Wisdom negates vanity. It forgives the red socks, the red silk skirt.

★ ★ ★

The Crown Princess bides her time. She is very old and very dead, so she ought not to be too impatient. Occasionally, perhaps, she wishes to prompt her hesitant emissary, who seems to have fallen into uncertainty and randomness. Maybe, she reflects, Viveca van Jost would have been a better vehicle of transmission? Maybe the energetic Viveca van Jost would by now have commissioned an opera or a ballet on the plot of the life of the Crown Princess and her Tragic Prince of the Rice Chest? There are so many different ways of telling stories, of perpetuating lives. But soon, one day soon, Barbara Halliwell will meet somebody to whom she will hand on the narrative. It will continue. It will not perish. One day soon, Barbara will meet, by design or by chance, a historian, or a psychoanalyst, or a criminologist, or a novelist, who will adopt the narrative, and allow it to continue its wandering exploration through the future. For the Crown Princess, old and tired though she is, has not abandoned her desire to make sense of her unique place in history. She is still willing to struggle on through eternity, even if the quest involves barbaric phrases such as 'contextual universalism' and 'postmodern relativism' and 'postcolonial Orientalism'. She cannot give up now.

Barbara Halliwell's social life has been restricted, not enlarged, by her move back to London. She turns down many invitations because getting about London is so fraught and so time-consuming. (Thus she narrowly misses a chance of meeting a woman novelist who would certainly have responded to the story of the Crown Princess.) She tries the Crown Princess and Prince Sado out on an elderly diplomat at a reception on the penthouse floor of New Zealand House, but, although he nods his head a lot as she speaks, she can tell that either he is too deaf or the noise level is too high for him to be able to hear her properly. He nods and smiles and gazes beyond her, at the panorama of the city and the turning London Eye, but, unlike van Jost in the Dutch Embassy overlooking Seoul, he does not follow the thread of her story.

Her story has a thread, a scarlet thread, but she does not know where it is leading her. She is looking for something, but she does not yet know what it is. She is looking for some resolution to her oriental journey, for some connection that will enable her to move on to the next chapter of her life. She is haunted by superimposed images, by palimpsests of memories. Time past and time present, London and Seoul, seem to be flowing through one another. They have not merged, they remain distinct, but they coexist, in some dreamlike time of correspondences. They do not fuse or melt. They seem to pass through one another, like clouds of bees, like distant galaxies. Which is real? Perhaps neither of them is real?

She is not accustomed to such swarms of ghostly apprehensions. She is a realist, a materialist, a modern woman, and she is far too young to have anything to do with the spirit world. Anyway, she comes from the wrong kind of culture, or so she tells herself, sharply, as she goes about her complex daily business. She has no access to any kind of belief system that can account for the tremulous connections between her grandparents' English garden, with its straggling gooseberry bushes and yellow tormentil and mauve mallow flowers, and the autumnal garden behind the Hall of Illuminating Ethics where she had strayed with Dr Oo. Why had she felt, there, that she had been on the verge of illumination? And why does she keep returning to the memory of the footbridge and the

426

pathway that had led to the royal Jongmyo shrines, and to the great sign marked 'Solemnity'?

She dreams of the footbridge over the ravine, and of the pathway to the shrines. She dreams of writing to Viveca van Jost. She dreams of the Chinese baby, waiting in vain for Jan van Jost to come for her. She dreams of van Jost, dead in her arms, and of the Coffin Prince, listening to the punishment of thunder.

She feels she is lapsing into solitude and eccentricity. Her future is opaque. She has lost a clear trajectory. She is in the early prime of her life, but she sees the mocking ghost of her ageing self, beckoning to her across the ravine.

She is waiting for a sign from the Crown Princess, who seems to be scrabbling around the pile of books on her table like a mouse, chewing and munching, munching and chewing, rustling and suggesting, suggesting and reminding, insisting and gnawing.

The old Edwardian houses of Cantor Hill are full of mice. The air of Cantor Hill, once famed as salubrious, is now perpetually disturbed by building works and loft conversions and road works. It is thick with the rising spores of the past. Ancient matter drifts and eddies. It fills the branching lungs and seeps into the convoluted folds of the brain.

The autumn leaves fall, in Cantor Woods and on Adelaide Park, as the year withers. The threatening season of Christmas approaches, with all its fabled ill will. Barbara recalls the slim and pretty vegetarian Buddhist guide who had

427

shown Dr Oo and Jan and herself round the Fortress of Grass at Hwaseong: this young woman, in September, had been dreading the advent of the Korean Harvest Festival of Chusŏk. Barbara does not dread Christmas unduly, for she spends it not unpleasantly in Orpington with her parents and her sister and her sister's husband and her sister's children. She is a good aunt, and comes to Christmas not uncheerfully, bearing gifts. But Christmas always reminds her of her childless state, and of the double negatives of her life. How could it not? She broods, a little, as the Festival of Christ's Nativity approaches.

One dark bright evening in mid December, on her homeward journey from a six o'clock guest lecture at the London School of Economics, her taxi comes to a protracted halt on the lofty thoroughfare of Gallax Bridge, which links the one-time old-world village of Highgate with the rapidly developing satellite suburb of Cantor Hill. Impatiently, she peers out of the window at the solid traffic before and behind, and at the immense drop from the bridge down to the busy four-lane motorway below. This is Lover's Leap, the site of the most favoured death plunge of North London, where tired bouquets of commemorative flowers are perpetually tied to the high iron railings that unsuccessfully attempt to inhibit the suicide bids of the desperate. (Its name, Gallax Bridge, is said, on unreliable authority, to be a corruption of Gallows Bridge.) Babs is not often detained here, stationary, for quite so long, and, as she gazes downwards, a

428

sign comes to her. Gallax Bridge reminds her of the footpath in Seoul, the footpath that is strung across the ravine, the footpath that links the Secret Garden of Prince Sado and the palace of the Crown Princess to the Royal Shrines. It has been at the back of her mind, this connection, for weeks, for months. This is what she has been looking for. This is the link. This is the bridge from death to life, from past to present. Below, above, ahead: this is the way, this is the path, this is the walk, this is the route that she needs to tread.

★   ★   ★

The Western year in the western hemisphere nears its shortest day, when the sap sinks. Babs Halliwell walks alone along the Woodland Walk from Cantor Hill to Finsbury Park, in the gathering gloom of a wintery Sunday afternoon. She walks towards the east. The route will, her map assures her, take her under Gallax Bridge. But how can it? Although she has made a sharp descent down wooden steps from a city pavement to reach this hidden path, and feels herself to be in the deeps, she also seems at the same time to be walking along a raised spine, past sunken back gardens of houses that exist in some other plane. This walk follows the route of an old, abandoned rail track, or so she has been told. She has never been down here, to this parallel underworld, sunk low beneath the surface, although she has driven above the fissure many times, on the high road above. She has never known how to reach it, or thought of trying to plunge down into it. Yet here she is, walking, beneath the layer of her daily life, beneath the level of the known.

It is potentially alarming but not quite deserted terrain, thinly populated by the emblematic figures of the modern urban wasteland. These apparitions do not perturb her, for she is tall and she is fit. One or two harmless solitary middle-aged joggers come towards her, pass her, and recede. She observes a bearded terrorist, immobile in the bedraggled bushes, speaking to an accomplice on his mobile phone, and a rapist, his back to a crumbling brick wall, fumbling at his flies. Large wolf dogs plod on with their sullen owners, their unmuzzled snouts hung low. A bag lady sits amidst her travelling luggage on the stump of a felled tree. These are the outcasts; these are the living ghosts of the city. The rusting and blackened skeletons of old motorcycles litter the undergrowth. She sees charred patches of cindery ash, memorials of last summer's conflagrations and cremations. She walks past high red railway arches, embellished with graffiti. A faint illicit odour of smoking hemp lingers in the evergreen leaves of the holly.

The path weaves onwards, now ascending, now descending, now ridged, now furrowed. Time past arches over and then threads its way beneath time present. The ancient and the modern coexist and bypass one another, like the curving spirals of a double helix, but they do not touch. They are simultaneous but discontinuous. The path is a metaphor of memory, of the interweaving of disparate strands.

Barbara Halliwell walks alone underneath the city. It is turning colder now, and a light powdery snow begins to drift and wander uncertainly downwards out of the dull iron upper air into the old railway cutting. This fine frozen dust of the sky will not settle on the trodden earth of the walkway, nor on the leafless branches of its brown and barren bushes, but its light flakes catch and rest weightlessly on the hooks of the wool of Babs Halliwell's grey winter coat.

She walks under Gallax Bridge, named for the gallows, and ahead of her she sees, in the trodden ravine, a hanging man. He dangles, from a wooden gibbet, a poor potato sack of a guy with a lolling head, playfully strung up with a dead magpie, a dead crow and some bunches of coloured feathers. Strange symbols are scrawled on the woodwork. The young of the undergrowth play strange games. She thinks of Prince Sado, prostrating himself in the snow before his angry father, and cowering when he heard the god of thunder. She flinches, like a coward, as she passes the dangling man, but then she stiffens her shoulders, and straightens her back, and strides boldly on, up the winding ramp, into the future.

At the next turning she will find an old-fashioned children's playground, with swings and a slide and a little roundabout. That is the sound of children's voices that we hear, as they play in the middle distance. They are not playing at hangman or funerals. They are playing pleasant games, childish games. She approaches

431

them. We hear the laughter of small children. It is not mocking laughter, the laughter that passing adults fear. It is indifferent; it is self-absorbed.

She sits on a wooden bench, and watches as the children play. They do not seem to see her. It is as though she were not there at all. She can see them, but they cannot see her. She is invisible. They look towards her, but they look through her. Not one of them can see her. No adults attend them. They do not look like the little English children with whom she had played in the green public parks and asphalted school-yards of Orpington. Not one of them looks towards her. They ignore her, as though she inhabited another world.

The white flakes drift, and fall, and rest, and melt, and vanish. She sits, as the seasons change. Spring comes, slowly, and the menace of the bleak walkway slowly vanishes under foliage and wild flowers. She rises, and walks onwards. She walks, and walks, and walks, through the hours, and through the days, and through the weeks. From time to time, she watches the children play. Then, one day, she goes home, and writes a letter to Viveca van Jost in Barcelona.

★   ★   ★

It takes months of intricate manipulation of Euro-legislation and of the Chinese quota system to procure the correct adoption papers for the Chinese orphan. The Chinese orphan is almost too old for adoption by the time the arrangements are completed. Van Jost, being dead, watches helplessly through these long delays. He could have done things better himself, had he managed to stay alive for just a little longer. The Crown Princess watches with curiosity: this is a promising development, though it is not quite what she had anticipated.

The orphan almost abandons hope, but she is a tenacious child, and she cannot believe that they will not come for her. She waits and waits. And, in time, they do come. She sees them as they walk the length of the long ward, with its rows of little institutional cribs. It is not as she expected, but it will do. From the large playpen in the corner, she fixes them with her compelling gaze, as she had fixed the travelling Dutchman. But the two women pass on, towards the supervisor's office at the end of the corridor: they do not as yet return her stare, as they are too confused and anxious to pause and take her in, and indeed she has not yet been identified to them, although she at once recognizes them. The women are in a state of shock. They are astonished by what they seem to have accomplished. They have taken a great risk, amidst great uncertainty, and here they are, with their almost-verified credentials, awaiting a final signature. They have no idea what will become of this enterprise.

It is partly to the hospital's credit that the Englishwoman and the Swedish-Spanish woman have made this long journey. Far from quietly pocketing the $1,000 deposit and attempting to resell the child to the next bidder, the hospital staff had done their best to track down the depositor. This search had taken time, but it had been accomplished, and here the foreign women are, to claim their child. These women are the heirs of the Dutchman, and the child they have inherited is called Chen Jianyi.

Viveca van Jost, as Barbara had half suspected, is not nearly as crazy as her husband had wished to suggest. She is eccentric, impulsive and volatile, but she is not mad. She and Barbara are good friends now, bonded by bureaucracy. Viveca will be First Mother, for she has the prior claim, but Barbara will offer regular and regulated support as Second Mother. Viveca has been much in need of support. As she has told Barbara many times, she would not have risked this enterprise on her own. Barbara's letter had fortified her. She had been on the verge of giving up her quest.

First Mother completes the final documents, and signs her name with a flourish. Is that it, then?

They are told that the child will be delivered to their hotel room in the evening, with her passport and her papers and her little bag of worldly goods. The homeward flight is safely booked. The women are to return to Europe the next day, with their new charge.

If Viveca and Barbara are frightened by their new responsibility, they do not display their fear to one another. They are possessed by a show of generous bravado. There is no retreating now.

Jan van Jost is impressed by their persever-ance. His women have proved themselves to be women of character.

434

The Crown Princess is also impressed. Her envoy has done well, and this is a child after her own heart, a child of determination and promise.

The child, when she is brought to the hotel, is silent. Her silence is uncanny. She does not cry. She makes no sound. She casts no lingering glance after the uniformed official who deposits her. She sits, in one corner of the hotel settee, and stares, and stares, and stares. She waits, and waits, and stares.

Is she hungry? Is she thirsty? Will she sleep? What is she thinking? Is she deaf? Is she dumb? What does this silence signify?

Chen Jianyi is disconcerting. The women do not know how to address her. She is small, and complete, but at the same time demanding. What does she want of them? Will she sit there, awake, staring at them from those great dark eyes, all night? She watches them as they move nervously round the room. She is wearing a little pale blue cotton outfit held together with white plastic press-studs. The women have brought some changes of Western-style clothes for her, but they do not know if she will accept them. Maybe she will be particular about her garments? However will they learn her ways? They have understood her to be potty-trained, but is this true? They have a small plastic pot in their luggage, but it would seem rude and crude to offer it so soon in their acquaintance.

Viveca cedes authority to Barbara, who had once had a child of her own, a child who had died at the age that this child is now. This new girl child succeeds Benedict, and steps into his shoes. Barbara is on the verge of panic, but she forces herself to be calm. It is only a small child, after all, a small child who had been dumped not long after birth at a bus station in a plastic bag.

Barbara sits down on the settee by the child, and dares to touch the soft skin of the child's dimpled hand. The child looks down at her own hand, impassively, and at Barbara's large fingers, and then looks up again, to meet Barbara's eyes. She tries to hold Barbara's gaze. Her expression is one of great solemnity. Still, she makes no sound. How will she respond to their foreign accents, their alien voices? They are not even sure how to pronounce her name. The gulf between them is immeasurable, and yet she stares across it, sucking out the soul of their attention.

Barbara has brought one or two toys, described as suitable for a two-year-old. She had bought them, on advice, at the Early Learning Centre, a store that specializes in practical and educational playthings. Diffidently, she takes from her shoulder bag a nest of simple hollow plastic coloured cubes, and offers it to the child. Politely, the child accepts the object, then puts it down on the settee. Barbara retrieves it, and demonstrates its properties. The cubes can make a nest, or, alternatively, a tower. The child watches, impassively, as big Barbara plays with the blocks. Barbara takes them out, and lays them out, and fits them back again into one another. She builds them up, then takes them apart again. It is impossible to tell if the child is interested or not. Will the child ever cry? Does she ever smile? Does she even know how to smile?

The blank slate, the empty vessel, the well of ink, the unwritten book. The universal, essential, patient, driven, unique, determined self.

Then, suddenly, as Barbara begins to despair of any interaction, the child reaches out her hand for the toy. She deigns to reach out for her gift. She looks at Barbara, enquiringly, as she reaches out her hand, and Barbara feels a shiver, a birth pang, deep in her entrails. Barbara gives the toy to the child. Soundlessly, seriously, the child unstacks the blocks, and lays them in a row. Then, silently, seriously, the child begins to put them together again, fitting one into another, one by one. She is dexterous and neat, and hardly falters in her selection. She understands the blocks, and how they are made to fit together.

The two women watch, spellbound, as the child demonstrates her skills. It is a miracle. This child is a survivor. This child is gifted beyond all other children the world has ever seen. She is a treasure, and she has condescended to allow them to bestow their care upon her. She has commanded them to come to her side, and they have answered her summons. It is a miracle; it is a mystery.

The child looks up from her childish cubes, and gazes from one woman to the other. She is wondering where that Dutchman has gone, that man with faded blue eyes who had sworn to return for her. She is too young to understand that he is dead. But she knows that these women

437

will do her bidding. She is imperial in her demeanour, and queenly in her expectations. The Crown Princess observes her new heir with satisfaction. Her interests will be safe with her.

★ ★ ★

There will be times, in her childhood, when Chen Jianyi will suffer moments of doubt about her eccentric upbringing and her rigorous education. But these will be few. On the whole, she will be confident that she has chosen the better part. These years, at the beginning of the second millennium, are good years for transcultural exchanges, and for clever multilingual children of mixed heritage. It is as well to be clever, in this sharp and fast new world of accelerating fusion and diffusion, but she is clever. She is very clever. She will direct her career with skill and style, and set her sights at the highest of goals. Maybe she will return to conquer her homeland of China, who knows? Maybe America will invite her to deploy her talents on behalf of its expanding empire? Maybe Europe, her foster mother, will manage to retain her in its service? As the posthumous stepdaughter of Jan van Jost, she will set her heart on degree after degree, piling them high upon one another like the tower of coloured cubes that was her first gift from the West. Her first doctoral dissertation will take the unification of North and South Korea as its topic: Jan van Jost and Kim Dae Jung will applaud from the grave, and Barbara and Viveca will applaud from the front

438

row. But a tower of degrees alone will not content her. Doctoral dissertations will not appease her restless and determined spirit. She has set her heart on power. She has endured enough of powerlessness.

When she comes in her eighth year to pay her annual July visit to Second Mother Barbara in London, the fulfilment of these long-term plans is still far in the future. But she has many short-term girlish plans in her head. She wants to go round on the London Eye, and she would like to see the crown jewels and their guardian jackdaws. She is keen to visit the widely advertised and allegedly sensational new installation at Tate Modern, which offers a breathtaking virtual journey through space and time. It is designed by a young Chinese sculptor whom Viveca had met in Stockholm, and it is called 'Silk Road'. She has also requested an out-of-town trip to Legoland or Stonehenge. Babs has encouraged her in all these wishes, for Babs is herself an ardent sightseer, eager to find an excuse to visit these attractions — the thought of Legoland she finds particularly intriguing, although she would never admit this to her colleagues. What *can* Legoland *be*? She has often wondered, and this will be her chance to find out. The Queen of England has been to see it, so why should not Barbara Halliwell and her honoured guest?

Chen Jianyi also wants to go shopping. First Mother Viveca has infected her adopted daughter with an awesome appetite and capacity for shopping. Babs, who is an episodic rather

439

than a perpetual shopper, looks forward, perhaps a little apprehensively, to taking her borrowed daughter on a shopping spree.

We see Babs watching eagerly, at the arrival gates, for the excitable Viveca and the small, resolute Chen Jianyi. Barbara Halliwell waves wildly, with both arms, like a windmill, when she sees them emerge from Customs. They see her at once. For even here, in England, amongst the English, Babs is conspicuous in a crowd. We see that she is looking well: her new, shorter, frizzle-curled hairstyle becomes her, and her skin is tanned and glowing with health. It has been, so far, a good spring, a good summer. It seems that the world is smiling on Dr Barbara Halliwell. On the way to the short-term car park, the child tightly, silently, holds the hand of Babs. The child's hand is warm and delightful and confiding and full of trust. This friendly sensation of contact is of the greatest importance to Barbara Halliwell. Chen Jianyi's gaze is often fierce, but her hand is always friendly. Babs continues to be surprised by the neat and proper manner in which their two hands fit together, the one so large, the other so small. The two hands seem to be made for one another. This must be an illusion, but it is a sustaining and benevolent illusion. They make an odd couple, as they make their way towards the car park. Viveca follows, meekly pulling the child's wheeled suitcase.

That night, Babs gives Chen Jianyi her favourite English supper, which consists of chicken korma from Sainsbury's, followed by homemade pancakes tossed to the ceiling, then covered in Tate and Lyle golden syrup. The depraved delicacy of Sainsbury's chicken korma is not available in Barcelona, and would not be permitted if it were, for Viveca is, at least currently, a food purist on a diet. Chen Jianyi looks forward to her chicken korma from visit to visit. Babs is not a good cook, but she knows what Chen Jianyi likes, and Babs enjoys making pancakes. Over her mild, pale yellow supper, Chen Jianyi, in her impeccably precise but very occasionally hesitant English, outlines her immediate needs. She is very anxious to acquire a new summer dress, like the one her schoolfriend Anna has recently acquired. This dress had been purchased in London, for her friend Anna is also a multi-ethnic infant, with indulgent diplomatic grandparents who live in somewhere called, Chen Jianyi believes, South Kensington. She does not know the name of the shop where it was purchased, but she believes the shop is also in South Kensington. Can they please go to South Kensington to look for a red dress just like Anna's?

Of course, says Babs.

It is evident that Barbara Halliwell has made an effort not only to provide a desirable meal, but also to tidy her apartment in preparation for the arrival of the child. Babs is still living in Cantor Hill, as she was when we last saw her, but she has cleared away most of the books that were piled so high upon her desk and scattered over her floors. Her Korean volumes are sitting neatly in a bookcase now, along with a growing collection of books on Chen Jianyi's native land.

The Korean texts are shelved, but not forgotten: they have done their work. And she has finished her book on triage in the NHS, for there it is, two shelves below the Crown Princess. (It cannot be claimed that it has had an immediate effect on government policy, but that was not its intention. Babs is not a politician: she is an academic.)

The apartment has been dusted, and swept, and polished. The mice have long since been evicted, for a fastidious child would not like to see the little brown droppings of mice. Insects, also, have been, in so far as it is possible, expelled. If the stoic and spoiled Chen Jianyi has a childish frailty, it lies in her horror of flies and spiders, and Babs respects this phobia. Chen Jianyi is irrationally afraid of insects, a weakness she has not been able to conceal. She has got it into her small head that they are spies and that they watch her during the night. Chen Jianyi, unlike Barbara, likes magpies, which she thinks are lucky birds, but she does not like flies and spiders. Babs has not been able to work out whether this phobia relates to some Chinese folk memory from early infancy — had not Chairman Mao once initiated a notorious anti-fly campaign? — or whether it springs, perhaps, from a confusion about the meaning of the vulgar word 'bug'. Perhaps all children are afraid of insects, and it is a normal universal childish aversion that she will soon outgrow? In vain so far has Babs tried to make Chen Jianyi more insect-friendly: the child still shudders, with involuntary distaste and alarm, whenever she sees a fly buzzing against a window pane, or, worse still, catches sight of a spider in the bathroom. Babs does not dislike spiders at all, but she has removed them from her apartment humanely by chasing them out of the window or capturing them in cups and releasing them into the garden.

She has also humanely removed any evidence of her current semi-resident lover. We have not been introduced to him, and the few traces he has left tell us little about him. It is impossible to guess from these traces whether he is a long-term or a short-term proposition. He may be another seven-foot manic-depressive megalo-maniac, with a face like the beak of a raven, though for her sake we hope that he is not. He may be another global intellectual with a heart condition, but again, for her sake, we hope that he is not. He has left a white towelling dressing gown hanging on the back of her bedroom door, but a dressing gown is no indication of height or of profile or of state of health. Nor is the monogram on its pocket likely to betray his identity: the large, navy-blue, machine-chain-stitched A is standardized, not personalized, so we cannot assume that he is called Adam, or Andrew, or Adonis.

We can, however, assume some sense of his taste in reading matter, for she has not felt the need to purge his bedside table of its bedside books. There lie his small-framed reading glasses, tucked away in a blue case. Through them, he has been innocently reading a guide book to Athens: may we be allowed the conventional hope that Barbara and this unseen man are planning a holiday together? Beneath the guide book lies an old Penguin Classic of the tragedies of Euripides. This in itself gives little away. Beneath Euripides lies the latest paperback Arden edition of *Macbeth*. The two, taken together, are a little more suggestive. Perhaps he is a playwright, and the Crown Princess is now planning a dramatic adaptation of her story? By the side of the three books, beneath the glasses case, we can see a postcard showing an Impressionist painting of a sloping meadow full of scarlet poppies in high summer. This is one of the most reproduced images of the age of mechanical reproduction, so perhaps it is sheer chance that it rests here. The poppies scatter like drops of blood, like a haze of blood. A woman and a small child walk for ever through the field of red, towards the ever-waiting eye of the spectator. The field of red is full of blood and joy. The woman is the artist's young wife, who was soon to die, though neither she nor the artist nor the child knew this when she was walking through this fair field in France.

The bottles of pills have disappeared from Babs's bedside table. The osteoporosis placebo trial is over, and the results have been fed in to the programme. Babs has forgotten all about it. She has shed this concern. Whether her bones are more or less brittle than they were two years ago is of no interest to her. She is no longer a guinea pig or a laboratory mouse.

When Babs has settled Chen Jianyi for the night, and sung the ritual song that she always

444

sings to her, she goes into her own bedroom, and sinks down heavily upon her bed. She is exhausted. The day has been stressful. Chen Jiangyi is a well-behaved child: indeed, most of the time, she is almost disconcertingly docile and self-contained. But a trip to Heathrow cannot be restful, and four hours with Viveca van Jost are more stimulating than restful. And Barbara Halliwell's ardent desire to please this small child is in itself exhausting. She is not accustomed to the company of small children, and, although she sees Chen Jianyi frequently, she feels always that she must be on her best behaviour, and offer the child the best of everything. Never can she ignore this surrogate daughter. Never can she scold her, or let her down. Can this be good for either of them? It is the best that she can do. The child is on loan. She is neither a gift nor a purchase, nor a substitution. She is a visitor and a guest.

Barbara runs through the week's plans, checking them for uncertainties and strategic difficulties. Will it rain on the day designated for the picnic on Hampstead Heath? Will they find the red dress on which the child had set her heart? Will Polly Usher have remembered the time that she has agreed to meet them at the Tate tomorrow, or should Barbara double-check?

Polly Usher and Barbara Halliwell are reconciled. Polly has conceded that her friend Barbara has acted not rashly, but, in her own way, properly. And, as Barbara knows, Polly is consumed by curiosity about the developmental progress of the Chinese orphan. She does not want to be left out of the plot.

She and Polly are meeting their new friend in the Tate. Their new friend is a novelist called Margaret Drabble, whom they had met a few months ago at the launch party for a book on medical ethics by a friend of a friend who was long ago at primary school with Margaret Drabble's children in North London. Polly and Barbara had known quite a lot of people at this launch, which was a low-key, ingrown and intimate affair in a specialist bookshop in Bloomsbury, but Margaret Drabble had seemed less well connected. It was not clear why she was there at all: did she accept every invitation she was sent, however out of the way? Had she nowhere better to go? They had observed her alone in a corner, wearing a long, red dress with small white spots on. She was eating a nutrition-free cheese-flavoured sawdust snack, and surreptitiously inspecting a display of psychoanalytic books. She was pretending to be busy. She was looking older than she did on her book jackets, but they recognized her through the disguise of age. They had boldly gone up to her and introduced themselves to her. They claimed that they knew her already, for it was she, in a manner, that had introduced them, all those years ago, in a pub in Lamb's Conduit Street, near the Great Ormond Street Hospital for Sick Children.

'We were both reading your book,' Babs had said, 'and so it was that we got talking.'

They did not tell her, at this stage, that they had argued about the book. Polly had liked it

446

better than Babs had liked it. Neither of them has read it since, and they have not kept up with her later output, but she won't know this, will she?

The lonely novelist had seemed pleased by this overture, and so, encouraged, they had told her more. She had subsequently met Babs for lunch in Museum Street, in a new Korean restaurant called Bi-Bim-Bap, and Babs had poured out much of her life's story. She had spoken about Peter Halliwell, and Benedict Halliwell, and Jan van Jost, and the Crown Princess, and Chen Jianyi. The novelist had seemed peculiarly receptive to this mixed and melodramatic material, as Babs had guessed she would be. The novelist had dutifully read the memoirs of the Crown Princess, and had professed herself as struck by them as Babs herself had been. In a way, Babs now feels she has handed over the Crown Princess to a suitable recipient and can forget about her. Let the lady nest and roost in a new dwelling. Let her nibble away at a new host. Babs has done her best for her. The Prince of the Rice Chest has appeared in the footnotes of the last, posthumous work of Jan van Jost, and his Princess can haunt and torment Margaret Drabble for a while, while Barbara Halliwell pursues her own life.

She and Margaret Drabble have become friends. Margaret Drabble seems to prefer Babs to Polly Usher, which, in the view of Babs, is as it should be. She says she is anxious to meet Chen Jianyi. (Everyone is anxious to meet Chen Jianyi.) So they will all meet on the morrow, in

447

Tate Modern, for a virtual journey along the Silk Road.

Novelists, the novelist had warned Barbara Halliwell amidst the ruins of Halicarnassus in Room 21 of the British Museum, are not to be trusted. They steal; they borrow; they appropriate. You should never tell them anything, if you want to keep it a secret.

Barbara Halliwell, sitting on her bed, thinking of all these things, yawns and sighs.

Medical ethics, literary ethics, maternal ethics. The ethics of multicultural adoption.

Will the child prosper? Who knows?

So be it, says Barbara Halliwell to herself, aloud. I have done my best.

So be it, she says.

As we watch Barbara Halliwell, a thought seems to strike her. She hesitates, about to rise, then rises, and crosses the room to the old-fashioned polished mahogany Edwardian chest of drawers by the window. She pulls open the top right-hand drawer, where she keeps her socks and her tights and her stockings, and she rummages round amongst them. After a while, at the back of the drawer, she finds what she is looking for. It is a tiny crumpled soft red ball. She takes it out, and sits down again, and solemnly unfolds the little pair of cheap red socks that van Jost had bought for her, on that hot autumn evening in Seoul. Small when new, they have puckered and shrunk to the size of socks fit for a doll's wardrobe. Wonderingly, she inserts a hand into one of them, and looks at the little woven butterflies. They are still there, still

448

distinct. She fingers the artificial fabric. She likes its unreal texture. It is frail, but it is imperishable, and its colour has hardly faded. It will outlive her. It may endure for centuries. Perhaps she is wondering whether she should give the socks to her adopted daughter, to go with her new red dress? Has her adopted daughter not a right to these socks? But no, as we watch, she rolls them up again, first fitting toe to toe, then rolling them, the one inside the other. She puts them back in the drawer. She hides the little red bundle safely at the back of the drawer.

Afterword

When I was a child, I had a little red velvet dress. It was my party dress. It may have been handed down, as many of my clothes were, but for a while it was allowed to be mine. I was very fond of that little red dress. It had a bodice made of a different and lighter fabric, covered in a pattern of little pink and red rosebuds.

If the Crown Princess had not mentioned her longing for a red silk skirt, I do not think I would have responded to her story as I did. It is an arbitrary connection. I am wearing a red dress as I write these words. If she had not mentioned her red silk skirt, I would not have been entrapped by her.

Margaret Drabble 17 July 2003

Acknowledgements

The four lines from the poem on p. 93/4 are taken from p. 46 of *Songs of the Kisaeng*, translated and introduced by Constantine Contogenis and Wolhee Choe, Boa Editions Limited, Rochester, New York, 1997.

The translation of Lady Sŏnhŭi's epitaph on p. 187/8 is by James Gale, the Canadian scholar and missionary, and is to be found in *James Scarth Gale and His History of the Korean People*, Royal Asiatic Society, Korea Branch: a new edition annotated by Richard Rutt, 1972.

A Note on Sources

The memoirs of the Crown Princess, 'Lady Hong', are well known and celebrated in Korea. The original manuscripts of the four different memoirs are believed to be lost, but there are several copies, which show variations in script, content and chronology. The memoirs are known in English under various titles, and there are at least three translations, taken from variant texts. (The translation by Thea Ŏ. Landry mentioned in my text is, of course, a fiction.) The earliest is entitled *Han Joong Nok: Reminiscences in Retirement* (1980), by 'Crown Princess Hong', translated by Bruce C. Grant and Kim Chinman: this is a full and readable version which has, appropriately, many Shakespearean echoes and resonances. It is prefaced with an explanatory note by Kwang-yong Chun, which gives a brief account of the chronology of the composition of the memoirs, and the version used, but the volume lacks notes and any other critical apparatus.

I first came across the memoirs in the year 2000, in the scholarly and carefully annotated version by JaHyun Kim Haboush, published in 1996. Professor Haboush is the recognized authority on the period, and I read and consulted her translation and other related works by her, in which she has carefully reconstructed much that would have been unavailable to the general reader. I also read the other two translations, and related works, in any language I could understand, that seemed to illuminate the reflections inspired in me by the Crown Princess's life. These sources include works of poetry, sociology, history and psychology.

I commend to the interested reader Professor Haboush's *A Heritage of Kings* (see below) which contains a firsthand witness account by a diarist, Yi Kwanghyon, of the Crown Prince's death. This document was discovered in the Yi family private royal family collection. Professor Haboush reproduces this, in translation (pp. 219–30), and discusses its authenticity in her Appendix 4 (pp. 251–3).

I would like to thank the Daesan Foundation for introducing me to Korea and its literature through its invitation to the First Seoul International Forum for Literature 2000.

Bibliography

'Crown Princess Hong', *Han Joong Nok: Reminiscences in Retirement*, translated by Bruce C. Grant and Kim Chinman (New York: Larchwood Publications, 1980). © Korea Literary Foundation.

Haboush, JaHyun Kim (ed.), *The Memoirs of Lady Hyegyŏng: The Autobiographical Writings of a Crown Princess of Eighteenth-Century Korea* (Berkeley: University of California Press, 1996).

Haboush, JaHyun Kim, *A Heritage of Kings: One Man's Monarchy in the Confucian World*, Studies in Oriental Culture, no. 21 (New York: Columbia University Press, 1988).

Haboush, JaHyun Kim & Martina Deuchler (eds), *Culture and State in Late Chosŏn Korea*, Harvard-Hallyam Series on Korean Studies, Harvard East Asian Monographs, no. 182 (Cambridge, Mass.: Harvard University Press, 1999).

'Lady Hong', *Memoirs of a Korean Queen*, edited, introduced and translated by Yang-hi Choe-Wall (London and Boston: Kegan Paul International Ltd, 1985).

Kyu-tae, Yi, *Modern Transformations of Korea* (Seoul: Sejong Publishing Company, 1970).

Lee, Peter H. (ed.), *Source Book of Korean Civilization*, vol. 11 (New York: Columbia

University Press, 1996).

Lee, Peter H. (ed.), *The Columbia Anthology of Traditional Korean Poetry* (New York: Columbia University Press, 2002).

McCall, John E., 'Early Jesuit Art in the Far East', *Artibus Asiae*, vol. 10, 1947–48.

McCann, David R., *Early Korean Literature: Selections and Introductions* (New York: Columbia University Press, 2000).

O'Rourke, Kevin (ed. & trans.), *The Book of Korean Shijo*, Harvard East Asian Monographs, no. 215 (Cambridge, Mass.: Harvard University Press, 2002).

Rutt, Richard (ed. & trans.), *The Bamboo Grove: An Introduction to Sijo* (Berkeley: University of California Press, 1971).

Tennant, Roger, *A History of Korea* (London and New York: Kegan Paul International Ltd, 1996).

Writing across Boundaries: Literature in the Multicultural World. Proceedings of the Seoul International Forum for Literature, 2000 (Elizabeth, NJ: Hollym, 2002). See Drabble, pp. 447–65. © Daesan Foundation.

We do hope that you have enjoyed reading
this large print book.

Did you know that all of our titles
are available for purchase?

We publish a wide range of high quality
large print books including:
Romances, Mysteries, Classics
General Fiction
Non Fiction and Westerns

Special interest titles available in
large print are:
The Little Oxford Dictionary
Music Book
Song Book
Hymn Book
Service Book

Also available from us courtesy of Oxford
University Press:
Young Readers' Dictionary
(large print edition)
Young Readers' Thesaurus
(large print edition)

For further information or a free
brochure, please contact us at:
Ulverscroft Large Print Books Ltd.,
The Green, Bradgate Road, Anstey,
Leicester, LE7 7FU, England.
Tel: (00 44) 0116 236 4325
Fax: (00 44) 0116 234 0205

Other titles published by
The House of Ulverscroft:

THE SEVEN SISTERS

Margaret Drabble

Candida Wilton arrives in London, alone, divorced and without much money. Yet she is strangely excited: what might happen to her now in her final years? She is prepared to fill her empty life with little events and pleasures, but she finds her horizons broadened by an unexpected windfall. Gathering together six travelling companions - women friends from childhood, from married life and after — Candida maps out the journey she has long dreamed of: to Tunis, Naples and Pompeii. Finally, she has realized that one can make anything happen, if one has the nerve . . .

THE PEPPERED MOTH

Margaret Drabble

It is 1912 and Bessie Bawtry is a small child living in Breaseborough, a South Yorkshire mining town. Unusually gifted, she studies hard, waiting for the day when she can sit the Cambridge entrance exam and escape the kind of life her ancestors have never even thought to question ... Nearly a century later, Bessie's granddaughter, Faro Gaulden, is listening to a lecture on genetic inheritance. She has returned to the depressed little town where Bessie grew up and all around her she sees the families who have stayed there for longer than anyone can remember. But has Faro really travelled any further than her Breaseborough kin?

THE WITCH OF EXMOOR

Margaret Drabble

A midsummer's evening in Hampshire, and the Palmer family — Daniel, Gogo, Rosemary, their partners and their children — are coming to the end of an enjoyable meal. As usual, their conversation is brought back to the more pressing problem of their famous and eccentric mother, Frieda, who has abandoned them and gone off to live alone on Exmoor. Frieda has always been a powerful and puzzling figure, a monster mother with a mysterious past. What is she plotting against them now? Why has she disappeared? Has the dark spirit of Exmoor finally driven her mad?

LORD JOHN AND THE PRIVATE MATTER

Diana Gabaldon

London, 1757. On a bright June day, Lord John Grey emerges from his club, his mind in turmoil. A nobleman and a high-ranking officer in His Majesty's Army, Grey has just witnessed something shocking. But his efforts to avoid a scandal that might destroy his family are interrupted by something still more urgent: the Crown appoints him to investigate the brutal murder of a comrade-in-arms, who might well have been a traitor. Obliged to pursue two inquiries at once, Major Grey finds himself ensnared in a web of treachery and betrayal that touches every level of society — and threatens all he holds dear . . .

THE COLOUR

Rose Tremain

Mid-nineteenth century: Joseph and Harriet Blackstone, along with Joseph's mother Lilian, emigrate from Norfolk to New Zealand, in search of new beginnings and prosperity. But the harsh land near Christchurch where they settle threatens to destroy them almost before they begin. When Joseph finds gold in the creek, he guiltily hides the discovery from his wife and mother and is seized by a rapturous obsession with the voluptuous riches awaiting him deep in the earth. Abandoning his farm and family, he sets off alone for the new gold-fields over the Southern Alps, a moral wilderness where many others are violently rushing to their destinies.